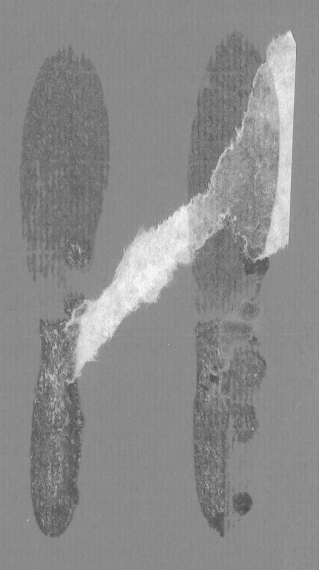

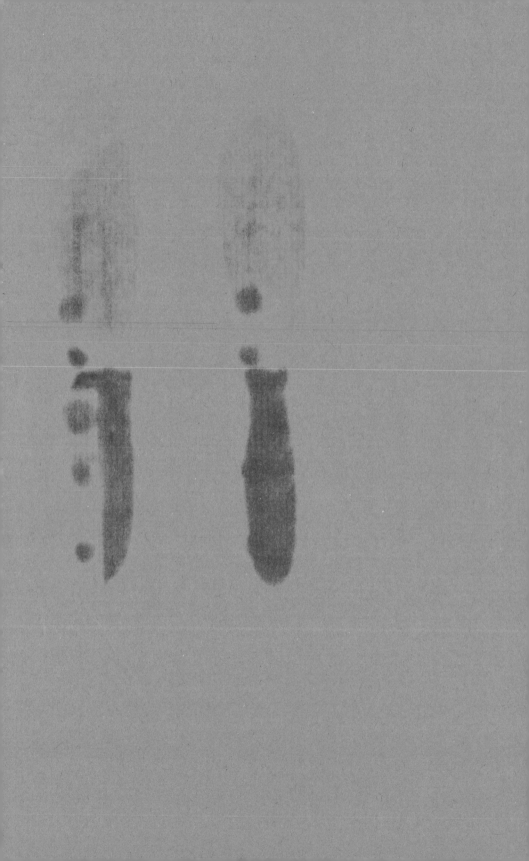

Leopold Stokowski

Leopold Stokowski. *Photo: Martha Holmes.*

Leopold Stokowski

Preben Opperby

MIDAS BOOKS
HIPPOCRENE BOOKS
New York

In the same illustrated Great Performer Series:
Sir Adrian Boult CH – A tribute. Edited by Nigel Simeone and Simon Mundy.
Maria Callas by Carla Verga.
Niccolo Paganini – Supreme Violinist or Devil's Fiddler? by John Sugden.
Arturo Toscanini by Denis Matthews and Ray Burford.

First published in 1982 by
MIDAS BOOKS
12 Dene Way, Speldhurst,
Tunbridge Wells, Kent TN3 0NX

© Preben Opperby 1982

ISBN 0 85936 253 1

First published in 1982 in US by
HIPPOCRENE BOOKS INC
171 Madison Avenue, New York, N.Y. 10016

ISBN 0 88254 658 9

Photosetting by Style Photosetting Ltd, Tunbridge Wells.
Printed and bound in Great Britain at The Pitman Press, Bath.

Contents

Foreword

Until the beginning of the twentieth century, the musical life of the USA was to a great extent dominated by German musicians and the German orchestral tradition. In many places the need for serious music was not greater than could be met by travelling artists, among them the real pioneers, Leopold Damrosch, Theodore Thomas and their orchestras. In fact, before the turn of the century only three major cities were able to support orchestras of an international standard, and that only because they had a handful of music-lovers devoted to culture and willing to make the necessary sacrifices.

Today conditions are quite different. There are now several hundred symphony orchestras in the USA, and at least ten of them stand among the greatest in the world. Stiff German discipline and old-fashioned orchestral playing techniques have disappeared; most musicians are educated in American music schools, and the best American orchestras have surpassed the leading European ensembles in efficiency and technique.

This transformation was to a great extent brought about by Leopold Stokowski. For more than half a century he was a central figure in the musical life of the USA, and all that time he constantly made front-page news, and became the object of much controversy. He has been of the greatest importance in the development of the modern symphony orchestra, and the time is ripe for an evaluation of his life's work. That is the purpose of this book. It is inspired by his perseverance, idealism and foresight.

However, I could not have done this without the assistance of innumerable persons and organisations, and for their courtesy and help I sincerely offer my thanks. I know that my memory will fail me and make me forget some of them, so I ask their forgiveness.

First, I am truly grateful to Elizabeth Hartman, former head of the music department of the Free Library, Philadelphia, and Anne Shepherd, Curator of the Cincinnati Historical Society, for their unselfish and indefatigable assistance in my research. Next, I wish to thank the many friends I have made through my interest in Stokowski for their help and encouragement: Oliver Daniel and Donald J. Ott, New York; Joseph Restifo, Nancy Shear, and Mr and Mrs Pearson Fischer, Philadelphia; Paul Hoeffler, Canada; Mr Ivan Lund, Australia; and Mr John Cruft, England.

My thanks are also due to the Royal College of Music, London, and its former and present music directors, Sir Keith Falkner and Sir David Willcocks; to the Arnold Schoenberg Institute, California; to many of the orchestras Stokowski was associated with through his career, not least the Philadelphia Orchestra, and to a great many recording companies for their kind assistance and generous gifts.

My greatest thanks, however, are to my wife, Mimi Opperby, for sharing my interest in Stokowski and my research into his work.

Copenhagen
January 1981
Preben Opperby

Chapter 1

Early Years

Leopold Stokowski's career is one of the most fascinating in the history of music, and involved practically all aspects of the musical life in the twentieth century. Consequently he became a public figure, but he always hated having his life delineated. To avoid this he told different stories about it, when he was asked, so parts of it have been veiled in obscurity and mystery. One ineradicable tradition has always made Stokowski Polish. Actually, he was born in North London at St John's Wood, on 18 April, 1882, and his full name is Leopold Anthony Stokowski. Some people wanting to disparage him, asserted that Stokowski was an assumed name, and that his fellow students in

Copy of Stokowski's birth certificate.

England called him Leo Stokes; but there is no truth in this. The copy of his birth certificate and entries in the files of the Royal College of Music allow no doubts about his identity.

His grandfather, Leopold Stokowski, was from Lublin, Poland. A fugitive from Russian officials, he came to London in the mid-1850's. Here he settled in Oxford Market and married an English woman. Their son, Josef Kopernicus Boleslaw Stokowski, earned his living as a cabinetmaker. In 1881 he met Annie Marion Moore, a pretty young woman said to have been grand-daughter of the famous Irish poet Thomas Moore. The young couple married in June, and the next year Annie gave birth to Leopold. Some years later came two more children; Lydia in 1885 and Percy John in 1890. Stokowski's father died in the 1920's, but his mother lived to the great age of 93, dying in 1952.

It was old Leopold Stokowski who introduced his grandson to music*. He sometimes took little Leopold to an immigrants' club, where he became fascinated by the songs they performed. It was here too that at the age of seven, he heard a violin for the first time. He became so fascinated by the violin that his grandfather eventually

Acacia Road, London. Stokowski lived in no. 18 with his parents 1896-9. The original house was torn down in the middle of the 1930s.

*This is the story Stokowski used to tell about his introduction to music, but according to some researchers, among others Abram Chasins, the old Stokowski died in 1879, three years before the birth of Leopold.

Stokowski as organist at St James's Church, London, in 1902. Attired in the same way as the choir-boys, he is seen sitting to the right of Reverend Canon Joseph McCormick.

presented him with one. His musical talent was obvious, and he received violin lessons, and later was taught the piano. The world of music was a revelation to him, as he described in his book *Music for All of Us*:

I can remember so clearly, when I was about eight years old, playing for hours every day the music of Bach, Beethoven, Mozart, Schubert, Brahms, Chopin, Debussy. I was not forced to do this, but did it of my own free will. Nor did it prevent me from enjoying such games as football with my friends. This daily communion with music gave me a vision of an ideal world of beauty with which I gradually became familiar, just as surely as I learned to know the material world of school and play. It gave me something of immeasurable value which will always be part of my inner life.

However, it was not long before Stokowski found the violin and the piano insufficient means of expression for his musical imagination and began to look for other possibilities. When he was ten years old, he wanted a chance to play the music of Bach on an organ. At that time he often played with a boy whose father was a Minister, and his friend obtained permission for Leopold to play the organ at his father's church. To begin with, Leopold could not reach the pedals, but within a year he was able to play all of Bach's organ pieces with the pedal. So in his early childhood the foundations were laid for the passionate interest in Bach's music which was so important in Stokowski's career.

Very early the desire to become a conductor grew, and when he was only twelve years old, Leopold got his first chance to conduct. He gave me the following account of this event:

I was at that time pianist for a chorus at an opera in London, and sometimes I also rehearsed the chorus. One night, when we were going to have a concert, the manager came up to me and told me that the conductor had become ill and was not able to conduct. "Can you do it?" he asked. And I, being a little boy and always so confident, only said, "Yes, of course I can." So we made the concert. I was so excited and thrilled, because this was a very unexpected opportunity for me to conduct, and I shall never forget how I felt that night. I could not sleep after the concert. I was thinking of the music all the time, and that my dream had come true, because I always wanted to be a conductor, and now I had become one.

Stokowski received a thorough musical training. In 1896 he entered the Royal College of Music, whose director at the time was the composer Hubert Parry. To begin with, Leopold's instruments were violin and piano, but later he chose the organ as his main instrument. He studied composition with Charles Villiers Stanford and counterpoint with Sir Henry Walford Davies. His mastery in these fields is partly due to those famous English composers. In 1898 he also attended the Royal College of Organists for a one-year course, and the same year Walford Davies invited him to be his assistant as organist at the City Temple. The organ intrigued Stokowski very much, and while Sir Henry was satisfied with his young assistant, Stokowski was not, and in 1905 he re-entered the College of Organists for a further course.

In 1899 Stokowski graduated from the Royal College of Music, and then, without taking up residence, matriculated at Queen's College, Oxford. On 19th November, 1903, with Hubert Parry, Charles Lloyd, and Frederick Read as examiners, he was awarded the degree of B. Mus. Each summer he went abroad for further studies, mainly to Germany. Particularly noteworthy were some master-courses in Leipzig in 1906, led by the famous conductor Arthur Nikisch, whom Stokowski greatly admired.

Those years were difficult for Stokowski. Although his grandfather was a Polish aristocrat, in England he had to earn his living as an artisan, and his father and mother were not prosperous enough to support him fully during his studies. In 1902, however, Stokowski was appointed organist at the fashionable St James's Church, Piccadilly, a job he was able to combine with continuing studies. He was also a frequent guest with a certain Godson family from the congregation. Now and then he earned money playing at restaurants or coaching singers. But the story he once told his friend, the late Charles

The organ of St James's Church, London.

O'Connell, that he later suffered from rickets, is probably spurious.

Stokowski did an excellent job at St James's, and in 1905 was heard playing by a visitor who was much impressed. This was Dr. Leighton Parks, the rector of St Bartholomew's Church, New York, who asked Stokowski to go to the USA and become organist and chorus-master at his church. Stokowski accepted and went to the USA for a post that was considered one of the best in its field in New York. According to those who knew him then, he was a strict and skilled chorus-master, and his highly individual personality was already evident. He was much in favour of theatrical staging of the liturgical parts of the service, and some of his own compositions, among them the

St Bartholomew's Church, New York.

Benedicite, date from this period. The congregation loved him, and it became fashionable to go to the church to hear him play. But the church-wardens were inclined to frown at his unpredictable ideas. Finally one day in 1908, when he concluded a service with Sousa's *Stars and Stripes*, with all the organ-stops pulled out, it was too much. If we can believe the account, he was simply fired.

At any rate, that summer Stokowski left his job in New York and went to Paris for further studies. But before this, in the home of a music patron from the congregation, he had been introduced to a talented young pianist called Olga Samaroff. She was born in San Antonio in Texas in 1882, and her name was really Lucy Hickenlooper, coming from a family of Dutch descent. Because of her talent, she was the first woman to be admitted to the piano classes at the Paris Conservatory, and after completing these she went to Berlin to study with Ernest Hutcheson. In 1905 she returned to USA to give her first concerts. It was during one of her stays in New York she met Stokowski.

At first they did not seem to like one another. Both were distinctive personalities absorbed in their respective careers. Besides that, Stokowski was a sworn bachelor, engaging only a male-cook in his household and devoting all his time to work and study. Music, however, became a binding force between them, and after several professional encounters they announced with short notice that they were going to marry on 24 April, 1911. Mme Samaroff gave this statement:

Mr Stokowski is the greatest orchestral conductor in the world, and I admire him professionally. If you must write a romantic story, say that he fell in love with my hands and I in love with his eyes.

At that time, Stokowski had already been appointed conductor of the Cincinnati Symphony Orchestra and he felt at home in the USA from the first day he arrived. 'I was powerfully stimulated by the freedom of life here, and the opportunity that is given to any man or woman with ideas and originality'. He certainly possessed both himself, and he also realised immediately that the USA was going to become one of the great music centres of the world. In 1914 he applied for American citizenship, and was naturalized in 1915.

Stokowski and his first wife, Olga Samaroff, in their summer residence in Munich. 1912. *Photo: Gebrüder Hirsch, Munich.*

Chapter 2

Cincinnati
Symphony Orchestra

Cincinnati has been a city with a musical tradition since the early 1870's, when the famous May Festival was established. But it did not get a symphony orchestra until 1895, when the Cincinnati Orchestra Association raised a guarantee fund and invited subscribers for three series of concerts, conducted by Frank van der Stucken, Anton Seidl and Henry Schradieck. After the first season Van der Stucken was engaged as sole conductor and remained for twelve years, giving ten pairs of concerts annually. In 1907, however, the Association ran into trouble with the Federation of Musicians, and rather than give way to their heavy demands it was decided to disband the orchestra. But the idea of reviving the orchestral concerts was kept in mind. During the next two years the Board of Directors endeavoured to raise a new guarantee fund, and finally in April, 1909, they were promised annual contributions of 50,000 dollars for five years. With this money they were able to engage musicians on full-season contracts, and it only remained to find the right conductor.

Assistance came from Herman Thumann, music critic of the *Cincinnati Enquirer*, who had heard good reports about the young organist and choir-master from New York, Leopold Stokowski. He was back again from Europe, and when he was approached as a possible candidate for the post he went to Cincinnati for an interview. The impression he made, among others on Mrs Christian R. Holmes, the President of the Association, was favourable, but there was some hesitation on account of his lack of reputation. No decision was made

THE CINCINNATI SYMPHONY ORCHESTRA ASSOCIATION announces the opening of the fourteenth season of Symphony Concerts, at Music Hall, on Friday afternoon, November 26th, and Saturday evening, November 27th.

The Board of Directors takes pleasure in presenting a new Conductor, Mr. Leopold Stokovski. Mr. Stokovski is young, talented, enthusiastic, and eminently qualified by experience to conduct a great-modern orchestra.

The Orchestra will number seventy-five musicians, all of whom are men with much orchestral experience, and have been selected with the utmost care by Mr. Stokovski. Many of them have played with us during former seasons and will be warmly welcomed back to our city.

Mr. Hugo Heermann, the concertmeister, is an artist of the first rank, with an international reputation. The Board feels it is to be congratulated upon securing his services.

The season will include twenty concerts—ten evening and ten afternoon. Attention is called to the fact that all concerts will be given on Friday afternoons and Saturday evenings of alternate weeks with two exceptions; between the second and third concerts, there will be an interval of one week only, and between the third and fourth concerts, during the holiday season, an interval of three weeks.

The original introduction from the programme of Stokowski's first concert in Cincinnati.

immediately, so Stokowski went back to Europe for further engagements. But none of the famous conductors would be available at such short notice to start a season the same year, so a member of the Advisory Board, Lucien Wulsin, from the famous Baldwin Company, on holiday in France, was asked to see Stokowski in Paris to decide if he would be the right man.

An opportunity came soon, on the occasion of Stokowski's official debut as a conductor. According to him he was coaching a singer for a concert with the Colonne Orchestra in Paris, but the conductor did not turn up, and at the last minute he was asked to take over at the concert on 12 May, 1909. This does not agree with the correspondence between Mrs Holmes and Lucien Wulsin, from which it is evident that Stokowski had already been engaged for the concert in April, probably with the help of Olga Samaroff, who was the other soloist at the concert. However, the concert was a great success, not least because Stokowski had natural authority, comprehensive knowledge, and a rare ability to make his intentions clear to the players. Lucien Wulsin had been sceptical of Stokowski's ability, but after this concert he waited backstage and asked if he was willing to go to Cincinnati. Stokowski accepted, and after the exchange of cables between Paris and Cincinnati was accordingly engaged for one year as conductor of the Cincinnati Symphony Orchestra. When the first season proved very successful he was offered a four-year contract to cover the entire guarantee period.

This was the beginning of Stokowski's long and illustrious career as a conductor. But even before he returned to the USA for his first permanent post he received fine reviews in Europe. On 18 May he had his British debut with the New Symphony Orchestra, in Queen's Hall, London. One of the critics wrote:

At the third concert given by Mr Francis MacMillen, Mr Leopold Stokowski made his first appearance in England as a conductor. Employing unexaggerated methods, he obtained excellent results from the New Symphony Orchestra, both in accompanying Mr MacMillen in Lalo's *Symphonie Espagnole* and Saint-Saëns's B Minor Concerto, and in contributing separate numbers. The most interesting of the latter was an orchestral suite by Mr Ippolitov-Ivanow, entitled *Caucasian Sketches,* which proved a pleasant piece of music based upon themes of Eastern character. The efforts of both violinist and conductor met with hearty approval.

In October Stokowski went back to the USA to prepare for his first season in Cincinnati. A silly story reports that he was so inexperienced that the leader had to explain the fundamentals of time-beating at the first rehearsal. Of course there is no truth in this anecdote; but it contains the essential fact that his career as a conductor began and

Stokowski raising his baton over the Cincinnati Symphony Orchestra in
Music Hall, Cincinnati, 1909. *Photo: Cincinnati Post.*

proceeded almost exclusively on American soil. In fact, the great
majority of American conductors of European descent have already
had an established career and international fame behind them before
coming to the USA – for example Koussevitzky, Mahler, Mengelberg
and Toscanini. But both Stokowski and Ormandy, associated with
building and leading the Philadelphia Orchestra, came to the USA as
unknown young men and succeeded not only in making glorious
careers for themselves, but also in influencing the American musical
scene more than most other conductors.

On 26 November Stokowski presented his first programme in Music
Hall, Cincinnati:

W. A. Mozart	Overture to *The Magic Flute*
Ludwig van Beethoven	Symphony no. 5 in C Minor
Carl Maria von Weber	Overture to *Der Freischütz*
Richard Wagner	Siegfried Idyll
Richard Wagner	Ride of the Valkyries

Probably never in the history of the Cincinnati Orchestra had
expectancy and curiosity before a new season been so great. But after
the concert there were no reservations, but enthusiasm from both the
audience and the critics. The greatest praise, however, came from
Stokowski's predecessor, Van der Stucken, who had attended the final
rehearsal. He said that the city need fear no decline from the high
ideals always striven for by himself, and that Cincinnati had found a
new leader to be proud of and to cherish.

From his first season Stokowski showed himself to be a personality.
He increased the proportion of modern music to classical music, and

many works by Strauss, Sibelius, Debussy, and Rachmaninov were now heard in Cincinnati for the first time. To conservative concertgoers at the time, such composers were quite unknown modernists. It must have been extremely shocking too when he presented programmes with all English or American composers, for instance Elgar, Walford Davies and MacDowell. But the audiences apparently gave way to him, and if they did not, he was not slow to lecture them, either on the contents of difficult music or on good manners for concert-goers.

Besides, Stokowski brought many fashionable soloists to Cincinnati, for example Kreisler, Rachmaninov and Elman; they, too, were full of admiration for the young conductor. In 1910 he accompanied Rachmaninov as soloist in his own 2nd Piano Concerto, which is how their life-long musical friendship started. Rachmaninov said that Stokowski was one of the most talented young men he had met, and Elman found him an ideal accompanist, because he respected the soloist's interpretation in a sympathetic feeling.

The activities of the Cincinnati Orchestra were extended in many other ways. After the first two seasons the number of subscription concerts was increased from ten to twelve pairs, and new series of popular concerts and music lectures at colleges were introduced. To exemplify his sublime view of music and its importance to the

Stokowski practising the piano in his home in Cincinnati 1910. *Photo: Cincinnati Historical Society.*

individual and society, Stokowski took the orchestra on tour to seven states and twelve cities, from Buffalo and Pittsburg in the east to Kansas City in the west, visiting many small places where people had never encountered a symphony orchestra before.

Stokowski's popularity was at a peak; he was considered a god by his many admirers. But he had not gained this position by any non-musical means. The best judgement can be made by examining his relations with the orchestra. Their general attitude was one of loyalty and admiration, as expressed by the concertmaster, Professor Hugo Heermann:

I am astonished and delighted at the magnificent work of our leader and the way the entire orchestra responds. All the men admire and respect him extremely both for his deep musical knowledge and his kindly, courteous treatment of them.

There was every indication that Stokowski's period in Cincinnati was going to be a fruitful and golden era, so it aroused consternation when it became known publicly in April, 1912, that he had asked the Board of Directors to be released from the final two years of his contract. But this was not a sudden decision. While the city had prospered under Stokowski's musical leadership, increasing friction had developed between him and the Board on certain questions of management. He said that negotiations with them were always difficult because they were reactionary and would never agree, so progress was very slow. This prevented him from building up a really great orchestra that could take its place among the best on the national scene. However, many members of the Board were offended by Stokowski's request, finding him much too arrogant. In an exchange of letters one member wrote that 'he is a nervous, hysterical young fellow who, at this time, like a naughty child, should have been well spanked and put to bed, carefully fed and rested, to bring him to a certain degree of sanity.'

However, it was finally decided not to grant Stokowski a release, and the Board wrote to him to tell that they expected him to complete the remaining two years of his contract. Stokowski answered that if they insisted, he would make the whole affair public in Cincinnati and elsewhere. Of course he would have to complete his contract, but enthusiasm for his work would be lost. Stokowski also asserted that there existed a verbal agreement between him and the President that in case of any dissatisfaction on either side, the contract could be dissolved at the end of any season. A special committee was now formed to look into his complaints, and after several dramatic meetings and a joint meeting with the Board of Directors it was resolved to get rid of him. On 5 April they wrote to him:

21

In view of the position which you have taken, which is one of hostility, not only toward the individual members of the Board of Directors, but toward the organization itself, it has been concluded that your efficiency as a conductor of the Cincinnati Symphony Orchestra has been seriously impaired and that you have become discredited with the public of Cincinnati, and as it is felt that you have consequently become valueless to the Association, the Board of Directors have decided to release you from your contract in accordance with your request.

Many music-lovers at the time did not agree with the management of the orchestra. An article in the *Cincinnati Enquirer* on 6 April ended:

For Mr Stokowski to give up his work here after two years of such great success would be a real calamity from Cincinnati's standpoint. The talented young conductor has a great opportunity here and the whole city wants him to remain.

So did the orchestra, but not even a declaration of loyalty from them could change his decision, and a few days later they went to see him off for New York, from which he went to Europe to do some guest conducting. The most important engagement was his debut with the London Symphony Orchestra, whose chief conductor was Arthur Nikisch. The concert took place on 22 May in the Queen's Hall, and the programme, which was repeated – and recorded – in the Royal Festival Hall at his sixtieth anniversary with LSO in 1972, was:

Richard Wagner...............................Overture to *Die Meistersinger*
Claude Debussy...............................Prelude à l'après-midi d'un Faune
Alexander Glazunov..........................Violin Concerto in A Minor
Johannes Brahms ....Symphony no 1 in C Minor
Peter Tschaikovsky ....Marche slave

The reviews of this concert certainly did not indicate that Stokowski was 'valueless' to an orchestra, but rather that he had become a great conductor, whose 'thorough knowledge of the music and of his own intention with regard to it was shown in the instant response of the orchestra to his requirements'.

Now America called for him again. In Philadelphia there had for a long time been bad relations between the Philadelphia Orchestra and its autocratic German conductor, Carl Pohlig. His relations with the Board of Directors had developed into a crisis which made it doubtful whether he would be required to complete his contract, which ran till 1913. After the last concert of his 1911-12 season Pohlig went to Europe as usual, but on 10 June he suddenly returned and offered to resign immediately. Surprisingly his offer was accepted by the management without hesitation. Pohlig gave this enigmatic statement:

Stokowski as he looked when he came to Philadelphia in 1912. *Photo: Bettmann Archive, New York.*

I left Philadelphia at the end of the last season with every expectation of returning to carry out my contract. In Europe I heard rumours which brought me back here to bring matters to a settlement. I tendered my resignation, which was accepted.

The rumours Pohlig had heard no doubt concerned Stokowski. One member of the Philadelphia Orchestra Board knew Stokowski, and had been commissioned to approach him, probably before he left for Europe in April, to find out if he would be interested in going to Philadelphia when Pohlig's contract ran out. Now that the situation had become acute, the Board was in fact relieved when Stokowski was once again engaged by cable. He accepted, not least because the Philadelphia Orchestra was considered to be one of the important posts in the USA. A few weeks before the season began he arrived in Philadelphia with his wife, to enter upon the leadership of the orchestra whose name has forever become synonymous with his own.

Chapter 3

The Philadelphia Orchestra

Before 1900 music had a barren existence in Philadelphia. Founded as it was by religious sectarians with an aversion to public amusements the limited demand for music was easily supplied by local associations and travelling ensembles. Most renowned was the Musical Fund Society, founded in 1820 and still active. Its goal was 'the relief of decayed musicians and their families and the cultivation of skill and diffusion of taste in music'. Both aims were for many years realised through concerts in the Musical Fund Hall for members of the society. But about the middle of the nineteenth century interest in orchestral music decreased while operatic performances increased in popularity, stimulated by travelling opera companies. In consequence, the Musical Fund Society stopped its concert seasons in 1857, and in the same year the Academy of Music opened to meet the requirements of the new age. It was originally planned partly as an opera house and concert hall, partly as a music school. The latter came to nothing, but the building is today the home of the illustrious Philadelphia Orchestra.

Philadelphia's demand for orchestral music was to a great extent met by travelling orchestras, and those few music-lovers in the 1890's who believed the city had attained a size where it should no longer depend on non-resident orchestras had to face the discouraging fact that even the famous Boston Symphony Orchestra, which gave five concerts in the Academy of Music each winter, often played to a sparsely-filled hall.

Academy of Music, Philadelphia. *Photo. Adrian Siegel*

Eventually, in 1900, they found a man who they hoped would be able to restore Philadelphia's prestige. Other great cities such as New York and Boston had for several years been able to support orchestras of their own. The man was Fritz Scheel, former assistant to Hans von Bülow, and later conductor in San Francisco. In 1899 he gave a series of concerts in Woodside Park, Philadelphia, where he was heard by some music-lovers. An agreement was drawn up with Fritz Scheel, who took responsibility for the following season using an amateur orchestra, on condition that he would have the opportunity to conduct a professional orchestra at the close of the season. This promise was fulfilled with two charity concerts, the success of which encouraged the committee to establish a permanent orchestra with Fritz Scheel as conductor. The first official concert took place on 16 November, 1900.

In those days it was a thankless job to maintain an orchestra in the USA. Every cent had to be raised privately, and during its first seasons the Orchestra Association had to call heavily on a few hundred guarantors to make up for ever-increasing deficits. In solving this severe problem Philadelphia developed a new and noble feature in American musical life. In the years 1902-4 groups of music-loving women formed committees to work for the orchestra. In her book *Twenty-five Years of the Philadelphia Orchestra* Francis A. Wister,

PHILADELPHIA ORCHESTRA

MR. FRITZ SCHEEL, Conductor

FIRST CONCERT

FRIDAY, NOVEMBER 16, 1900, AT 8.15 P. M.

PROGRAMME

Carl Goldmark	- -	Overture, "In Spring," Op. 36
Ludwig von Beethoven	-	Symphony No. 5, C minor, Op. 67

      I. Allegro con brio 2-4
      II. Andante con moto 3-8
      III. Allegro 3-4
      IV. Allegro 4-4

INTERMISSION OF TEN MINUTES

Peter Ilitsch Tschaikowsky	-	Concerto for Pianoforte, No. 1, B flat minor, Op. 23

      I. Allegro, non troppo e molto maestoso . . 3-4
      II. Andantino simplice 6-8
      III. Allegro con fuoco 3-4

Karl Maria von Weber	-	"Invitation to the Dance," Op. 65

Orchestration by Felix Weingartner

Richard Wagner	-	Entry of the Gods into "Walhalla," from "Das Rheingold"

SOLOIST

Mr. OSSIP GABRILOWITSCH

EVERETT PIANO USED

First programme of the Philadelphia Orchestra.

former president of The Women's Committees for the Philadelphia Orchestra, tells of these committees' untiring work to find subscribers for the concerts and new guarantors for the deficits, and of numerous receptions and public events for the orchestra and its visiting artists. During a visit to Philadelphia in February, 1960, I spoke to some veteran members of the committees about this work. I am filled with admiration for the affection and loyalty these women display in their work for the orchestra, and for music in Philadelphia.

Fritz Scheel was a skilled musician. He worked untiringly to improve the quality of the orchestra and its programmes, and by his death had a faithful, but limited audience. Stokowski was full of praise for the first conductor of the orchestra:

I am very grateful to Fritz Scheel, who founded the Philadelphia Orchestra. He selected splendid players, they were mostly German players – in fact, we rehearsed in the German language in those days. Fritz Scheel found for example the great first horn player – his name curiously enough was Horner, Anton Horner. He also found the great timpanist for us, Oscar Schwar, also a German, and many other wonderful players, so when I came, I was fortunate enough to inherit all that Fritz Scheel had done to lay the foundations of the orchestra.

Carl Pohlig, from Würtemberg, engaged after Fritz Scheel's death in 1907, left no lasting influence on the Philadelphia Orchestra. He is remembered only as Scheel's successor and Stokowski's predecessor. Apart from an increase in the number of subscription concerts, his five years in Philadelphia were characterised by stagnation. An accusation which cannot be made against his illustrious successor.

Stokowski's first concert in Philadelphia took place on 11 October, 1912, and the programme was as follows:

Ludwig van Beethoven ....Leonore Overture No. 3
Johannes Brahms ....Symphony No. 1 in C Minor
Michail Ippolitov-Ivanow ....*Caucasian Sketches*
Richard Wagner..............................Overture to *Tannhäuser*

The concert was a complete success. *The Philadelphia Public Ledger* reported the next day:

Leopold Stokowski made his debut yesterday afternoon at the Academy as conductor of the Philadelphia Orchestra, in the opening concert of its thirteenth season. Every seat was taken and the extra chairs had been placed within the orchestra rail. There was much enthusiasm, manifesting itself at the beginning in prolonged applause as Stokowski came forward with bowed head, evidently pondering the content of his musical message. Those who went forth to see a hirsute eccentricity were disappointed. They beheld a surprisingly boyish and thoroughly business-like figure, who was sure of himself, yet free from conceit, who dispensed with the score by virtue of an infallible memory, and held his men and his audience from first note to last firmly in his grasp . . .

'Mr Stokowski's conducting is after the order of Nikisch, whom he frankly admires. He does not tear a passion to tatters. He holds his thunders and the winds of Aeolus in a leash. His gestures are graphic, the arcs and parabolas he describes tell of a kind of geometrical translation going on in his mind,

Fritz Scheel, first conductor of the Philadelphia Orchestra. *Photo: Bell and Fischer, Philadelphia.*

whereby he visualizes the confluent rhythms in outward action. At impassioned moments his movements have the freedom of a violinist's bow arm; at other instants he brings his fists against his shoulders with vehement concentration, or his uplifted eloquent left hand pleads with some suppressed choir to come forward and assert itself in power. There is, from first to last, no langour or slackened moment; he directs with a fine vigor and intensity that mounts to ecstacy, yet does not lose its balance or forget its sane and ordered method.

This contemporary review portrays an unusally effective and mature musician, and the fathers of the Philadelphia Orchestra had no doubt that they had found the proper man to carry it forward to new musical achievements. But they hardly realized that his was the start of one of the most unique partnerships the world of music has known, and the creation of an orchestra the sound and technique of which was without peer. Even today, more than forty years after Stokowski left it as permanent conductor, it still has an easily recognizable sound of its own, although during the 1960s and 1970s, when most of the members of Stokowski's original orchestra had retired, it changed from a golden sonority into a more polished, opulent tone. Renowned also for its immediate response, its ability to produce a perfect straight crescendo, and the pure intonation and diminuendo of its brass and woodwinds. Such outstanding results can only be achieved by the greatest conductors, and not without great talent on part of the orchestra. Stokowski conceded that a poor orchestra often plays better under a great conductor, but he believed that great music can only be produced by musicians with a thorough education and a deep cultural background. But this alone is not sufficient to account for the special sound and technique that characterizes all the orchestras Stokowski has worked with closely. There are many other orchestras composed of excellent musicians, but lacking these qualities. The ultimate explanation is found in Stokowski's own person, in his ever-aspiring intellect, never satisfied with the status quo, constantly searching for new ways of improving performance. These qualities also led him to introduce a new technique, which left plenty of opportunity for the players to express themselves individually within the ensemble.

The Board of Directors had certainly found a unique conductor for their orchestra. But they also soon realised that Stokowski was a man with an unusually strong will, and so full of new plans that they were often anxious what his next project might be. After a short time in office, for instance, he insisted that all rehearsals must take place in the Academy of Music. Until then they had been held in various halls with inferior acoustics, and the conductor could not possibly know how the orchestra would sound at the final concert. The problem was that the Academy of Music was an independent institution, which was only rented for the concerts. It is still a separate organization, but now with the essential difference that the Philadelphia Orchestra Association has bought the majority of the stock to secure a permanent residence for the orchestra. Stokowski threatened to quit, and soon got what he wanted, probably because the discussion was overheard by a concert-goer of much commonsense and great influence. His name was Edward Bok.

Stokowski was also much concerned about the size of the orchestra. Certainly, it was larger than the Cincinnati Orchestra when he joined in 1912, but he was not satisfied with its size as a major symphony orchestra. So the number of personnel was rapidly increased. From an original size of 85, it had grown to 95 members in 1915, and in 1921 it numbered 104, reaching the size it remains today.

A brief glimpse at the programmes for the years 1912-15 shows many new pieces, for example, Elgar's First Symphony, excerpts from Richard Strauss' opera *Feuersnot*, Rabaud's Second Symphony, and Scriabin's *The Divine Poem*. But these were nothing as compared with the shock Stokowski gave the Board of Directors by suggesting a performance of Gustav Mahler's Eighth Symphony. He had attended the first performance of the work in Munich in 1910, and since then he had been contemplating a performance of the gigantic work for an American audience. The symphony requires 1068 performers, including two choruses totalling 950 members, and Stokowski estimated the cost of a performance to about $15,000. The Directors reacted to this amount, and many were against the plan, anticipating bad reception of the performance. But others believed that the appearance of the Philadelphia Orchestra at such an extraordinary musical event was so important that the performance was ultimately sanctioned.

The story of this performance, which is still alive in the memory of those who attended it, is dramatic from the very beginning. Stokowski was in Munich in August 1914 to secure the rights from the publishers for the first American performance when the First World War broke out. Olga Samaroff had just finished a concert tour through Austria-Hungary and came to Munich to accompany her husband home. Stokowski was still a British citizen, and his presence in Germany after the outbreak of the war was dangerous for him. For three days he and his wife had to roam about, incessantly changing trains because the transport of troops occupied the railway system. But at length they managed to escape across the Dutch frontier and from there home to the USA.

The performance of the symphony had originally been fixed for spring 1915, but owing to difficulties in having missing parts sent from Europe, it had to be postponed till the next year. Rehearsals with the choruses began in the autumn of 1915. The first chorus was the newly-established Philadelphia Orchestra Chorus, which was trained by Stokowski. The other chorus, composed of The Philadelphia Choral Society, The Mendelssohn Club, The Fortnightly Club, and a chorus of 150 children from the public schools in Philadelphia, was trained by Henry Gordon Thunder, for many years one of the finest choral conductors in the city. The rehearsals with the two choirs were

The performance of Gustav Mahler's Eighth Symphony, March 1916.
Photo: Philadelphia Orchestra.

conducted with great severity. Singers who stayed away from a single rehearsal were excluded, and when the performance drew near, nerves were strained to breaking point. But singers who patiently persevered the whole winter developed a deep and lasting devotion to the man who made this great event possible.

Three performances were announced for Philadelphia and in collaboration with the Society of the Friends of Music one performance was arranged for New York, to take place at the Metropolitan Opera House on 9 April. Applications for tickets came from all over the USA, and the demand was so great that the box-office manager had to increase his personnel to keep up with demand.

The performance was a shattering success. Musicians and critics were dumb-struck at the brilliant accomplishment of the performance. *The Philadelphia Public Ledger* gave the following review the day after the first performance:

Every one of the thousands in the great building was standing, whistling, cheering and applauding, when Leopold Stokowski, his collar wilted, and his right arm weary, but smiling his boyish smile, finally turned to the audience in the Academy of Music last night.

He had scored, so famous musicians agreed, the greatest triumph of his career, the greatest triumph the Philadelphia Orchestra has known in its sixteen years of life, and he had done it on a stupendous scale with the American première of Gustav Mahler's Eighth Symphony. He carried along with him to triumph an orchestra membering 110 musicians and a chorus of 958 singers, to say nothing of the city's music lovers and scores of musical pilgrims from other cities.

After the concert Alexander van Rensselaer, president of the Philadelphia Orchestra Association, gave a wreath to Stokowski as a memento of the great event, praising him for his great musicianship. Stokowski accepted the wreath, and when the applause had come to an end, said:

It is impossible for me to put into words my emotions tonight. This stupendous and noble work was written six years ago. For six years I have been meditating the possibility of its performance and hoping, some day, to have the opportunity of giving it, although I knew the requisite forces would be extremely difficult to obtain.

Through a generosity for which I can never sufficiently express my gratitude, Mr van Rensselaer and the directors of the Philadelphia Orchestra Association made the great undertaking possible at last. The dream still would have remained unfilfilled, however, had it not been for the hard work and willingness of the orchestra, of all these dear people in the chorus, who

Stokowski and Alexander van Rensselaer together with the soloists in Mahler's Eighth Symphony. From left to right: Margaret Keyes, Susanna Dercum, Inez Barbour, Clarence Whitehall, Leopold Stokowski, Alexander van Rensselaer, Florence Hinkle, Reinald Werrenrath, Adelaide Fischer, and Lambert Murphy. *Photo: RCA.*

Stokowski and the Philadelphia Orchestra in Carnegie Hall. *Photo: RCA*

have worked for more than a year, training for this night, of all the soloists, and of Henry Gordon Thunder, who has supported and helped me with most wonderful generosity.

My final and greatest debt, a debt so great that I feel I never can express it, is to you, the public, for your warmth and understanding at the first hearing of this great work. It is a great inspiration.

News of the sensational Mahler concert spread all over America, and reports of it reached Europe. Interest in the work and in the performing artists was so great that four extra concerts had to be arranged. In spite of this, 1500 people had to be refused entry. Nothing like it had ever been experienced. During its first decade the orchestra had played to a less than half-filled auditorium, but under Stokowski's many years' leadership the orchestra nearly always played to full houses, a testimony to the magical powers with which he was able to bind his audience.

After the last performance of the Mahler symphony in Philadelphia all the artists and equipment were transported to New York in two special trains for the final performance, in the Metropolitan Opera House. Every seat had been sold long before, and the touts demanded up to 25 dollars for a single ticket.

Until now the Philadelphia Orchestra had always been looked on with the utmost scepticism in New York. At its guest appearance in Carnegie Hall in November 1907, a New York critic asked what the idea was of bringing the Philadelphia Orchestra all the way across New Jersey, since the city was already supplied with scores of the kind of concerts it gave. Even Stokowski's previous appearances in New York had not attracted much attention. But after the Mahler concert the response was quite different. Even after the first movement, there were excited outbursts of enthusiasm, and after the second movement it seemed that there would be no end to the applause. The Philadelphia Orchestra was now accepted without reservation, and interest in Stokowski as one of the coming leaders of American musical life was immense. One of the critics advised Philadelphia to take great care of him, if they believed him to be of importance to its musical life.

This concert also influenced the appearances of the Philadelphia Orchestra in New York. During its first seasons it only gave one or two concerts in the Carnegie Hall, receiving little public attention. But in 1918 they were increased to five afternoons, changed into five evening concerts in 1919. In 1921 the number was increased to ten, and since then the orchestra has remained the most frequent and popular guest at Carnegie Hall.

During its first years the Philadelphia Orchestra was exclusively a local organization, but under Stokowski's leadership it developed into an ensemble of international standards and it was acknowledged by leading critics to be the best orchestra in the USA. The time had come for such a valuable asset to be put on a more permanent economic basis. Until then, the ever increasing deficits had been met by a few hundred publicly devoted philanthropists, among them Henry Wheelen and Alexander van Rensselaer, who held leading positions in the management until their deaths in the 1920s and 1930s. This method of financing was very unsatisfactory, because all the money was spent every year, and more new guarantors had to be found. In this work the Women's Committees made a valuable contribution, but time and again financial crises threatened to stop or curtail the activity of the orchestra. The idea of a permanent interest-bearing fund had often been contemplated but rejected, since it was difficult to ask for money for yearly deficits and for a permanent fund at the same time. But in May, 1916, an anonymous benefactor offered to meet the deficits for the next five years, provided an endowment fund of 500,000 dollars was raised, and that Stokowski's leadership of the orchestra was guaranteed for these five years. The unknown benefactor was apparently Edward Bok, the editor of *Ladies' Home Journal*. Since intervening in the dispute between Stokowski and the manager about the rehearsal problem in 1913 he had taken a fervent interest in all the musical affairs, and become one of the most devoted friends of the Philadelphia Orchestra.

Everyone connected with the orchestra, including the many Women's Committees, at once set out to raise the huge amount, and promises of contributions soon surpassed 500,000 dollars. It was decided to prolong the campaign by two years, and it was given the title 'The Seven Year Endowment Fund'. At the close, in 1923, the capital had reached 788,400 dollars.

In the meantime another difficulty had appeared. In 1917 the USA entered the First World War. The orchestra found itself deprived of many of its musicians, and it was next to impossible to replace them. It was now quite obvious, too, that with fast-increasing costs, the endowment fund would not meet the annual deficits. Edward Bok suggested that on the twentieth anniversary of the orchestra another campaign should be launched to provide extra capital of 1,000,000 dollars. The campaign was exciting. Would they succeed in getting the money, or was the Philadelphia Orchestra to succumb? This last possibility was inconceivable. The orchestra was now Philadelphia's greatest cultural asset, and nobody wanted to lose it. Stokowski participated in the campaign. In the programme for the concert on 17 October the audience read the following message from him:

We are facing two possibilities today. Shall we continue the Orchestra as it is, or shall we reduce it? Let me tell you exactly what these two things mean, so that we will know exactly what we are leading to.

Suppose we reduce the Orchestra, which we must do if we do not raise this Endowment Fund. That means that your first men in the orchestra, the chiefs of each section, would not remain, because there are orchestras being formed all over the country now, and these orchestras will naturally take away the splendid first men that we have in our Orchestra.

You would naturally have to replace those men with second-class men. You would have to do this because the relation of supply and demand of orchestral players is tremendously intense. There is far more demand than there is supply of really great players. Having second-class men in those positions, you would have a second-class orchestra.

Then you could not allow such an orchestra to go outside of Philadelphia. You could not permit a second-class orchestra bearing the name of the city to travel to the West, to New York, Washington, Baltimore, Pittsburg, Toronto, and the various places where we play. It would be too much to our shame. We could not do it. So all the tours would have to be cut out.

In Philadelphia itself we should not be able to give concerts of the first quality, and you would naturally become dissatisfied. And after these second-rate concerts had gone on for one or two seasons, you would say to yourself, this must stop; we must have again an orchestra like what we used to have; we must have a first-class orchestra. You would begin all over again to rebuild your Orchestra once more, and do you realize how long it takes to build or rebuild an orchestra?

Do you realize that it took me personally all the seven years that I have been in Philadelphia to get three first-class artists for just one section of the Orchestra? And you have ninety-seven men in your Orchestra. That gives you just an idea of the work involved.

Will Philadelphia give its Orchestra its needed fund, avoid the calamity I have tried to outline and let the Orchestra go on as it is, and as the generations go on, and we go from this life, we will have the feeling that its influence will go on, that it will accumulate tradition, that it will go on maturing, and that it will become more and more beautiful.

In the next week's programme Stokowski described how things would be if the orchestra had its fund:

We would naturally not only continue the Orchestra as it is, but we would go on developing it every season to a higher quality, for in art there is no end, since as soon as you reach the horizon which you saw a year ago, new horizons appear and new fields of beauty. The end never comes, because you are never satisfied; that is the wonderful thing about art.

From the Endowment Fund Campaign. Broad Street, Philadelphia, 1919. *Photo: RCA*

Let us carry this fund through. We are not asking for a fund that is raised and spent. Not a penny of the million dollars is to be spent, every dollar is to be invested and put away. Twenty, thirty, forty years from now it will still be there, always working, bearing interest. And only this interest is to be spent. Is this not a good investment for yourself, your children, and your city? Upon this twentieth anniversary I plead for this birthday gift to the Orchestra.

On 31 October the object was far from accomplished, but the campaign committee was untiring in its efforts and ingenuity to convince people of the need to invest money in the orchestra, and the campaign was prolonged by one week. Finally, on 14 November the programme announced that the goal had been reached. The Philadelphia Orchestra was saved.

Since then finances have varied according to good and bad times. The cultivation of the arts has never been lucrative, and even if Stokowski with his unending struggle for new musical conquests performed the miracle of keeping up public interest for the entire period of his leadership, the Orchestra Association at best barely made receipts and expenditure balance. In the 1940s and 1950s a further rise in costs made the economic resources of the orchestra insufficient, and new appeals to the public were necessary. Most recently, and still rare in American musical life, the City Corporation of Philadelphia has displayed an understanding of the cultural importance of the orchestra by contributing a permanent annual subsidy. But the amount only just meets the deficit for a series of popular concerts at reduced prices.

To Stokowski music was not art for connoisseurs only. It was always of vital importance to him to bring the best possible music to as many people as possible, especially to young people. He explained this himself:

It is difficult for adults to take in new ideas and impressions contrary to those they have already received. They are formed for life. Children are more elastic, more receptive. In a few years they will form a new generation, a new audience.

In 1921 Stokowski arranged, in co-operation with the public schools of Philadelphia, the first orchestral concerts for children. No adults were admitted to these concerts except in company with one or more children. With an understanding of children's quite different tastes in music, he arranged very short programmes with much participation by the children. He was himself the fascinating narrator on these occasions.

In 1932 with the superintendent of the schools he planned radio broadcasts of modern music for children, believing that with their unprejudiced view of life they were the best audience for that kind of

Stokowski at work for the NBC Network. *Photo: RCA.*

music. Many people were opposed to the idea, among them the late Walter Damrosch, who declared that such experiments were criminal. But time has justified Stokowski. Modern music is not the worst basis for children's introduction to music; there is also the hope that the best modern music will get a position similar to that of older music.

The greatest difficulty about the children's concerts was not to attract youngsters, but to keep them away, as they grew too old. There was a clear demand for programmes for young people who had become too big for the children's concerts, but who were not yet mature enough for the adult concerts. In 1933 Stokowski decided to fill this gap and instituted the youth concerts, with age limits of thirteen and twenty-five years. By involving the youngsters in the work of programme-making, announcing, decorating, and ushering Stokowski achieved perhaps the most loyal audience he has ever had. He offered them only the best music, including first performances, so today that generation constitutes a great part of the faithful audience at the Philadelphia Orchestra concerts.

The invention of the radio and the gramophone had a revolutionary influence on the diffusion of music. Stokowski was one of the few who immediately understood the immense possibilities these inventions offered to spread music to bigger audiences than ever. In the autumn of 1929 the Philadelphia Orchestra made history with three radio broadcasts over fifty American stations and several European and Asian short-wave stations. The concerts came from a studio without an audience, and thanks to Stokowski's insight into the technical and scientific principles of the reproduction of music, plus a big staff of engineers from the National Broadcasting Company, a broadcast quality far ahead of its time was obtained.

Soon Stokowski developed doubts about the changes broadcast music might suffer as a result of technicians' manipulations at the control-board. Therefore he had his own control-panel installed in front of the podium in order to control the broadcast music himself. It is said that on one occasion the technicians took revenge by disconnecting the conductor's panel and taking over control of the broadcast. Whether the anecdote is true, I do not know, but it was only in the infancy of radio that the technicians frowned on the intrusion of the meddlesome conductor into a territory which they looked upon as exclusively theirs. Most technicians later learned to respect him.

Soon Stokowski abandoned his control panel, and the chief engineer was seated like a member of the orchestra in front of the conductor.

Stokowski and Dr Harvey Fletcher at the early stereo experiments in 1933. *Photo: Bell Laboratories.*

But for the next season a control room was installed in the Academy of Music, and for the first time the concerts were broadcast with the audience in the hall.

The culmination of this pioneering period came when Stokowski began to cooperate with the Bell Laboratories and Dr Harvey Fletcher about the reproduction and transmission of sound. Dr Fletcher suggested that they set up a complete laboratory in the basement of the Academy of Music and research into recording and transmission during rehearsal and concerts. Consent was given, and after a period of experiments the technical staff developed a method of broadcasting concerts with much less distortion than earlier, and also stereophonically, at that time called 'auditory perspective'. Entirely new amplifiers and loudspeakers were designed, and by using two independent circuits from the telephone company it became possible to give a concert at the Academy of Music while a specially invited audience was listening in Constitution Hall, Washington, via a control-panel and two loudspeakers. About this experiment, on 27 April, 1933, Stokowski said:

Not only was the music reproduced in Washington with all its initial expressive qualities, its tonal perspective, its varied sonorities, but the eloquence of the music was increased by new dynamic possibilities that wired transmission gives to music. The music of the future will undoubtedly take advantage of these new possibilities.

Stokowski participated in the history of the gramophone almost from its infancy to his death at the age of 95. He had the greatest influence among all musicians on the development of modern recording techniques. He made his first recordings with the Philadelphia Orchestra in Victor's studios in Camden on 22 October, 1917, but later, when electric recording made it possible, the recording sessions were transferred to the Academy of Music, the acoustics of this fine hall contributing greatly to their quality.

All Stokowski's shellac-recordings with the orchestra were made by RCA Victor. In 1943 the orchestra made an exclusive contract with Columbia, but the recordings with this company were not always equally successful. While the early Victor recordings are remembered for their balance and realism, the Columbia recordings have sometimes been marred by a certain flatness and uneven sound-quality. Consequently the recording sessions were transferred, first to the ballroom of the Broadwood Hotel, from about 1957 to 1960, and then to the large auditorium of the Town Hall. In this way a brighter sound and a longer reverberation period were achieved, but the beautiful acoustics of the Academy of Music were painfully lacking.

Recording session with the Philadelphia Orchestra in February 1960. *Photo: Columbia Records.*

In 1968 the orchestra returned to RCA Victor, and recording sessions to the stage of the Academy of Music. RCA Victor proudly announced that they would recreate the sound of the orchestra as the public knew it in the 1920s and 1930s. Unfortunately, they did not have the courage to produce the natural sound of the Academy, but substituted an ugly electro-acoustic sound, reinforced by help of the adjoining Ball Room. This only lasted for one season, and the next year RCA Victor also resorted to the auditorium of the Town Hall, so we have still not got back the original Philadelphia Orchestra sound.

Records have always been the hallmark of the orchestra and one of its chief sources of revenue. Even in Stokowski's day it was a top-seller of classical records, and after the invention of modern recording techniques sales have grown greater than ever.

Stokowski's repertoire was very wide, and far more varied than most conductors', and naturally a great part of it originated from his years with the Philadelphia Orchestra. A large portion of it consisted of the music of Bach. This is in the first place due to his initial career as an organist, and when his orchestral transcriptions began to appear in the early 1920s, Bach topped the repertoire with 9 per cent, as compared to 2 or 3 per cent with other American orchestras.

Stokowski in 1931. *Photo: Bettmann Archive, New York.*

Sometimes it has been stated that with its massive sound the Philadelphia Orchestra was unfit for the performance of the classical music. That is not true, nor is it true that Stokowski was a mediocre interpreter of the Viennese masters or that he was little interested in the music of this period. But it is true that neither Stokowski nor the Philadelphia Orchestra are satisfactorily documented on records in this kind of music. I think this is limited by the wide-spread tendency to identify them as specialists in narrowly defined fields of music.

Of course the many great 19th century composers occupy a large part of Stokowski's repertoire. Slavonic music was near to his heart with a high proportion of Tschaikovsky, Moussorgsky, and Rimsky-Korsakov. Among the German composers, Brahms and Wagner held leading positions. His interpretation of Brahms is impassioned, moving (called hectic by detractors), and devoid of German heaviness; and he has recreated Wagner's melodic symbolism and incandescent harmonies in a brilliant series of orchestral transcriptions of extracts from the great operas.

The most unanimous recognition of Stokowski has been reserved for his pioneering work in the field of twentieth century music; even his antagonists have admitted his superiority in the performance of this music. With the Philadelphia Orchestra he has given first American performances of numerous works by Sibelius, Rachmaninov, Stravinsky, De Falla, Shostakovitch, Schoenberg and many others.

Many of these composers became Stokowski's personal friends, among them Rachmaninov and Schoenberg. Through his communications with them he gained a thorough understanding of their character and musical ideas. This was a great inspiration, but he never became dependent on these relationships in his interpretation of their compositions. He always relied first of all on his own musical judgement.

Time has often justified his determination to play the music of composers who were in their prime when he set out on his own conducting career. Many of their pieces have already become classics, some even in their composer's lifetime, for example Stravinsky, others, for example Schoenberg, only after their death. However, he has only performed music in which he honestly believed. He had several friends among modern composers whose music he never performed because it is what he considered to be just 'paper-music'.

America's own composers had a devoted advocate in Stokowski. Many of those whose music he played formed the first independent American school of composers, for example Aaron Copland, Henry Cowell and Walter Piston. But it was not exactly the right diet for the ladies from the Main Line of Philadelphia to have Morton Gould's Chorale and Fugue in Jazz for the dessert at a concert in 1936. Even more outrageous was the performance in 1934 of William Dawson's Negro Folk Symphony at a time when serious black artists still had no place in most of America's musical life. But Stokowski did not care,

Rachmaninov conducting the Philadelphia Orchestra in his own work in the 1930s. *Photo: RCA.*

43

and those who did not agree were invited to leave before the controversial music was played.

In the opinion of some Stokowski was too generous in his advocacy of American music, since many works have had only a single hearing before sinking into oblivion. But to Stokowski, the first aim was to give the composers encouragement and experience, which only a performance of their music can give. Only Serge Koussevitzky has given a larger number of performances of American music:

1925 – 35: Boston 3% – Philadelphia 2%
1935 – 45: Boston 8% – Philadelphia 6%

The increasing percentages over the two decades can be ascribed to the growing maturity of American audiences, and this in turn to the great pioneering work of these far-seeing musicians.

Stokowski never one-sidedly favoured one period or composer. On the contrary, in his programme-making he endeavoured to create a better balance between the different periods than most conductors. In line with his view of music as a living art, he has always devoted a high proportion of the repertoire to contemporary music, while an average repertoire, even today is considerably biased to classic and romantic music. The percentages are roughly

Stokowski:		Average:	
Baroque	15	Baroque	10
Classic	15	Classic	30
Romantic	30	Romantic	40
Modern	40	Modern	20

The great importance Stokowski attached to contemporary music brought about a curious relationship with his audience. They dared, in time, to defy their musical teacher, and at length there developed quite a tug-of-war between conductor and audience about the range, nature and legitimacy of the contemporary music. Stokowski acknowledged the right of the audience to disapprove of the performed music, but he demanded equal respect for those who found pleasure in it. Therefore he requested the dissatisfied to give up their subscription to the many hundreds on the waiting list. Later he agreed, as a concession to conservative music-lovers, to place the dubious works at the end of the programme. This did not prevent several subscribers remaining in the auditorium for the start of the controversial music, some because they found Stokowski irresistible whatever he was doing, others just to get a substantial reason for their indignation. He had to remind them that the arrangement had been made to give them an opportunity to leave the concert before, and not during the performance of that kind of music.

Innumerable controversies took place during Stokowski's long leadership, but none of a serious nature. Opinions were not directed against him, but against the music, and the applause was always enthusiastic. Special indignation was aroused by the first performance of Arnold Schoenberg's *Five Pieces for Orchestra* in 1921. The Philadelphians hissed, the Washingtonians smiled, the New Yorkers laughed loudly, and the critics stated that the orchestra was degraded in performing such music. Today hardly anybody hisses at Schoenberg, but changes in taste occur slowly. As recently as the 1940-1 season there was again hissing when the first American performance of the same composer's Violin Concerto took place. After the first movement Stokowski interrupted the performance:

Shall we forever make the same foolish, narrowminded unsportsmanlike blunders, upon only hearing a thing once.' – Silence – 'Certainly Schoenberg is one of the greatest musicians alive today. His music is extremely difficult to understand. We do not ask you to like or dislike it, but to give it a fair chance. That is America.

The results of Stokowski's educational work did not fail to appear. He taught his audience to listen and to appreciate every kind of good music. This was fully demonstrated at his appearances in Philadelphia in 1960, and it was confirmed by Mrs S. Leonard Kent, a member of the Women's Committees, who told me:

Caricature from *Saturday Evening Post* 1929.

Stokowski has taught his audience complete silence, so that they may appreciate to the utmost the music they are hearing. Also throughout the city there is to-day a great appreciation of fine new music, due to the educational work he did when he was conductor of our orchestra. He was intrepid in educating his audience, and perhaps they were not in sympathy with all he played for them, but they soon learned to appreciate his programmes.

Stokowski regarded the performance of contemporary music as a personal obligation to the composers. About this he said:

One cause of distortion and unbalance of orchestral music is that composers do not have enough opportunity to hear their orchestral compositions and readjust those parts of the orchestration that are out of focus. This was true in the eighteenth and nineteenth centuries and is often equally true to-day. The ideal way to make this better is by periodically broadcasting the most outstanding new compositions of younger composers, so that all music lovers over the whole country can hear them and have an opportunity to follow these latest developments of their national art. These broadcasts should be recorded, and the records given to each composer. He will be able not only to hear the music when broadcast, but to study it constantly afterwards from the records.

Stokowski's insatiable need to experiment often made his concerts in Philadelphia front-page news in the daily press. The public always wondered what caprices they would be exposed to the next time they attended.

One day in 1926 they could read in the programme-book that in the future the Academy of Music would be shrouded in darkness during concerts. Stokowski gave the following explanation:

The conviction has been growing on me that orchestra and conductor should be unseen so that on the part of the listener more attention will go to the ear and less to the eye. The experiment of an invisible orchestra is for the moment impossible – so I am trying to reach a similar result by reducing the light to a minimum necessary for the orchestra and its conductor – Music is by its nature remote from the tangible and visible things of life. I am hoping to intensify its mystery and eloquence and beauty.

But the listeners missed seeing what took place on the stage, and after a couple of weeks it was announced that the experiment had been a failure, and that the lighting would be as before.

The same year the audience experienced a performance of Rimsky-Korsakov's *Scheherazade*, accompanied by coloured patterns produced by an instrument called a clavilux projected onto a big screen covering the orchestra. This instrument was invented by the Danish scientist Thomas Wilfrid, who controlled it with a kind of keyboard with which he could produce and blend different forms and colours in rhythmic patterns. It intrigued Stokowski so much that he also got the idea of staging Scriabin's *Prometheus* according to the original score, which contains a complete twelve-note part for colour-organ to be played together with the music in a gigantic work of total art. The response from the public was very cool, however, so these performances remained isolated events.

Very early Stokowski became interested in electronic instruments. He believed that in the future the tone will be produced electrically so that musicians would be released from the difficulties of intonation of our present instruments, and concentrate on the inner qualities of music. As a foretaste of such a golden age he occasionally introduced new electronic instruments to the audiences in Philadelphia, for example the thereminvox and martenot. In the Ondes Martenot, the Frenchman Maurice Martenot, the tone is produced by electric circuits and controlled from a keyboard. In 1930 the instrument was featured by the composer Dimitri Levidis, who played his new composition, *Poème Symphonique pour Solo d'Ondes Musicales et Orchestre.*

Experimental composers have often found a generous protector in Stokowski. The Mexican Julian Carrillo, who wrote some of his works on an octave divided up into 96 intervals, had his Concertino for Violin, Guitar, Cello, Piccolo, Harp, and Orchestra performed at a concert in 1927. The solo-instruments were constructed specially to produce the sixteenth-intervals, whereas the orchestra played with ordinary tuning. The same applied to a Quartertone Concerto for Piano and Orchestra written by the German-American Hans Barth and first performed in 1930.

In 1929 Stokowski was approached by the chairman of the League of Composers, Mrs Claire Reis, who wanted to know if he would produce some stage works for them. With his insatiable appetite for new activities he accepted the invitation, and on 25 April he conducted the first American stage version of Stravinsky's *Les Noces* at the Metropolitan Opera House, New York. This co-operation brought him new friends from the theatre world, particularly the stage designer Robert Edmund Jones, whose work he much appreciated.

The next year he won the consent of the Philadelphia Orchestra Board to present a double bill for the league, staging Schoenberg's *Die Glückliche Hand* with Ivan Ivantzoff and Stravinsky's *Le Sacre du Printemps* with Martha Graham as the principal dancer and Leonide Massine as choreographer. The success of these performances – three in Philadelphia and two in New York – led to another double bill the next season: Stravinsky's *Oedipus Rex* and Prokofiev's *Les Pas d'Acier.*

Stokowski enjoyed the challenge of these performances, and now wanted to present some operas of special merit for his Philadelphia audiences. His interest was greatly stimulated by a visit to Russia in 1929, where he acquired a copy of the original version of Moussorgsky's *Boris Godunov*. While preparing the next season with the Philadelphia Orchestra he experimented with presenting 'Boris' in concert version, complete with chorus and soloists, at the concerts on 29, 30 November and 2 December.

For his new interest in stage works, Stokowski depended on talented students or graduates for the Curtis Institute, founded on his advice in 1924 by the wife of Edward Bok. Here he met a talented young pianist called Sylvan Levin. This was just at the time he had brought home all the material for *Boris Godunov*. He showed the score to Levin, who immediately found errors in some of the orchestral parts. This decided the matter; Stokowski assigned him to select and train the singers for the performance, and to prepare the chorus for the final rehearsals.

The next season Stokowski wanted to do a real stage production again, and this time chose Alban Berg's *Wozzeck* for its American premiere. The preparations were almost as sensational as those for the memorable Mahler performances in 1916. More than one hundred rehearsals were necessary to realize the complicated score, and for six months everybody was busy in teamwork that also involved the entire Curtis Institute. In all this Sylvan Levin proved indispensable to Stokowski, who appointed him his assistant conductor. Halfway through preparations, Stokowski tested his audience with three excerpts from the opera at a concert on 15 November, 1930, but the stage premiere did not take place until 19 March, 1931. About this, the *Public Ledger* said:

Before one of the most brilliant audiences that ever assembled in Philadelphia, the American premiere of Alban Berg's 'Wozzeck' was given by the Philadelphia Orchestra at the *Metropolitan Opera House with Leopold Stokowski conducting his first appearance as an operatic conductor in this city.

The music which Berg has set to this sordid tale is highly original in most respects, and there is no questioning either the sincerity of the composer nor his ability as a composer and orchestrator.

The performance itself was splendid in every respect. The persons selected for the cast were admirably adapted in every way to the very difficult tasks imposed upon them, not only by the almost unsingable music, but also in the dramatic development of character.

*Only the name is identical with that of the New York opera. Actually, Philadelphia's Metropolitan Opera House was built on Broad Street in 1908 by Oscar Hammerstein in competition with the New York opera. After three unsuccessful seasons the building was turned to other use.

Of Mr Stokowski's conducting it need only be said that he evidently knew every note of the tremendously complicated score, and that he dominated the entire performance as absolutely as he does those of the Philadelphia Orchestra symphony concerts – which, after all, is the function of any conductor of a great ensemble.

Original programme with the cast of 'Wozzeck'.

The last comment reveals a shocking attitude, which apparently prevailed, taking the presence of Stokowski as a matter of course; an attitude dangerous for the future of the orchestra.

In 1932 there were no stage productions, but in 1933 Stokowski celebrated Easter by giving a complete concert performance of Wagner's *Parsifal*; on account of its length, the three acts were given separately on 31 March, 1 April, and 3 April.

Stokowski's presentation of operas and other stage works, and the discontinuation of the annual Metropolitan Opera guest performances at the Academy of Music tempted the Board of Directors to initiate a regular opera season, with performances of *Carmen, Der Rosenkavalier, Falstaff, The Marriage of Figaro*, and many others under the direction of Fritz Reiner and Alexander Smallens. In this way they hoped to make more money from their orchestra, but instead they acquired a disastrous deficit. There also arose a violent dispute between Stokowski, Arthur Judson, manager of the orchestra since 1915, and the board. Stokowski was against a regular opera season as he believed the orchestra should be primarily a symphonic ensemble, but Arthur Judson was in favour of opera performances, and was backed by some of the directors.

Stokowski threatened to resign, giving a shock to the whole musical world. What would the Philadelphia Orchestra be without Stokowski? For a generation he had been the most important person in Philadelphia, and this had also been acknowledged in 1922, when, after a tenure of ten years, he received the Edward Bok Award for services to the community. The Board of Directors had to face the fact that Stokowski's resignation might mean the end of the orchestra. Arthur Judson realised he had lost the argument and resigned. But no problems were solved, as is evident in the open letter Stokowski sent to the Board of Directors on 6 December, 1934:

I am writing this to you as an open letter, because I feel that I am speaking not only to the members of your board, but also to my colleagues in the orchestra, our audiences everywhere, our youth group, and our radio listeners. Last spring my contract with the Philadelphia Orchestra expired, and you offered me a new five-year contract. I thanked you, but asked for a year's leave of absence for study.

Later you asked me to help out by conducting for the three opening months of this season, and in that spirit I signed a contract to conduct all the concerts from October 1st to December 26th.

You asked me to conduct opera also, but I declined because I wished to have us produce certain operas in new ways, and there was not time to prepare the new methods. These new methods were partly begun by us in "Wozzeck", in Schoenberg's "Glückliche Hand", and Stravinsky's "Oedipus Rex", but since then important new possibilities have been developed.

In October you asked me if I would be willing to sign a further continuing contract to begin September, 1935, with no time-limit, either part free to terminate it at a given date each year. I expressed my willingness to do this, provided the work for the next season could be done according to certain principles I have stated in a letter to you. You accepted these principles in your letter of November 20th.

Meanwhile a new element had entered. Mr. Arthur Judson had resigned as manager on October 8th. From that time I have repeatedly stressed the importance of your selecting the new manager for the next season, so that he and I could develop the general conception of the next season's work, establish the principles upon which we could base our planning, and bring practical execution of the plans to a point where the executive director would be able to carry them on after I leave Philadelphia on December 31st for the other work that I have postponed last spring at your request.

You have not been able to engage an executive manager that is acceptable to you and me, and so I have not been able to make the essential arrangements for the next season and to relate opera and symphony concerts to each other as a whole unit for the coming season.

For this reason I cannot possibly assume the musical responsibility for the next season. From the legal standpoint we are both free, because you have not presented a written contract to me, and no contract has been signed by either of us for the next season.

Because of the loss of time which cannot be made up, I cannot accept the new contract you have offered me for the next season. I shall of course completely fulfill my present contract and leave my department in good order. I wish to pass over in silence and forget our deep lying differences of opinion and remember only the beauty and inspiration of the music we have made.

I write this with pain in my heart.
    Leopold Stokowski.

Stokowski's resignation aroused a storm of indignation. The Board of Directors received an indignant letter from the Committee of the Youth Concerts with more than three hundred signatures telling them on no account to let this resignation be carried out; and the applause after the concert on 8 December was demonstrative and rousing. Stokowski let it be known that he did not consider all ways out closed, and said to the audience:

I am hoping that some day we shall find a way to continue. But it looks impossible to me now.

There was uprising within the orchestra management. Inspired by a statement by Stokowski about 'new blood in the Board'. President Curtis Bok, Edward Bok's son, tried to get the entire Board to resign, leaving himself free to appoint a new board which would be more capable than the old one of understanding and negotiating with

From a youth concert in the Academy of Music. *Photo: Philadelphia Orchestra.*

Stokowski. However, he was voted down, and resigned from the Board.

A new president was elected, and the number of board members reduced from 24 to 15. Some of Stokowski's strongest antagonists disappeared, two representatives from the audience were added, and on 15 December the Board was ready to meet Stokowski on his own terms. Philadelphia-born Reginald Allen, an executive at RCA Victor, was suggested as the new manager, and before leaving for a study tour Stokowski promised to conduct the orchestra for three months of the 1935-6 season. But negotiations about a new contract were postponed till the next year. Stokowski left for the rest of the season, and when he returned late in 1935 everybody thought things were going to be all right; but it appeared that the reconciliation was only temporary. In the spring of 1936 Stokowski declared that he was definitively finished with the Philadelphia Orchestra, but agreed to conduct the beginning and end of the following seasons. This arrangement continued until 1941, when he conducted the orchestra for the last time, in a great performance of Bach's St Matthew Passion.

The separation between Leopold Stokowski and the Philadelphia Orchestra was one of the greatest tragedies in the recent history of music, but it was inevitable. Only a few open-minded Board members had ever followed Stokowski in his great visions, and during the great depression in the early 1930s the Board pursued a short-sighted policy of consolidation. Before the 1933-4 season there was a veritable war between the two parties, the Board saying that the next season's programmes would be devoted to acknowledged masterpieces of orchestral music, and Stokowski saying that for the coming season he planned both old and new music. Actually, Stokowski won the first round, and played as much modern music as usual. But in the long run he felt, with increasing bitterness, that nothing more was to be accomplished in Philadelphia. This view was confirmed as late as 1940, when he made the remarkable world premiere of Schoenberg's Violin Concerto. At the beginning of the season this work was not listed in the schedule, and on inquiries from the soloist, Louis Krasner, the manager answered that it was not to be performed because there was no money available for soloists. Stokowski admitted that there were problems, but assured him that the concerto would be performed. So it was, but afterwards it transpired that Stokowski had paid Krasner out of his own pocket.

However Stokowski's resignation was never caused by one single problem. It was the clash of two opposed minds. Stokowski's was Faustian, the Board's Philistine; and Stokowski was never a man to settle down to an endless routine with an orchestra where no new achievements could be made. This is to the eternal shame of Philadelphia, which has boasted of the orchestra as its most valuable cultural asset, but rarely given more than half-hearted support to the man who made it so.

Chapter 4

After the Rupture

Making concert tours, at home and abroad, is one way by which an orchestra can gain prestige. For the Philadelphia Orchestra this was not necessary. As early as the 1910s it had achieved a national reputation, which developed in the 1920s and 1930s into world-wide fame, especialy when the gramophone and radio secured it a new innumerable international audience. Nevertheless, it is the dream of every orchestra to go abroad and play to new audiences, to feel their response, and to discover new experiences. Even in Fritz Scheel's early years the Philadelphia Orchestra toured the eastern states, but it was not until Stokowski's tenure that plans for foreign tours were discussed. In 1927 a tour through Britain and France was contemplated, and in 1933 plans were made for a tour of Russia, but impassable economic obstacles, difficulties of transportation, and finally the war overthrew the plans. The European and the Russian tours were not realised until 1949 and 1958 respectively, and then it was too late to let Europe witness the unique co-operation between Stokowski and the Philadelphia Orchestra.

On the other hand, before his final retirement, Stokowski fulfilled a long-entertained wish for a transcontinental tour with the orchestra. Under the sponsorship of RCA Victor, the orchestra gave 36 concerts in 27 cities, and Stokowski was assisted by his first trumpet-player Saul Caston, and his friend Charles O'Connell. The tour was a great success. Gigantic audiences appeared, the artists were met with ear-splitting ovations and several of the concerts seemed as popular as

Saul Caston. *Photo: RCA.*

baseball games. 20,000 people heard the orchestra in Hollywood, the Tabernacle of the Salt Lake City was filled to the seams, and the final concert in Madison Square Garden, New York, was heard by an audience of many thousands.

For the future, however, the orchestra could not do without a permanent conductor. In full agreement with Stokowski, the Board of Directors engaged the promising young conductor of the Minneapolis Symphony Orchestra, Eugene Ormandy, for a period of three years, beginning with the 1936-7 season. As Stokowski still insisted on resigning, Ormandy was appointed musical director in 1938. From many sides, the young conductor was advised to stay in Minneapolis. To succeed Stokowski, it was said, would be artistic suicide for a young conductor; but encouraged by his friends Charles O'Connell and Arthur Judson he accepted the demanding post.

It was no easy task for Ormandy to succeed Stokowski. Certainly he was already a very fine musician, but not such a personality as Stokowski, partly because, like his idol, Toscanini, he had few interests other than music. The fact is that Stokowski built up the Philadelphia Orchestra not only on extraordinary musical talent, but also by virtue of great personal qualities, many-sided cultural interests, an uncanny instinct for talent, and a deep engagement in all problems associated with music and its performance. Without possessing similar qualities, Ormandy nevertheless asserted himself on a solely musical basis, and even if he has not been able to, nor wanted, to conquer new

Eugene Ormandy and the Philadelphia Orchestra. *Photo: Adrian Siegel.*

territory, he has at best maintained the inheritance he took over from his predecessor at the same high level.

As expected, at the accession of the new leader there was a decline in the number of subscribers for Philadelphia Orchestra concerts, particularly in New York, where many disappointed Stokowski adherents changed their subscriptions to other orchestras. But gradually a new audience was built up, mainly of people who came not to experience a certain conductor, but to hear ordinary music. Nor were they disappointed. Ormandy's programmes have usually been of a musical and pleasant character, with something for everybody, while Stokowski, with his daring first performances and experiments, sometimes challenged even his most faithful adherents, making them feel deprived of musical pleasure.

Another fear was that the sale of records, for many years one of the best sources of revenue, would decline appreciably at Ormandy's taking office. This did happen, and to maintain the receipts from recording until Ormandy had built up a new record repertoire, Charles O'Connell suggested engaging Toscanini as guest conductor for the 1941-2 season, with the intention of recording some of his repertoire.

This was carried out, and Toscanini appeared to be at his very best. Relations between him and Stokowski had always been of mutual distant respect and admiration, so he went to his job in Philadelphia with great pleasure and expectations – and was not disappointed. The orchestra carried out his intentions willingly and flexibly, and the audience was rewarded with some memorable performances of works by Debussy, Mendelssohn, Schubert and Tschaikovsky.

There is no doubt that Toscanini was also intent on demonstrating that he could make the orchestra sound even better than Stokowski had been able to, and the records were to prove it. But he could not, partly because he had never been willing to learn from Stokowski's unorthodox playing techniques and recording methods, so when he heard the test copies of his recordings with the orchestra, and found they did not match Stokowski's, he obstinately refused to approve any of them. As a result, the masters have remained for many years in RCA Victor's archives in Camden, and had it not been for Walter Toscanini's untiring work to preserve recordings of his father's performances, we should most likely never have heard any of them. The first result of this work was the release on LP of the recording of Schubert's C Major Symphony (Victor LM 2663). The performance is perhaps the best Toscanini ever rendered of this work – fine, well-balanced tempi, rhythmic exactness, and a superb sense of tone and form, and the recording quality is surprisingly good. To be sure, there is little of

Toscanini and the Philadelphia Orchestra, 1941. To the right, Charles O'Connell. *Photo: RCA.*

Stokowski's legendary balance of sound and harmony, but there is fine Toscanini, unmistakable Philadelphia Orchestra playing, and the excellent acoustics of the Academy of Music. In 1976 RCA finally released the rest of these historic recordings, and all the false myths about them were finally exorcised.

In 1941 the Philadelphia Orchestra had to dispense with Toscanini's help. But it did fairly well, and it will remain doing so as long as the legacy of Stokowski is managed with talent, and as long as there is a demand for great music in the city which fostered it.

Stokowski's separation from Philadelphia in 1941 was so complete that he did not return to the city until 1960 where for many years he had made his home. Nor did he conduct the orchestra, or even hear it until the summer of 1958. At that time the Philadelphia Orchestra and Stokowski happened to be in Russia simultaneously, the former as the first American orchestra to visit Russia, and the latter as the first American to conduct Russian orchestras. They met in Kiev, where Stokowski attended the last concert of the Philadelphia Orchestra. In this way the connection was resumed, and in the autumn of 1959 the sensational announcement was made that Stokowski would return to Philadelphia in February 1960 as guest during Ormandy's mid-winter vacation.

Stokowski and the Russian State Orchestra at the Moscow Conservatory in 1958. *Photo: Nordisk Pressefoto.*

Photo signed for the author in 1960

In musical circles in Philadelphia the event was anticipated with the greatest expectation. Nearly all tickets were sold half-a-year before, and on the day of the first concert there was a long queue of people all way round the Academy of Music, standing in the hope of unclaimed tickets. However every one stood in vain. Many also telephoned Mrs Hatfield, president of the Women's Committees, offering 50 dollars for a single ticket; but not one seat was to be procured.

The first programme was played at the concerts on 12, 13, and 15 February, and on 16 February it was repeated at the Carnegie Hall, New York. I was present at the three performances in Philadelphia and experienced the great moment when Stokowski mounted the podium and lifted his hands for the first work in the concert, the Overture to Mozart's *The Marriage of Figaro*. The old magic worked anew, and time was set back 19 years with the great performances he gave of De Falla's *El Amor Brujo*, Respighi's symphonic suite *The Pines of Rome*, and Shostakovitch's Fifth Symphony. The applause was rousing, and justly. It is unlikely that Stokowski ever achieved greater results in orchestral sound and musical interpretation. The daily press was unanimous about this, and *The Evening Bulletin* had the following comment on 13 February:

'Since he was last here, Mr Stokowski has acquired the advantages and benisons of age, rather than its infirmities. Still alert and springy of step, he radiates a new-found dignity, an intellectual grasp of the music which is informed with authority and serenity.'

During the concerts I had the opportunity to speak to members of the audiences, and learned of the deep and lasting affection they had for Stokowski over the years. Certainly there was great satisfaction with Ormandy as conductor, and he was highly esteemed for his musical skill, but recollections of the Stokowski era will never fade. This is also evident from the following statement in *The Sunday Bulletin*, made by one of the city's music-lovers:

Stokowski interviewed for radio at his guest appearances in Philadelphia in February 1960. *Photo: The Philadelphia Inquirer.*

It is to Philadelphia's undying shame to have let Leopold Stokowski slip through its fingers some twenty years ago. It does not matter now whose "fault" it was that he left the orchestra, and doubtless both Stokowski himself and the board must share in the blame. The simple fact remains that we are all the losers, and the whole world of music has suffered at the loss.

That Stokowski is one of the greatest conductors of all time is beyond question. Stokowski and the Philadelphia Orchestra were a combination unique in the history of art, one of the musical miracles which the world may never see again. He forged an instrument which, in spite of his absence, continues to play as he created it – with an unmatched standard of excellence, technical virtuosity and beauty of tone which perpetuates itself. This is perhaps the most astonishing tribute to his genius, and Mr Ormandy can be thanked for keeping "the world's greatest symphony orchestra" as the master who created it.

Stokowski made no secret of the fact that he looked forward to his engagement in Philadelphia, and at the end of the first concert the applause would not come to an end until he raised his hands as a sign that he wanted to say a few words. In these he gave expression to his feelings:

As I was saying about nineteen years ago' – laughter – 'it is a thrilling pleasure to make music with this magnificent orchestra and for such a sensitive public, listeners, as you are. I want to thank Mr Ormandy and the board of directors for inviting me to come back home to the Academy with the beautiful new ceiling' – laughter – 'it was always there, but it was so nice and dirty' – laughter – 'and to tell you it is an unbelievable thrill to make music with masters of their instruments so that every technical thing that the music demands they can give with ease, but much more than that, they can express the spirit and the soul and the deep message that is in great music. What a thrill.

To the orchestra itself Stokowski's guest appearances were also an event of great emotional significance. Many of the musicians, thirty-nine of whom were members of Stokowski's original Philadelphia Orchestra (and most new members had at one time played in orchestras under his leadership), confessed that they had played with tears in their eyes, and that they had never played better. The first flautist, William Kincaid, who had played in the orchestra since 1921, said in an interview:

I was afraid that after nineteen years things would not be the same. They were not. Stokowski was better than ever.

On 23 February Stokowski gave a concert for the Pension Foundation of the orchestra. The programme on this occasion

William Kincaid, first flute with the Philadelphia Orchestra 1921-60.
Photo: Philadelphia Orchestra.

consisted of three of his own Bach transcriptions, Brahms's C Minor Symphony, and The Love Music from Acts 2 and 3 of Wagner's *Tristan and Isolde,* also in Stokowski's transcription. I was invited to two of the rehearsals, and during them realised the degree to which orchestra and conductor were mutually inspired to sublime achievements. It was a unique experience, and I am much indebted to Mr Stokowski for that rare opportunity.

During the following years, Stokowski's appearances in Philadelphia developed into regular events and, for many among the audience, one of the climaxes of each season. On 7 February, 1962, he conducted the third Pension Foundation Concert of the season, and during the intermission he was presented with honorary citizenship of Philadelphia by city representative Fredric R. Mann. In his speech Mr Mann referred to Stokowski as 'the Prime Minister of Music.' 'Prime Minister,' replied Stokowski, 'I am glad I am only a musician.' And while the audience applauded, Mann quickly answered, 'Maestro, so is the whole world.'

In this way the old rupture between Stokowski and Philadelphia seemed to have been happily settled; but in 1966 new discord arose. At the beginning of the new season, the orchestra started a long strike for a better contract with the Association, and when it had been going on

Albert Wilhelmi. *Photos: courtesy the Leopold Stokowski Society.*

Rehearsal with the Philadelphia Orchestra, February 1963. *Photo: Adrian Siegel.*

for a whole month, it began to threaten the existence of the orchestra. A committee of citizens was set up to arrange a concert for the benefit of the orchestra's strike fund, and, to the annoyance of the Association, Stokowski agreed to conduct. An audience of 9,000 filled Convention Hall, and the orchestra was saved from dissolution. Of all Stokowski's triumphs with the Philadelphia Orchestra in the 1960's, none was more magnificent than his production in 1960 of Schoenberg's *Gurrelieder*. The soloists were Zambrana, Rankin, Petrak, Hoffman. Stokowski's mastery of large-scale choral works always produced great enthusiasm from audiences all round the world: it is curious that so few were recorded.

Chapter 5

Film work

It is beyond doubt that his attachment to the Philadelphia Orchestra was the greatest love-affair in Stokowski's life; but the final divorce in 1941 was inevitable. Since then the same question arose again and again: 'Was he ever happy after he left Philadelphia?'

No one but Stokowski could tell us, and he never did. Yet I think the answer is 'yes', because he was always the master of his own fate. In fact his career was not the result of coincidences, but of plans he had carefully made for his work, characteristically totally denying the reality of age and the decline of life. What therefore in 1935 appeared as an indignant protest against unwise management and improper interference with his artistic integrity may also partly have been his own work. At any rate, he took the opportunity to realise his plans to reduce his heavy concert schedule to spend a greater part of his time on travel, studies, and research into the reproduction of music on radio, gramophone and film.

The first sound film appeared at the end of the 1920s, and Stokowski soon saw the possibilities of bringing classical music to still more people. In 1936 he went to Hollywood at the invitation of Boris Morros, musical director of Paramount, who wanted him to appear in an episode of *The Big Broadcast of 1937*, in which he conducted Bach's chorale *Ein feste Burg* and the *Little G Minor Fugue*. Several critics referred to the lighting which played upon his face and hands, and then revealed in turn the different sections of the orchestra, and said that his appearance was theatrical. But they altogether missed his intention to show people who had never attended a concert how an orchestra and its conductor work.

Stokowski himself was quite aware of this sort of criticism when he wrote about his film debut:

I have often been called a showman, and I hope some day to merit that title, in the best sense of the word.

After this modest start to Stokowski's film career, there were rumours about a fantastic plan to make a film on the life of Richard Wagner, with Stokowski in the role of the composer and as conductor of all the music. This project came to nothing, however, perhaps being too ambitious and expensive. But the same year he was engaged by Universal to perform the music and a speaking part in Henry Koster's *A Hundred Men and a Girl*.

Mr Koster had been responsible for the debut of the young film-star, Deanna Durbin, in *Three Smart Girls*, and he was now looking for an idea to utilise Miss Durbin's singing talent. When he heard that Stokowski was in Hollywood, he suggested to his company that they approach him to ask him to undertake the conductor's role in a story with the young singer. The management was at first greatly opposed to the idea, partly because they did not believe the public would go and see a film with classical music, partly because they thought that Stokowski would never agree to act. Eventually Mr Koster won the argument, and Stokowski was invited to a conference. And no more was needed. Everybody was taken by his charm, he did not appear in the least difficult, and soon the contract was a reality.

Stokowski and Deanna Durbin in 'A Hundred Men and a Girl'. *Photo: Universal.*

In the early spring of 1937 Stokowski received and approved the manuscript, but insisted that the music recordings were made with the Philadelphia Orchestra using advanced multichannel techniques. So in April the entire technical staff turned up in Philadelphia, and under Stokowski's guidance set up nine sound-track machines to cover all the sections of the orchestra. Deanna Durbin was also there, but when it came to her parts, she appeared so scared that they had to give up her singing for the time being.

Later that year the scenes were shot in Hollywood. On the film Stokowski conducted a band of extras, but they were real musicians. He was not an actor, but he played his role as the conductor with both dignity and human warmth, and contributed greatly to a happy atmosphere in the studios. This set Deanna Durbin so much at ease that she was finally able to record her singing parts. They were made separately, and then mixed with the nine orchestral channels on a single soundtrack.

The musical arrangements were made by Fridrich Holländer, an emigré German musician, and consisted of the Fourth Movement of Tschaikovsky's Fifth Symphony, The Hungarian March from the *Damnation of Faust* by Berlioz, the Prelude to Act 3 of Wagner's *Lohengrin*, and the Hungarian Rhapsody no. 2 by Liszt, in addition to accompaniments for Miss Durbin's parts, *Alleluja* from Mozart's *Exultate Jubilate* and the *Drinking Song* from Verdi's *La Traviata*.

A Hundred Men and a Girl was not only a fascinating and charming musical story. Through its theme, it also gave an elementary understanding of the social importance of music, and many people who saw it were permanently enchanted, both by classical music and by Stokowski, among them the author of this book. I recently saw the film again on television, and wondered, after so many years, if my memory had played a trick on me. But the impact was tremendous, even greater than in my younger days.

But the greatest musical adventure on film was yet to come. It began at a restaurant in Beverly Hills. Stokowski was spending a period in his little summer residence there, and one day, when he was dining alone, Walt Disney entered the same restaurant and sat down close by. Disney was contemplating an animated film based on Dukas's *The Sorcerer's Apprentice*, and when he saw Stokowski, he suggested that they dine together. Stokowski accepted, and when Disney revealed his new idea to him, it appeared what kindred spirits they were. Disney would like to have Stokowski conduct the music for him, and Stokowski in turn had long dreamed about making a film with Disney, integrating the visual and aural arts.

They agreed to keep in touch, and at the beginning of 1939 the recording of *The Sorcerer's Apprentice* was made. But they did not stop

Mickey Mouse as 'The Sorcerer's Apprentice'. *Photo: Disney Productions.*

there. Stokowski had become so intrigued with the project that he persuaded Disney to change it into a full-length picture based on a concert of classical masterworks. This is how the great film *Fantasia* came into being.

In *Fantasia* music was for the first time in the history of motion pictures the primary art; the pictures had the secondary function of interpreting its contents through colour, form and movement. To maintain the illusion of a concert, titles on the screen were entirely abandoned; instead the well-known American music-critic and commentator Deems Taylor, introduced the works in his instructive and popular manner.

Sweatbox session from the production of 'Fantasia'. The participants are Disney, Deems Taylor, and Stokowski. *Photo: Disney Productions.*

Since the appearance of the film there has often been lively discussion on the suitability of illustrating classical music. The objections seem to come from those who think that they have a monopoly in high-class music; and whether you know the music or not, you cannot avoid being captured by the imagination and sparkling humour of Disney's musical stories. Besides, like Stokowski's other musical-films, *Fantasia* has basic appeal to people only distantly related to the art of music, and that alone is enough justification for its existence.

Nothing was spared to make *Fantasia* a perfect film. First of all, Disney held a long series of meetings with all his staff-directors, together with Stokowski and Deems Taylor, listening to records of every conceivable masterwork to decide the music for the film. After several weeks they decided upon seven works, besides the one that had been the cause of it all. Now the real work could begin.

The music was divided up into seven sequences, and each sequence got a sub-director, responsible for production. Co-operation was achieved through regular weekly staff-meetings ('sweatbox-sessions'), at which new ideas and suggestions were exchanged. They were invaluable for intimate correlation of music and pictures. Stokowski had a remarkable understanding of this problem, and it is to his credit that the small musical adaptations necessary for the film were both justifiable and acceptable.

In the spring of 1939 all the music was recorded by Stokowski and the Philadelphia Orchestra in the Academy of Music, and then the work with the film began to speed up. Until that time, the artists had only had previous recordings to depend on; but now they had the original music to work from.

RCA Victor was in charge of the recording, and the new methods applied were far ahead of contemporary practice. Instead of recording on wax-matrices, like the masters of gramophone records, it was decided to record the music on sound-film. Nine sound-cameras were used, one for overall blend of orchestral sound, and eight for close-ups of important details from the eight instrumental groups into which the orchestra had been divided. In this way the music was picked up by thirty-three single microphones distributed on eight channels, reduced to five or three sound-tracks on the final film, depending on the sound-system in the cinema.

By the new recording methods distortion of the music was reduced, and the orchestra was heard with a brilliance and depth never before experienced, particularly in cinemas with loudspeakers all round the auditorium. Evidence of the advanced techniques are the records with the music from the film made in the 1950s after the invention of the long-playing record. Of course, they cannot match present-day high fidelity or stereophony, and the instruments have a tendency to 'wander' from one side to the other. But there is a lot of tonal

Stokowski mounting the dummy podium for the sequences of 'Fantasia' where he appears on the screen. *Photo: Disney Productions.*

perspective in them, and they are still miracles of orchestral sound and recording technique (Disneyland (S) WDL 4101 A-C).

In his book *Music for All of Us* Stokowski delights in some of the new possibilities the recording of *Fantasia* offered in orchestral balance:

Recording music for motion pictures can be of such high quality that certain important features of the music only dimly heard or even inaudible in a concert hall can be brought out with the full eloquence and richness of tone which is their true nature. For example, in the thunderstorm part of Beethoven's Pastoral Symphony are certain intense phrases for bassoon, clarinet, and oboe which have an urgent agitated expression. These phrases are almost inaudible in the concert hall because the rest of the orchestra is playing loudly and furiously. In 'Fantasia' we were able to give these important passages their true value by making the melodic lines for bassoon, clarinet and oboe soar above the rest of the orchestra without emasculating the rushing stormy music of all the string instruments. Because of the inherent lack of balance in the orchestration, I have never before heard these phrases given their due prominence and tonal importance.'

The programme for the music of *Fantasia* was the result of happy teamwork, but it was Stokowski's audacity that led to including such difficult music as that of Bach and Stravinsky:

J. S. Bach: Toccata and Fugue in D Minor
(Sequence director: Samuel Armstrong)
Peter Tschaikovsky: Selections from 'The Nutcracker'
(Sequence director: Samuel Armstrong)
Paul Dukas: 'The Sorcerer's Apprentice'
(Sequence director: James Algar)
Igor Stravinsky: 'Le Sacre du Printemps'
(Sequence directors: Bill Roberts and Paul Satterfield)
Ludwig van Beethoven: Symphony no. 6 in F Major
(Sequence director: Hamilton Luske)
Amilcare Ponchielli: 'Dance of the Hours' from 'La Gioconda'
(Sequence director: T. Hee)
Modeste Moussorgsky: 'A Night on the Bare Mountain'
Franz Schubert: 'Ave Maria'
(Sequence director: Wilfred Jackson)
Production supervisor: Ben Sharpsteen

The greatest difficulty was presented by Bach's Toccata and Fugue with its abstract character. In the Toccata, Disney gave us glimpses of the different sections of the orchestra, and the elegant figure of the conductor in fantastic hues and angles, whereas the Fugue was illustrated by quasi abstract forms and beautiful colours in motion.

Stravinsky was the only living composer whose music had been chosen for *Fantasia*, and he took great interest in the way his score was

'A Night on the Bare Mountain'. *Photo: Disney Productions.*

used. Originally *Le Sacre du Printemps* described the consecration of spring in pagan Russia through the adoration of the earth and the sacrificing of a virgin to nature. But Stravinsky had no objection when Disney chose to illustrate it with a series of episodes from the evolution of the earth. The final Sacrificial Dance was omitted and replaced by the theme of the Introduction.

Acting as the Sorcerer's Apprentice was Mickey Mouse. It was a stroke of genius, and Disney's story was quite in agreement with both Goethe's poem and Dukas's congenial music.

Less proper, but absolutely irresistible, was the sparkling imagination Disney displayed in Beethoven's Pastoral Symphony and in the ballet of the animals which accompanied Ponchielli's 'Dance of the Hours'. For the film coupling *A Night on the Bare Mountain* and *Ave Maria*, Disney carried us to a desolate mountain in southern Russia, where the Evil One was the central figure of a fierce witches' sabbath, which ended abruptly at daybreak. The evil powers were called down, the Evil One yielded to the light of day, and a long row of pilgrims bearing torches appeared in the distance. As the procession advanced, nature changed into a lofty cathedral, and the darkness of the night yielded to the dazzling sun. Stokowski used his own excellent version of *A Night on the Bare Mountain*, and its last part led in a remarkable way direct into Schubert's *Ave Maria*. Together they gave a grandiose vision of the fight between the light and the darkness, and the triumph of good over evil.

Fantasia became a great success and was shown to filled cinemas in the USA for more than two years, and again later when the film was re-processed for stereophony. In Europe, however, it had a mixed reception. In many countries it was the object of severe criticism, and was often received with indifference. This was to some extent due to European distrust of things American.

Fantasia won many prizes for its producers, and Stokowski also received his due. In 1942 he received a special award from the Academy of Motion Picture Arts and Sciences for his contribution to the development of music in film.

The next time Stokowski appeared on the screen was in *Carnegie Hall*, a motion picture made by Federal Films after the fiftieth anniversary of the opening of the famous concert hall. Around a slight plot we heard and saw glimpses of many of the artists who have appeared there. Both with the Philadelphia Orchestra and later with a series of New York orchestras Stokowski contributed immensely to the history of the Carnegie Hall. In the film he conducted the New York Philharmonic Orchestra in the Second Movement of Tschaikovsky's Fifth Symphony. His hair had become a little whiter and his features older since *Fantasia*, but he was the same youthful, sensitive artist, and – believe it or not – the Philharmonic sounded much better under his powerful hands.

Stokowski's belief in the future of film as an art was fervent. He thought that when the time is right for it to take its place among the arts, music will play an important part of it.

Stokowski conducting the New York Philharmonic in the Federal Films production 'Carnegie Hall' in 1946. *Photo: Keystone Press.*

Chapter 6

All American
Youth Orchestra

When Stokowski finally left the Philadelphia Orchestra at 59, several detractors triumphantly declared that his career was over. This was merely wishful thinking, based on the assumption that his career had been the result of publicity. However, a career in serious music cannot possibly be based on mere publicity. The demands on an artist nowadays, when the performance of music has been brought to a perfection unknown in past centuries, are far too great. Stokowski's contributions to the musical life of our century are so significant that nobody can deny them without at the same time denying the leading role the USA has had in the development of the modern symphony orchestra and in the performance of orchestral music.

Up to the Second World War this leadership depended to a great extent on buying up all the best musicians from Europe, and much less on the use of national talent. Today things are quite different. America now educates a great number of skilled musicians, and it is no longer an exception to find American born and trained conductors, among them Leonard Bernstein, Thor M. Johnson and Saul Caston. This turn of the tide is due to devoted Americans who realized that dependence on Europe is both unworthy and unnecessary. Stokowski was one of these Americans.

In the early 1920s he was the guiding spirit in the foundation of the famous Curtis Institute music school in Philadelphia. During its first years he led its student orchestra, and by using members of the Philadelphia Orchestra as teachers, Stokowski had a great influence on the education of American musicians. Whenever there was an opportunity, both at concerts and recordings, Stokowski made use of the Curtis Institute Chorus, and now and then some of the vocal students got their debuts as soloists. This is how, for instance, Rose Bampton started her remarkable career as an opera singer, first in Manuel de Falla's *El Amor Brujo*, and later as the Wood Dove in Schoenberg's *Gurrelieder*.

However, the fight for economic equality of music with other social activities has always been difficult. As late as 1956 Stokowski made an urgent appeal to the American public to give music better conditions. Otherwise the nation would face a serious shortage of first-class musicians for keeping up musical life. Young talents would prefer more profitable and safe professions. In this way their natural ability would be lost to the nation, and Stokowski was of the opinion that there was a great wealth of national musical talent. This conviction led to his work with the All American Youth Orchestra 1940-1.

The origin of this orchestra goes back to 1937, when Stokowski expressed a wish to organise a youth orchestra to demonstrate the results which could be achieved with national youth talent, but the plans did not materialise until 1940. At that time Germany and Italy seemed to be winning the war, and the USA was trying to fight German influence and propaganda in South America by making a political and cultural offensive there. Stokowski's youth orchestra would fit perfectly into such a plan, but the State Department had not a penny for such purposes. So Stokowski's personal representative went to New York to secure the financial support of RCA Victor, who were quite enthusiastic about the project, and promised to sponsor a South American tour with the orchestra, and make records from it.

The work started with the recruiting of the players. Out of 15,000 young students from music-schools all over the country 560 were selected. Stokowski listened personally to them, and finally selected 90 players for his youth orchestra. All the states were represented, and there were no restrictions of race or colour. The only restrictions were that the players had to be between 15 and 25. Rehearsals took place in Atlantic City, which made available the Convention Hall and hotel rooms for the members of the orchestra. After three weeks of rehearsals the debut of the All American Youth Orchestra took place in Convention Hall on 21 July, and it got very fine reviews. One critic wrote, 'The orchestra has a unanimity and precision hardly surpassed by the foremost organizations. There is vitality and enthusiasm, flexibility and responsiveness.'

Now the orchestra was ready to start on its South American tour, accompanied by eight veteran members of the Philadelphia Orchestra, among them first bassoonist Sol Schoenbach, harpist Edna Phillips, and solo-trumpet and co-conductor Saul Caston, who promised Stokowski to support the young players on the tour. In the meantime, however, a serious problem had arisen. RCA suddenly backed out of the project, because its president, David Sarnoff, decided to send Toscanini and the NBC Symphony Orchestra to South America instead of Stokowski. This went quite against the idea of a tour for American culture, as Toscanini was Italian and many of the musicians foreigners. The State Department was furious, but Stokowski had too much respect for Toscanini to fight him, so he got Columbia Records interested in the tour instead. They seized the opportunity to get Stokowski on their artistes list, and underwrote part of the tour and the recordings with the orchestra.

During the summer of 1940 Stokowski toured more than twenty cities in Brazil, Uraguay and Argentina, and it was a triumph. A large amount of contemporary music was played, expecially American music, and Stokowski often insisted on playing contemporary composers when they came to a community where people knew little music. He said, 'When they have never been at a concert before, then let us play Shostakovitch's Fifth Symphony. They will accept this as just as valid as something older.'

After the South American trip Stokowski gave a final concert with the Youth Orchestra in the Carnegie Hall, and he received official thanks for the good-will he had created for USA with his unusual venture. The young players also felt that the tour had given them a lot of experience, and the following summer it was decided to re-form the orchestra. They now made an extensive tour of Canada and the western part of USA, stopping in Los Angeles for some final recording sessions.

At the end of the year USA entered the Second World War, and many young musicians were called up. The orchestra could not continue. When the war was over, many of the young people returned to fill important positions in the leading symphony orchestras. Among them, for instance, James Chambers, solo French horn of the New York Philharmonic, Ralph Gomberg, solo oboe of the Boston Symphony Orchestra, Manuel Zegler, solo bassoon of the New York Philharmonic, and many others. They have all testified how much their work with Stokowski meant to them in their future careers. For Stokowski himself, the All American Youth Orchestra was also a great personal experience, and his pleasure at meeting some of his players again was not less than theirs:

Everywhere I go in the United States to conduct orchestras, I find players who were in one of the two Youth Orchestras. They usually are the first players of their sections, and in each instance it is a great pleasure to both of us to work together again.

Chapter 7

NBC Symphony Orchestra

An integral part of Stokowski's plans for the future involved research into broadcasting music, culminating in a few exclusive radio concerts each year. It fitted well with these plans when he was asked by the National Broadcasting Company to conduct the NBC Symphony Orchestra for part of its season at Radio City, New York. The engagement began with the 1941-2 season since its conductor, Arturo Toscanini, had left abruptly – and stayed away for a whole year – after one of the many explosions which were so characteristic of him. It was most rewarding for the musicians to play under a man like Stokowski, who understood radio better than anybody.

The NBC Symphony Orchestra had been established in 1937 to secure Toscanini's return to the musical life of America after he left the New York Philharmonic Orchestra in 1936. He had promised the Philharmonic Society that he would never enter into competition with it and in fact he did not. The orchestra was founded exclusively for broadcasting, and Studio 8H in Radio City only accommodated a few hundred listeners with special admission tickets.

The NBC Symphony Orchestra was no ordinary radio orchestra, but had been recruited from the best available musicians, in many cases bought regardless of financial considerations from the leading orchestras of the country. Among former Philadelphia Orchestra players were Mischa Mischakoff (concert master), Frank Miller (cello), Robert Bloom (oboe), and Arthur Berv (French horn). In many respects, the orchestra could easily compare with the best American orchestras, and its concerts under Toscanini were matchless in musical planning; but for radio broadcasts his repertoire was limited, mainly comprising Haydn, Mozart, Beethoven, Brahms, Wagner, Rossini and Verdi, besides a few Italian composers whose works are not much played outside Italy. The majority of contemporary composers he scorned, and of American composers he said, 'When I first came to America, composers had no technique. Now they have technique, but no heart.' And about the future of American music, 'There will be composers in time.'

But there would never be any future for the composers of America if all conductors ignored contemporary music as Toscanini did. Therefore it was necessary to use other conductors, and the engagement of Stokowski as co-conductor secured a successor for the unpredictable and ailing Toscanini, and provided for a comprehensive repertoire with the best possible performances, especially of the neglected pre-classical and modern music. This division of the repertoire was an implicit agreement between the two conductors, but it did not prevent Toscanini from snatching from Stokowski the performance of a contemporary work, if he discovered it was of current interest. This was the case, for instance, with Shostakovitch's Seventh Symphony, the 'Leningrad Symphony', composed in the critical days of the siege of Leningrad 1941-2.

Stokowski had already prepared a performance of the work and made arrangements for recording, when Toscanini suddenly realized its propaganda possiblities and insisted on the right of the first American performance. A polite correspondence was exchanged

The NBC Symphony Orchestra in Studio 8H, Radio City, New York. *Photo: RCA*

between the two conductors. Stokowski pointed out that he had played Shostakovitch's music since the late 1920s, and given most of his symphonies their first American performance; but Toscanini replied that for twenty years he had fought Fascism and Nazism, so he too had a background for performing the work. In addition, the conductor of the Boston Symphony Orchestra, Serge Koussevitzky, entered the scene; with his numerous premieres and commissions of modern music he claimed a performance of the work. At last a compromise was agreed; Toscanini got the first broadcast, Koussevitzky the first public performance, and Stokowski the first recording of the work. However, Stokowski never got any pleasure out of this arrangement. The broadcast of the symphony took place on 19 July, 1942. But only three days later a total ban on recordings with organised musicians was enforced on account of disagreements between the record companies and the musicians' union. When the ban was finally lifted more than two years later, interest in the work was gone, and the recording came to nothing.

However, Stokowski did perform the Leningrad Symphony with the NBC Symphony Orchestra, at a concert on 13 December, 1942. It is interesting to compare this with the one Toscanini gave, because they demonstrate the immense differences between the two conductors' understanding of orchestral sound and musical phrasing. In the First and Fourth Movements, Stokowski takes much care with harmonic balance and tonal colour, while Toscanini reveals a childish delight in stressing the monotonous repetitions of the March Theme and the massive Coda; but both reach exciting climaxes. The Scherzo and the Adagio contain some of the most substantial material of the symphony, and here it is obvious that Stokowski's technique is far superior to Toscanini's. Especially where the high strings move in large intervals, in the first theme of the Adagio, for Toscanini the music disintegrates, whereas with Stokowski's technique it is moulded into a powerful recitative of utmost beauty.

Of course, Stokowski gave many other remarkable performances of contemporary music with the NBC Symphony Orchestra; for example Vaughan Williams's Fourth Symphony, Prokofiev's *Alexander Nevsky* Cantata, and the premiere of George Antheil's Fourth Symphony. He also had a very fine rapport with members of the orchestra, who enjoyed the feeling of being respected as individual artistes, not exposed to the humiliating invectives they were accustomed to with Toscanini.

During the entire 1941-2 season Toscanini stayed away from all the regular concerts, after a big controversy with the management. But he would sometimes turn up at rehearsals; and when he saw Stokowski's seating of the orchestra, he exploded and rushed over to an NBC

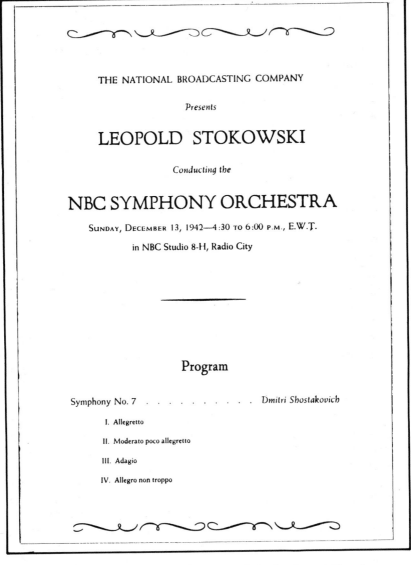

THE NATIONAL BROADCASTING COMPANY

Presents

LEOPOLD STOKOWSKI

Conducting the

NBC SYMPHONY ORCHESTRA

Sunday, December 13, 1942—4:30 to 6:00 p.m., E.W.T.

in NBC Studio 8-H, Radio City

Program

Symphony No. 7 . . . . *Dmitri Shostakovich*

    I. Allegretto

    II. Moderato poco allegretto

    III. Adagio

    IV. Allegro non troppo

Original programme from the performance of the Leningrad Symphony.

executive, shouting furiously, 'He is ruining my orchestra.' However, his ears told him something different, and from the beginning of the 1942-3 season he took up his work again. But he never understood Stokowski's unorthodox methods, and what he did not understand he hated. Although there was no argument between them, that decided the matter.

After two seasons with the NBC Orchestra Stokowski received no offer of a new contract. This fact is incredible, since several American musical organisations would have been delighted to benefit from his work. It was claimed that he played too much American music; but this cannot be the true explanation. It was a clear agreement that Stokowski was to take care of modern music; and besides, his programmes never contained more than one-third modern music, whereas the remainder consisted of works from the standard repertoire. Charles O'Connell, who had an intimate knowledge of the affair, asserts that the reason was to be found in the Toscanini group's fear of Stokowski as a rival. Stokowski did not deny this, but he rarely entered into controversies. He confined himself to a diplomatic statement, the long and short of which was:

'It is the old trying to stop the new – Europe trying to dominate America.'

At the beginning of 1954 Toscanini retired after his famous last radio broadcast, during which it became obvious to all that he could not conduct the NBC Symphony Orchestra any longer. RCA immediately dismissed the orchestra, and it officially ceased to exist. In this way a unique opportunity was lost to secure Stokowski, who was a free-lance at that time, for the musical life of New York.

However, the NBC Orchestra in fact continued to exist under the name of 'Symphony of the Air'. The musicians refused to disband, and continued on a private, co-operative basis. But this did not enable them to offer whole regular seasons, and the host of guest conductors could not maintain it among the foremost orchestras in America. A frequent guest was Stokowski, who utilised the orchestra for his mid-season concerts in New York, and for various recording duties during his period in Houston in the years 1955-61.

In the summer of 1960 he also led its first European tour, which was also his first visit to Europe with an American orchestra. The tour was sponsored by the American International Foundation, and the orchestra gave concerts in Italy, France, Holland, Belgium, Spain and Portugal. A climax was reached during the visit to Toscanini's native town, Parma, where the musicians paid a musical tribute to their late conductor. In another respect too the European tour turned out as a homage to Toscanini; the revenue from the concerts was given to a Toscanini Memorial Foundation for the education of young Italians, and for the benefit of the boys' towns in Italy.

In this period the famous Carnegie Hall in New York was marked down for demolition in connection with the erection of the new Philharmonic Hall as a home for the New York Philharmonic Orchestra. However, public opinion soon spoke out in favour of preservation of the hall. One of the most fiery advocates of the old hall was Stokowski, who found it incredible that a large and rich city like New York could not maintain more than one major concert hall. Finally it was decided to set up a committee to look into the problem, and when the financial questions had been solved, Carnegie Hall was restored to its former glories. A scheme was set up to make Symphony of the Air permanently resident in the building, and there was also to be a comprehensive programme of visiting ensembles and artistes. Stokowski was named the new permanent conductor of Symphony of the Air, but unfortunately this project came to nothing. Apparently Stokowski did not find its future adequately secured, and the orchestra gradually disappeared. Circumstances put an end to one of the great orchestras of America, because it failed to secure the only man who could have given it a glorious future.

Carnegie Hall, New York. *Photo: Carnegie Hall Corporation.*

Chapter 8

New York City Symphony Orchestra

Although Stokowski dedicated much of his time in the 1940s to study, it was by no means his intention to retire from public appearance. Without committing himself permanently, he found opportunity each winter to give public concerts, in 1944 with a new orchestra, the New York City Symphony Orchestra.

The origin of this orchestra goes back as far as 1925, when the New York City Center of Music and Drama was built. On a private basis performances of symphonic and dramatic music were given, yet only in the first year with an orchestra that belonged to the Center. In 1943 the building was bought by the City Corporation of New York. The Mayor, Fiorello La Guardia, made serious and determined efforts to raise the cultural prestige of his city, and at his request Stokowski formed the New York City Symphony Orchestra with the object, as he expressed it himself in *The New York Times Magazine* on 5 March, 1944, 'to make available the best music for the most people at the least cost'.

Because it was wartime, it was difficult to build a new orchestra from scratch. Of course, there were many unemployed musicians, but very few first class players. Many of the best younger musicians had been called up, and were playing in the bands of the army or the navy. However Stokowski found a rich reserve among women players, and succeeded in a short time in creating an orchestra that could match many of the best American orchestras, even if the brass section was not of the high quality we were accustomed to with Stokowski.

On 6 March the orchestra had its debut, and several critics welcomed it as among the best ensembles to be heard in New York. It filled a large gap in the musical life of the city, which was largely based on subscription, excluding many people with a genuine demand for music, especially younger people. For the first season, however, there was not sufficient time to plan more than six concerts. But it was Stokowski's intention to increase the number of concerts in the next season, and when the war was over, he envisaged a new city centre building with a larger auditorium and performances of opera and ballet, students' concerts and recitals of chamber music; in other words, a civic centre, which he has described vividly in his book, *Music for All of Us*.

The New York City Center project was a real challenge for Stokowski in his search for new fields of activity. The outrageous

Stokowski rehearsing his players of the New York City Symphony Orchestra in March 1944.

NBC affair had made a considerable rift in his plans, and that explains to some extent the readiness and enthusiasm with which he accepted La Guardia's invitation. But there was also much idealism in the project, and Stokowski offered his services on condition that he was not to receive anything in return because:

'I wish to make this work an ideal expression of the art of music unhampered by any professional considerations.'

But music cannot exist, even less survive, on idealism alone. The New York City Center had a very small budget to operate on, so Stokowski had to contribute generously out of his own pocket to create an interesting 1944-5 season, with new works and first-class soloists. Nor did he get the support he had expected from La Guardia, who did not understand why they could not just reduce the orchestra to make the budget balance. Stokowski realised that he could not go on under these circumstances, so in the middle of the next season he resigned. The young Leonard Bernstein, who had recently made his debut with the New York Philharmonic as substitute for Bruno Walter, agreed to take responsibility for the rest of the year, and continued for three seasons, without any salary. Then the orchestra died. New York was not yet big enough for a second full-time orchestra beside the Philharmonic.

Chapter 9

Hollywood Bowl
Symphony Orchestra

One year before he brought to an end his engagement with the New York City Symphony Orchestra Stokowski accepted a three-year contract as musical director for the Hollywood Bowl summer festivals, to be effective from the 1945 season. He might easily have fulfilled both assignments, but disappointed with the meagre results of his idealistic work in New York he decided that from now he would both make money and music at the same time, and still have time for travel and enjoyment.

Hollywood Bowl is the world's largest amphitheatre, with a seating capacity of 20,000 people. It is situated in one of the beautiful valleys in the mountains south of Hollywood. From a huge concert platform with room for a full-scale symphony orchestra, choir and soloists the music is reflected from the famous shell to the lower seats in the valley, as well as to the upper seats farther up the mountain slopes. Nature and the almost miraculous acoustic and climatic conditions make the music a grandiose and poetic experience.

The possibilities for music here were seen as early as 1919. After the acquisition of the area a committee of music-lovers in Los Angeles founded The Hollywood Bowl Association in 1922, and under the management of the 'Symphonies under the Stars' organisation there have been for many years eight-week summer seasons with performances of classical and popular music. Lacking a permanent orchestra, the organisation has mainly made use of the orchestras of San Francisco and Los Angeles, under their respective conductors.

With the accession of Stokowski as musical-director, it was almost inevitable that something new would happen. Hollywood Bowl was going to have its own orchestra, and Stokowski knew where to get it from. In the first place he engaged some of the members of the Los Angeles Orchestra, whom he knew from earlier appearances. He also knew that for a decade the film industry in Hollywood had attracted hundreds of the best musicians in America and Europe, not least by high salaries, but also with working conditions which were far better

Los Angeles, 1945. *Photo: Otto Rotschild.*

than in the big symphony organisations. So from the ranks of these artists he was able to pick some of the best players for important positions in the orchestra. Finally he arranged auditions for young musicians from California, and chose eight or ten gifted young players, among them a sixteen-year old violinist and a nineteen-year old flautist.

Another new feature of the seasons was that Stokowski invited some of the resident composers to write fanfares to be played backstage each Tuesday night five minutes before the beginning of the programme. Among the contributors were Igor Stravinsky, Arnold Schoenberg, Robert Dolan, Jerome Kern, George Antheil and many others. Schoenberg's contribution to the festivities was a sketch built on three motifs from the third part of *Gurrelieder*, scored for brass instruments.

On 10 July Stokowski inaugurated his new orchestra in the presence of an audience of 14,000 with the following programme:

J. S. Bach/Stokowski..........................Passacaglia and Fugue in C Minor
Richard Wagner/Stokowski................Love Music from Act 2 and 3 of
Tristan and Isolde
Peter Tschaikovsky ....Symphony no. 6 in B Minor

Not advanced, but a typical Stokowski programme, and a dignified start for his new conductorship. Later there was more novelty, among other things Virgil Thomson's film score *The Plow That Broke the Plains* and Stokowski's first public performance of Shostakovitch's Seventh Symphony. The season was successfully concluded with Beethoven's Ninth Symphony.

The following season the Hollywood Bowl celebrated its silver anniversary, and Stokowski envisaged a great festival starting with a performance of Gustav Mahler's Eighth Symphony. This came to nothing, probably because the preparation of such a gigantic work needs a full season's work; but otherwise it was just as great a season as the previous one. A great deal of the repertoire was recorded by RCA Victor, in Republic Studios, Hollywood.

The conductorship of the Hollywood Bowl seemed to fit well into Stokowski's plan to gradually retire from the strenuous work of full year concert-seasons, only giving a few exclusive concerts and recordings a year, so it was thought that he had now found another permanent situation. But after the 1946 season he announced that he was not able to carry out the last year of his contract. There had been some of the usual disagreements, among them some criticism by Stokowski of the famous shell. He asserted that it was constructed in such a way that it did not reflect the music equally well in all directions, and wrong angles inside made for some distortion of the sound. He was in favour of having it pulled down and the orchestra reinforced by electric amplification. This, however, was not the stumbling block; and how much the management was taken by surprise at Stokowski's decision is revealed by the fact that no new musical director was appointed for the 1947 season, which was covered by guest conductors. Was it just coincidence that Stokowski's successor for the 1948 season was Eugene Ormandy?

Stokowski in the Hollywood Bowl.

Chapter 10

New York
Philharmonic Orchestra

At the beginning of the 1947-8 season the New York Philharmonic stood in the serious position of being without a chief conductor. The Board of Directors managed to secure six prominent conductors to share the podium as guests. The conductors involved were Leopold Stokowski, Efrem Kurtz, Charles Münch, Dimitri Mitropoulos, George Szell and Walter Hendl.

Ever since its foundation the orchestra has had to shift conductors too frequently, and therefore has not always been among the best orchestras in America. The most important event in its history was the amalgamation with the New York Symphony Society in 1928, and Toscanini's leadership of the renovated orchestra in the years 1929-36. During these years it was capable of equalling the more reliable orchestras in Philadelphia and Boston. When Toscanini resigned in the spring of 1936, the young Anglo-Italian conductor, John Barbirolli, received many warnings not to accept the vacant position, which had been offered to him. For a conductor at the beginning of his career it might spell catastrophe to succeed a musician of Toscanini's stature. However, Barbirolli took the plunge, and without trying to imitate his illustrious predecessor he succeeded in realising his own musical gifts and gaining an audience who appreciated his honest endeavours. But Barbirolli's leadership was a period of stagnation. His own career was saved, but not that of the Philharmonic. Only by new artistic conquests and the firm guidance of a foresighted organiser is an orchestra able to maintain a high musical standard. Such a conductor was Arthur Rodzinski, who was engaged when Barbirolli left in 1942 to become conductor of the Hallé Orchestra in England.

It was Stokowski who found Rodzinski in Warsaw way back in 1925 and invited him to America to become his assistant in Philadelphia. In 1933 Rodzinski was engaged as conductor of the Cleveland Symphony Orchestra. By building this insignificant organisation into an orchestra of national reputation, and later in his selection and preparation of the new NBC Symphony Orchestra, he made a reputation for himself as an excellent organiser and orchestra-builder. These qualities he developed further as musical director of the New York Philharmonic Orchestra. By a radical purge of musicians, an essential renewal of the repertoire, and engaging the best guest conductors and soloists he led the orchestra to a musical and technical perfection which bode well for its future. Unfortunately, his supremacy as a musician led him into a series of controversies with the Board of Directors, and in 1947 the situation became so intolerable that Rodzinski resigned. The New York critics deplored this interruption in the growth of the orchestra, but Rodzinski stood by his decision, complicating the situation further by accusing the manager, Arthur Judson, of interfering with his decisions, as president of Columbia Artists as well.

The Board of Directors were now reluctant to give a new man the same authority as Rodzinski, and there then came a peculiar interregnum with six guest-conductors but no musical-director.

It was not the first time Stokowski faced the New York Philharmonic. In the 1930-1 season he and Toscanini had exchanged orchestras for two weeks, and it did not pass off without incident. While Toscanini's appearance in Philadelphia was idyllic, Stokowski had trouble with the Philharmonic, and some of the musicians were expelled from the orchestra for the whole period. The explanation is to be found in the relations between the two conductors and their players. Stokowski's discipline was based solely on musical results and left room for individual technique and personal responsibility on part of the musicians. They never felt oppressed or exhausted – they retained their artistic integrity. Consequently, guest conductors were always gratified to discover the flexibility and adaptability of Stokowski's musicians. With Toscanini it was quite different. His discipline was based on tradition and uniformity, and he utterly exhausted his musicians. Conductors often felt betrayed conducting orchestras Toscanini had worked with. The musicians appeared obstinate and unwilling to co-operate, apparently feeling that the new conductor was not in possession of the same knowledge or authority as Toscanini. However, Stokowski soon made the Philharmonic understand that he knew what he wanted and how to obtain it; after that there was no trouble. The second time Stokowski was guest with the orchestra was in the 1941-2 season, when Bruno Walter, Fritz Busch, Walter Damrosch, Dimitri Mitropoulos, Arturo Toscanini and other prominent musicians were invited to conduct the orchestra on the occasion of the hundredth anniversary of its foundation.

According to the critics, his work with the New York Philharmonic was among Stokowski's best and most balanced since his resignation from the Philadelphia Orchestra. Finally a long-standing wish to secure him for New York had been fulfilled. Apparently he was also much at ease in the capital of American music, and gave many peerless performances of works for which he had always been highly praised in Philadelphia, besides, as usual, a generous number of premieres of new works. Here is, for instance, part of a review by Virgil Thomson for a concert on 3 January, 1947:

Tomas Luis de Victoria ....Motet 'Jesus Dulcis Memoria'
W. A. Mozart ....Overture to 'Don Juan'
Paul Hindemith ....Symphony no. 1
Eduard Lalo ....Symphonie Espagnol
Claude Debussy ....'Prelude a l'apres-midi d'un faune'

As for Mr Stokowski's conducting, it was a pure miracle from beginning to end. Often in the past, critics, the present included, have protested at errors of taste on this conductor's part. Last night there was none. Everything was played with a wondrous beauty of sound, with the noblest proportions, with the utmost grandeur of expression. The perfection of tonal rendering for which Stokowski and his Philadelphia Orchestra were so long famous was revived last night with the Philharmonic men in a performance of Debussy's Afternoon of a Faun that for both beauty and poetry has been unmatched for many years, if ever, in my experience.

However, the many conductors harmed the orchestra to some extent. It missed the organic unity which can only result from a single conductor's artistic supremacy. Stokowski undertook an important part of its activities by taking it on concert-tours, in the spring of 1947 to the southern states, in September 1948 to the northern states, and in April 1949 again to some of the southern states. Such journeys are an indispensable part of the life of an orchestra. They give it an outlook and experiences which may benefit its daily work.

In the 1949-50 season Stokowski and Mitropoulos were the only conductors to occupy the podium. Under these dynamic conductors the orchestra reached new artistic heights. At the close of the season, on 7 April, 1950, Stokowski repeated his life's greatest triumph with a performance of Mahler's Eighth Symphony. The vocal parts were performed by the Westminster Choir, Schola Cantorum, a children's chorus from the Manhattan Public School no. 12, and eight soloists from the Metropolitan Opera. About the performance Virgil Thomson wrote:

Gustav Mahler's Eighth Symphony, as directed last night by Leopold Stokowski in Carnegie Hall, was a glorious experience to one who had not heard it before. Its sculpture of vast tonal masses at the end of each of the two movements was handled by the conductor in so noble a manner that the sound achieved monumentality while remaining musical. The effect was unquestionably grand.

One is grateful to Mr Stokowski and to his assembled forces for letting us hear it. Also for giving it to us with such great care for musical decorum. Such handsome loudnesses as took place in both perorations one does not encounter often in a lifetime. The soloists were excellent too. It was a glorious performance of a noble but not wholly satisfactory work.

If Stokowski had been willing to undertake a whole season's work during these years, he might have repeated his illustrious Philadelphia era with the Philharmonic. But after the 1949-50 season he resigned, and Mitropoulos became chief conductor of the orchestra.

Stokowski always mentioned Mitropoulos as a friend, but he did not appear with the Philharmonic a single time during Mitropoulos' period as musical-director in the 1950-8 seasons. This was also a period of artistic decline; but with the accession of Leonard Bernstein in 1958 Stokowski appeared with the orchestra again, on a few rare occasions, almost like a laureate conductor, the last times on 11, 12, 13 and 15 April, 1968. True to his nature the programme contained the world-premiere of Virgil Thomson's *Shipwreck and Love Scene* from Byron's *Don Juan*.

Chapter 11

Leopold Stokowski
Symphony Orchestra

In 1947 Stokowski began to make recordings for RCA Victor with an orchestra without a name. The record-labels said only 'Leopold Stokowski and his Symphony Orchestra', but did not conceal any of the established orchestras. In fact, it never gave a concert and seemed to have no existence at all.

At this time Stokowski was conductor of the New York Philharmonic, and since this orchestra had an exclusive contract with Columbia Records, it was not possible for him to make recordings for RCA Victor with any of the existing orchestras. Therefore he selected ensembles from the best players in and outside New York exclusively for his recordings with RCA. With those groups of 20-100 musicians, he organized a regular orchestra.

These orchestras were a striking evidence of the truth which Stokowski had asserted on various occasions, that the established symphony orchestras were not always the best. They had several of the well-known qualities which characterized the Philadelphia Orchestra and other orchestras which Stokowski had worked with: a virtuoso woodwind section, an effective brass section, and strings with a noble tone which made them rank among the ten best American orchestras. But in addition they always had an intensity of playing which illustrated their enthusiasm.

In one way, however, I think the Maestro took us in, or perhaps it was owing to natural modesty that he left one essential fact unstated. Through his many years of musical activity he had gradually created a

'Stokowskian' playing tradition, which meant that wherever he gathered a group of musicians for ensemble playing, there was always a firm basis to rely on.

Among the members of his orchestras there was usually a more or less permanent core among whom were oboist Robert Bloom and the cellist Frank Miller, both former members of the Philadelphia Orchestra. In addition from the New York Philharmonic there were violinist John Corigliano and trumpet player William Vacchiano, and the matchless flautist Julius Baker. All these, and for that matter the rest of the orchestra, represented the élite of American musicians. Stokowski selected them from his files, in which he recorded information on practically every player from whom he might expect high technical skill and co-operation.

This co-operation was so perfect that as soon as the players assembled in the studio, recordings began immediately without any rehearsals. The musicians always knew beforehand what works they were going to record and after three takes there was always enough material to work on. After each run-through Stokowski and the orchestra would listen to the results and then make the necessary corrections. Usually the third take would be the master, with just a few corrections from previous takes. Right after the session the players would spread out across the USA again, and the orchestra dissolve into anonymity.

In some of his recordings for Capitol, Stokowski used orchestras with the same title and the same excellent qualities as his RCA Victor orchestras. However, they were not identical; they were different orchestras, representing his personal choice among the best available players in New York or Los Angeles, depending on where the recordings took place. But common to all these orchestras were the qualities which Stokowski always conjured up: subtle intonation, excellent phrasing, perfect solo-playing, and unique sound balance. These qualities in most cases have been perpetuated in excellent recordings.

Chapter 12

Guest Performances

Stokowski always had an insatiable appetite for travel and study. During his first years in the USA he returned to Europe every summer to study, and when he settled down in Philadelphia he longed to travel to other parts of the world to experience the different cultures, art and folk-music. In the 1920s he got leave of absence to go to the Far East, and in the 1930s he was off again to remote places. 'I think we can learn a lot from the music-culture of other countries, especially in rhythm, which is often much more developed than ours, and they in return can learn from us the use of polyphony.'

In 1939 he also began to appear as guest-conductor with European orchestras. He visited France, Sweden, Denmark and Poland, and he was in Poland when the war broke out. His life was often in danger when the Germans bombed trains in which he was trying to escape the country. The war put a total stop to his appearances in Europe, but when it was over he became a frequent guest at the music-festivals in Salzburg, Vienna, Luzern and Bergen, at Maggio Musicale in Florence, at La Scala Opera, at festivals in Britain and Holland, and with radio orchestras in London, Cologne and Hamburg.

His programmes on these occasions were not so bold as those at home. In addition to the standard repertoire of Mozart, Beethoven, Brahms, Wagner, Tschaikovsky, Berlioz, Debussy, Ravel and Sibelius he presented some of his own orchestral transcriptions of music by Bach, Gabrieli and Palestrina. He also performed works by recognized Americans such as Griffes, Copland, Riegger and Villa-Lobos, and

Stokowski in Stockholm 1939. *Photo: Nordisk Pressefoto.*

usually he added interpretations of works by composers from the countries he visited, for instance Fartein Valen and Harald Saeverud in Norway, and Edmund Rubbra and Kenneth Leighton in Britain.

Stokowski always appreciated working with foreign orchestras, and enjoyed the various national differences in sound and technique. Communication with the players was no problem for him as he mastered German, French, and Russian, and when he came to countries where none of those were understood, he did not consider that a barrier. 'Music is an international language,' he declared, 'and we all understand each other.' Some critics have expressed their doubts whether the foreign orchestras always understood Stokowski's methods, and whether he was completely happy as a guest-conductor, when he could hardly achieve the same authority as he could with many years' work with a single orchestra. In some places there were strictly closed rehearsals, but the results were always great, and stamped by the same dramatic power and beauty which we know from his recordings.

One of the more difficult concerts took place in Copenhagen in 1939. Denmark is one of the countries where his intentions and methods have never been properly understood. Even at the first rehearsal there were disagreements. The Royal Opera Orchestra resented being rehearsed playing an A Major chord over and over again to achieve the intonation he wanted, and an old player got so angry at being criticised for crossing his legs, which Stokowski believed restricted his control of the violin, that he got up and left. Stokowski left the hall, too, but after negotiations and intense rehearsals he was gradually appeased. He was even tempted on a picnic with the musicians, and he expressed his pleasure at the countryside and the beautiful castles. Driven by his curiosity, he also got to know Knudaage Riisager, composer of ballet-music, and Niels Bohr, the famous Danish physicist, and studied the Egyptian collections at the Glyptotek.

On 8 June the concert took place, and, even though the days before had not been promising, the night turned out a success. Works by Bach, Moussorgsky, Debussy, Wagner, and Brahms were played, and after Brahms' C Minor Symphony Stokowski showed he was satisfied with the achievements of the orchestra.

In 1967 he was in Copenhagen again to open the Danish Ballet and Music Festival to celebrate the 800th anniversary of the foundation of

Stokowski at the reception in the City Hall, Copenhagen, after the concert in 1967. *Photo: Nordisk Pressefoto*

the city. On this occasion he conducted the Danish Radio Orchestra, a much younger ensemble than the Royal Opera Orchestra. (The latter is considered to be the oldest symphony orchestra in the world, dating back several hundred years as the court orchestra of the Danish kings.) But there were no great problems with the Danish Radio Orchestra, as there had been in 1939.

The concert included Carl Nielsen's Second Symphony, and considering how difficult it is for foreign conductors to play Carl Neilsen to the satisfaction of Danish music-critics, this is perhaps the highest recognition he could get:

He opened the concert with Carl Nielsen's Second Symphony. It was a rare, unreserved performance. It was so exceptionally distinctive, sometimes bitter, as Carl Nielsen might be, but worked in every little detail. The originality and daring of the symphony were maintained from first to last by orchestra and conductor.

During the interval Stokowski gave an interview for Danish Radio and said:

I would like to see the ruins of Gurre and I would like to perform and record here the "Gurrelieder" of Schoenberg, an extraordinary composition, and the poem, of course, by one of your great poets.

A very clear suggestion, but there was no response from Danish Radio, to whom it would have been of enormous value to get on the international market with a conductor of Stokowski's stature. Besides, we might then have the modern recording of *Gurrelieder* with Stokowski which we lack so painfully.

As a rule, Stokowski's work with foreign orchestras was not difficult. In 1951 he took up relations with Great Britain after a gap of 39 years, when he was invited for a series of concerts and tours with the Royal Philharmonic Orchestra. His reception was very enthusiastic, and the critics found it 'stimulating in the extreme to have such a music-maker among us.' There were also engagements with the BBC for four consecutive seasons, and finally in 1957 he was invited back by the London Symphony Orchestra after an absence of 45 years. He came to the orchestra when it was at rather a low point, but his work was an inspiration, and of the British orchestras the LSO became 'his' orchestra, both at concerts and in recordings. Some of their greatest moments were reached at the Edinburgh Festival in 1961, where they played Arnold Schoenberg's *Gurrelieder* and Michael Tippett's Concerto for Double String Orchestra. Schoenberg's widow, who was present at the festival, declared that Stokowski's

Stokowski opens the Edinburgh Festival 1961 with Schoenberg's 'Gurrelieder'. *Photo: The Scotsman.*

performance of 'Gurrelieder' was the greatest she had heard. Michael Tippett was also in the audience, and after the performance of his Concerto he seized Stokowski's hand and kissed it.

Generally speaking, English musicians admired and respected Stokowski, both as an interpreter and a disciplinarian. Of course, they did not always agree with him in all he did with a score, but his impact was so great that they were ready to accept his ideas, also the individual playing technique, which has unquestionably resulted in greater flexibility in the playing of the British orchestras.

In 1963 he was invited by the BBC for two of the Promenade Concerts at the Royal Albert Hall, and in 1964 for two more. He was much at ease at these events, inspired by the young, responsive audience, and he gave wonderful readings of works by Beethoven, Sibelius, Vaughan Williams and Mahler.

He was originally to have conducted Mahler's Eighth Symphony in 1963. However, due to lack of time the Second Symphony had to be substituted. Considering Stokowski's legendary performances of the Eighth Symphony this was a great disappointment; but his reading of the Second Symphony turned out to be one of the most sublime and glorious he ever made. The audience gave him a standing ovation, and, living up to the occasion, he turned to them, asking in his typical mock-humorous manner, 'Would you like to go home now?' 'No,' was the unanimous answer. 'Would you like to hear the finale again?' he inquired. 'Yes,' was the answer from thousands of throats. So part of the work was repeated with endless applause at the end.

During the 1950s Stokowski was a frequent guest in the winter-seasons at many of the major orchestras in the U.S.A. and Canada. In the 1951-2 season he visited the University of Illinois in Urbana for for two weeks and trained the students' orchestra and chorus for a festival concert. Two major broadcasting series he dedicated to contemporary music, namely 'The Columbia University CBS Radio Contemporary American Music Festival of the Air' in 1952 and 'Twentieth Century Concert Hall' in 1954.

In 1952 he completed his seventieth year, and in the interval of one of the concerts in the Columbia University Radio Festival he received the year's 'Alice M. Ditson Award to an American Conductor for Distinguished Services to American Music'. The Vice-President of the University, Dr Grayson Kirk, presented the award with the following citation:

The Alice M. Ditson Award to an American conductor is being given this year to Leopold Stokowski. Born in London, England, he came to this country in 1905 and became an American citizen in 1915. Since 1909, when

Stokowski rehearses a Promenade Concert in St Pancras Town Hall, London, in 1963. Listening in the background his daughter Lyuba and her son Richard. *Photo: Keystone Press.*

he commenced his conducting career as leader of the Cincinnati Orchestra, he has been one of the most brilliant and distinguished figures in American music. A champion of the new and the venturesome, he has devoted his remarkable talents to the improvement and extension of modern means of performance such as the radio, the phonograph, and the motion picture; to the recognition of new and experimental idioms of composition; to the encouragement of young performers, as founder and conductor of the All American Youth Orchestra, and towards the development of an American school of composition by frequent and eloquent performances of American works.

Stokowski accepted the award and the citation with the following statement:

American music is a nationwide development. I would like to see Washington realise that the American musician, painter, sculptor, poet, and artist of every kind is an important part of our national cultural life. Washington helps the farmer, and rightly so. Washington should help the creative American artist in every field of art. Our cultural life is an important part of our standard of living because it strengthens morale, and only through morale will we as a nation survive.

In 1959 Stokowski made some totally different guest-appearances, as conductor of opera. It was the first time he had conducted opera, since the exciting productions in the early 1930's. The New York City Center Opera, which had succeeded the New York City Symphony Orchestra at the old City Center, asked him to undertake a production of Carl Orff's *Carmina Burana* and Stravinsky's *Oedipus Rex*. Both works Stokowski had been closely associated with during his career, giving the first east coast performance of *Carmina Burana* in Boston in 1954, and the first American stage production of 'Oedipus Rex' in 1931. The productions were a great success, and the next season Stokowski was invited back for another double-bill, this time Monteverdi's *L'Orfeo* and Dalla-Piccola's *The Prisoner*. Some critics resented Stokowski's use of modern and ancient instruments together in the Monteverdi, but they all agreed as to the impact of the performance of *The Prisoner*.

The culminiation of Stokowski's opera work came, however, in the 1960-1 season, this time at the invitation of the Metropolitan Opera. A new production of Puccini's *Turandot* was planned for the latter half of the season, and Dimitri Mitropoulos was to conduct it. But on 5 November, 1960, he suddenly died from a heart-attack on the podium of 'La Scala', Milan. This was an emergency for the Met; but one of the officials knew that Stokowski had just left his post as musical-director in Houston and was available. He accepted a contract for the

Stokowski rehearses the Metropolitan Opera Orchestra for the production of 'Turandot' in 1961. *Photo: Louis Melancon.*

rest of the season. More drama was ahead, however. Stokowski had a serious accident at the end of the year and broke his right hip; and everybody thought this was the end of *Turandot*. But no! Stokowski lived up to his reputation for the dramatic and turned up at the Met on crutches for the rehearsals. With amazing vitality, he gave meticulous attention to *Turandot*, with Birgit Nilsson and Franco Corelli in the principal roles.

On 24 February the curtain went up for what a critic described as 'one of the greatest shows ever seen on Broadway', and the old Met resounded with the most sumptuous orchestral and choral sound. But Stokowski was not satisfied. He wanted more control of the staging than it was customary for an opera conductor to have; so he soon got into controversy with people, including the stage-director and the prompter, and after conducting all ten performances of the season, declared he would not continue with the production unless the lighting of Act 1 was considerably improved. This was just an

Stokowski discusses Liu's part in 'Turandot' with Anna Moffo. *Photo: Louis Melancon.*

arbitrary detail about which he chose to make an issue. In fact he was dissatisfied with many things, particularly the inadequate number of full rehearsals. After the first two performances of the next season he declined to conduct *Turandot* any more.

This marked the end of Stokowski's work with opera. He always loved opera, but he rarely found the right conditions to work with it, and when things began to turn out to his dissatisfaction, he had only one answer, to quit. On the whole, he preferred to conduct symphonic music, where he had complete control of everything. In an opera house, too many things can go wrong. Authority is divided between conductor and director, never clearly defined; and staging and lighting can be poor. There are insufficient rehearsals, and after a time substitutes appear on the stage and in the orchestra. Then the whole performance begins to deteriorate; and Stokowski would never accept routine or mediocrity.

Chapter 13

Houston
Symphony Orchestra

The sceptics were reckless in prophesying that Stokowski's career was over when he left Philadelphia. They left out of account the fact that the Philadelphia Orchestra was his work; and after his separation he demonstrated that his great musical ability unfolded wherever the conditions for making music were present. Through many years guest-conducting in the USA he had become regarded in the public eye as a free-lance conductor; so it was a great surprise when in the autumn of 1955 he undertook the position of musical director of the Houston Symphony Orchestra, in Texas.

The history of the orchestra goes back to 1913, when an ensemble of thirty-five musicians gave concerts under Julian Paul Blitz. Interest in the concerts led to a more permanent organisation, the Houston Symphony Society. The First World War caused the dissolution of the orchestra, but the Symphony Society continued its activity and arranged performances of chamber music. It was not until 1930 that the orchestra was reorganised, and under conductors such as Uriel Nespoli, Frank St Leger, Ernst Hoffmann and Efrem Kurtz it achieved a certain maturity. For several seasons it had to do without a permanent leader, and meet the various demands of a series of guest-conductors; for instance in the 1947-8 season no less than twelve, among them Leonard Bernstein, Charles Münch and Tauno Hannikainen. After Efrem Kurtz completed a period of four years, there followed in the 1954-5 season a not-very-successful interlude with the German-Hungarian conductor, Ferenc Fricsay, and after that the orchestra was again without a conductor. The Board of Directors then opened negotiations with Stokowski, and under his leadership the orchestra went through an artistic growth which brought it to the level of many of the great American orchestras.

Many wondered what made Stokowski engage himself once more in the demanding work of leader of a big symphony organisation. There is no doubt that the great interest in youth, one of the features of cultural life in Houston, was a powerful attraction for him. He himself had the creative imagination and emotions of youth, and its ardent belief in life and the future. With an average age of thirty-three, the Houston Orchestra was one of the 'youngest' American orchestras. From two earlier guest appearances, he also knew that it was already a good orchestra, and with its youthful flexibility and enthusiasm Stokowski would be able to mould it in his own image, just as he had done with the Philadelphia Orchestra and the All American Youth Orchestra.

True to character, Stokowski made a lot of changes when he came to Houston. With his persuasive eloquence, he sketched the alternatives for the future. It might become a good orchestra, an excellent orchestra, or one of the best orchestras in the world, depending on whether the management was willing to make the necessary sacrifices. From 90 musicians, Stokowski raised it in a short time to the same size as the other great American orchestras and, with relatively few changes of solo-players in the string section, he raised the quality. He

Stokowski at rehearsal in Music Hall, Houston. *Photo: Jim Thomas.*

also had an acoustic reflector installed in The Music Hall to his own design.

The backbone of the orchestra's activity is the subscription concerts. The original number of ten pairs was increased to fifteen, and from the 1960-1 season to sixteen. Youth concerts are planned in collaboration with the schools, who receive the programmes beforehand and go through them with the music students. Stokowski performed separate programmes for different age groups, and arranged special concerts with short programmes for children between the ages of four and nine, because it was his conviction that children are responsive to music much earlier than generally supposed.

Every year there were auditions for music-students, and the best qualified got an opportunity to appear as soloists at the youth concerts. The Ima Hogg Scholarship Fund granted the most talented students the privilege of getting private lessons with members of the orchestra, and Stokowski monitored their progress at the end of each season, deciding whether their scholarship should be extended. Interest in youth was not confined to the performance of music. Creation of music was encouraged too. Stokowski suggested in 1955 the establishment of a commissioning fund, and laid the foundation with a substantial gift. Through this fund the Houston Orchestra commissioned works by Texan composers, among them José Serebrier, and gave them their first performances.

Stokowski engaged Walter Süsskind as assistant conductor; besides his work as conductor in Canada Süsskind led the orchestra in its out-of-town activities. These covered many cities in the south-western part of America with no orchestras of their own.

From 1955 to 1958 Maurice Bonney was associate conductor. Former viola-player in the orchestra, and founder of the New Symphony Orchestra in New York, he had responsibility for most of the youth concerts. Maurice Bonney considered co-operation with Stokowski the culmination of his life:

'The privilege of sharing the podium with him is a rare one, and I am profoundly grateful for the opportunity.' In the autumn of 1958 he left Houston to take over leadership of the Alberquerque Civic Orchestra, and as his successor Stokowski engaged Ezra Rachlin, conductor of the Austin Symphony Orchestra.

The Houston Orchestra co-operates closely with the Houston Chorale, an excellent chorus, founded in 1947, and whose 150 members are trained by Alfred Urbach. Stokowski was glad to work with this chorus and did not hesitate to give it demanding tasks, among them Beethoven's Ninth Symphony, Bach's Mass in B Minor, Brahms' *Ein Deutches Requiem*, and *Trionfo di Afrodite* and *Carmina Burana* by Carl Orff.

With his keen interest in contemporary music, Stokowski made many innovations in the repertoire of the Houston Orchestra. He considered it natural that the music of modern composers be performed today, just as the music played in Mozart's and Beethoven's time was of contemporary composers. Stokowski divided his programmes between modern and old music, and even in his first season he planned two first-performances, two American premieres, and six first performances in Houston. He asserted that although music-lovers who appreciate modern music are a minority, this minority has a right to hear this music. Besides, his compelling performances have won many new adherents for contemporary music.

For the subscription concerts of the 1957-8 season the division between old and new music was:

Old Music		New Music	
Composer	Number of Works	Composer	Number of Works
Anonymous	2	Barber	1
Bach	6	Bartok	1
Vivaldi	1	Debussy	2
Mozart	2	Krenek	1
Haydn	1	Le Flem	1
Beethoven	2	Mennin	2
Berlioz	1	Orff	1
Brahms	1	Panufnik	1
Liadov	1	Prokofiev	1
Moussorgsky	1	Rachmaninov	1
Rimsky-Korsakov	1	Ravel	1
Tschaïkovsky	2	Revueltas	1
Wagner	3	Serebrier	1
		Shchredin	1
		Shostakovitch	2
		Sibelius	1
		Stravinsky	5
		Vaughan Williams	1
		Villa-Lobos	2
Total	24	Total	27

Period	Percentage
Baroque	18
Classic	10
Romantic	19
Modern	53

This was an even better balance between old and new music than in the Philadelphia-era. But of course times have changed. What was at

Stokowski and the Houston Symphony Orchestra 1958. *Photo: Richard Pervin.*

that time considered daring, is today looked upon as an obligation to the music of our time.

The Houston Symphony Orchestra is now one of the big orchestras in America, and many foreign conductors, among others the late Sir Thomas Beecham, consider it one of the best, both in technical skill and co-operation. Virgil Thomson wrote about it in the *New York Herald Tribune:*

The Houston Symphony Orchestra is a virtuoso group, comparable throughout to the Northern orchestras. A powerful and solidly-blended string body, completed by excellent woodwinds and brasses and topped off by impeccable soloists in all the sections, gives the colour range completeness and flexibility.

There is no doubt that Houston was flattered that the famous Stokowski had accepted the permanent leadership of its Orchestra; but after the expiration of the first three-year contract some of the enthusiasm disappeared on both sides. Stokowski carried on his usual policy of featuring new music, but the traditional audience disliked or even laughed at most of the novelties. Stokowski, on his side, never seemed to engage himself totally in Houston. He never settled down there, but spent half of each season in New York, partly for concerts, partly with his little sons. On the other hand, it was only through his inspiring work that the Houston Orchestra had entered the spotlight of the musical scene, and some excellent recordings for Capitol and

Everest – the only ones made with the Houston Orchestra before or after the Stokowski-era – even pointed to an international reputation. The Board of Directors wanted to renew the contract with him, although they had to rely on guest conductors for a large part of the mid-season concerts and for the tours, but in the 1960-1 season clouds began to appear on the horizon. The Board, having an idea that Stokowski might soon retire, secretly approached John Barbirolli to ask whether he was willing to take over the orchestra from the next season.

Nobody said anything to Stokowski, but in November he suggested engaging a black choir in the city for one of the choruses in a new production of Schoenberg's *Gurrelieder*. The suggestion was turned down, obviously on racial grounds, and soon after Stokowski left for New York for his mid-winter engagements. A few days later he sent a telegram saying that he would not be able to carry out the remaining part of his contract, and asked to be released. The Board issued a formal regret of his decision, but this was pure hypocrisy. The truth is that Houston had always been half-hearted about all Stokowski's plans, and half-heartedness is death to the arts. When I met Stokowski in Philadelphia in February 1960, he still talked about his Houston engagement and his plans for the coming season with enthusiasm. But the next year, when I spoke to him at the Edinburgh Festival, Houston already seemed far from his mind. He only gave me this general statement about his resignation:

I left there because of racial prejudice. I am opposed to racial prejudice of every kind, and I think it is very dangerous to the future of the United States, because we must be together, we must not be separated into groups which are hating each other, but we must be in one great strong group.

Chapter 14

The American Symphony Orchestra

There were never any long pauses in Stokowski's musical activity. So it was no surprise when, on 15 October, 1962, he presented to the public an entirely new orchestra, the American Symphony Orchestra, as he stated, 'to afford opportunity to musicians of great gifts, irrespective of age, sex, or colour, and also to give concerts of great music in the range of possibility for everybody'.

For some years he had received letters from young musicians, who complained that it was next to impossible to get an opportunity to play in an orchestra. Many of the great cities in the world such as Vienna, Paris and London, supported several full-time orchestras; why shouldn't a great city like New York be able to house and support more than one? So, encouraged by music patrons and with support from the Kaplan Fund and the Samuel Rubin Foundation, he set to work on giving New York its second orchestra.

We consider nothing impossible,' said Mr Rubin, 'because Stokowski considers nothing impossible. He is an inspiration to people with whom he works, he explores new ideas, he is bold, and he is adventurous. He makes everyone feel young, and we respond accordingly.

Stokowski donated his services as conductor and music-director, and a large sum of his own money was needed to help the new project over its first year.

As soon as his plans became known, young musicians from all over

Stokowski announces the foundation of the American Symphony Orchestra at a press conference in New York, 25 April, 1962. *Photo: United Press International.*

the country began to flock to his Manhattan apartment for auditions. He listened to all of them, and finally hired the thirty-odd outstanding players, putting the rest on a waiting list. Then he consulted his files for sixty-odd experienced and noted instrumentalists to make up the rest of his orchestra. He believed that older musicians can give something of their experience and methods to young musicians, while the latter may convey some of their youthful enthusiasm and creative power to older colleagues.

The orchestra was a living illustration of Stokowski's unprejudiced attitude towards musicians and orchestras in general. The American Symphony Orchestra is open to anybody, he said, but only if they are good players. And he meant it. If they did not work concentratedly and intelligently, he turned them out and had others in instead. Nor did he believe in permanent membership of an orchestra. 'There are orchestras,' he said, 'who have played together for years and remained bad orchestras, and there are players who have only been together for a few weeks who are among the greatest in the world.' On the other hand, there are also players who become better with age, so it was not surprising to find veteran musicians with Stokowski in the new orchestra, such as Arthur Berv (horn) and Bernard Portnoy (clarinet), both former Philadelphia Orchestra players.

There have also been more than thirty women in the orchestra for most of its seasons. 'They are just as gifted musicians as men are,' Stokowski said, 'and they have both feeling and imagination, indispensable in performing music. They are not better than men, not worse, but just as good players as they are.' As clear evidence that the same is true of different races, the orchestra counted among its members musicians of Negro, Japanese, Chinese, Korean and Indian descent.

Stokowski's aim was not only the training of orchestral players, but also the training of young conductors. He felt that there was a serious shortage of experienced conductors to take over the great orchestras after the deaths of most of the big giants like Mitropoulos, Koussevitzky and Toscanini. It was also his opinion that good results could only be obtained by giving them the opportunity to conduct rehearsals. To achieve this he engaged three young associate conductors, namely Warner Bass, David Katz and José Serebrier, to help him conduct rehearsals with the orchestra. These rehearsals were intended as an advanced school for student conductors, who were invited to discuss methods and to ask questions and to conduct the orchestra. In this way Stokowski attempted, for the first time in his long career, to transmit systematically some of his rich experience in conducting to the younger generation, putting aside his own ego, and making the encouragement of young talent one of the objects of his activity.

On the whole, Stokowski valued rehearsals very highly. 'The greatest results are achieved at rehearsals,' he said, 'and if anything goes wrong, we can do it all over again.' He was not so interested in concerts, but both managers and the public demanded concerts, and therefore he had to do them, he added mischievously.

And concerts he certainly gave. From modest beginnings of six Monday nights in Carnegie Hall during the first season, the orchestra increased the second season to eight pairs of subscription concerts, and in the 1970-1 season the peak was reached with two different series, in Carnegie Hall and Philharmonic Hall, with eight pairs of programmes for each series. Besides these, there were children's concerts, youth concerts and visits to other cities.

Programmes were demanding and varied, with a balance of two to one between old and modern music, a balance which Stokowski thought right for present day programmes. Among the modern works there has been a substantial diet of American composers, maintaining the reputation Stokowski always had as an advocate of contemporary national music, including works by Henry Cowell, Peter Mennin, Paul Creston, Warner Bass, William Schuman and Charles Ives. Concerning Ives, on 26 April, 1965, Stokowski gave the world

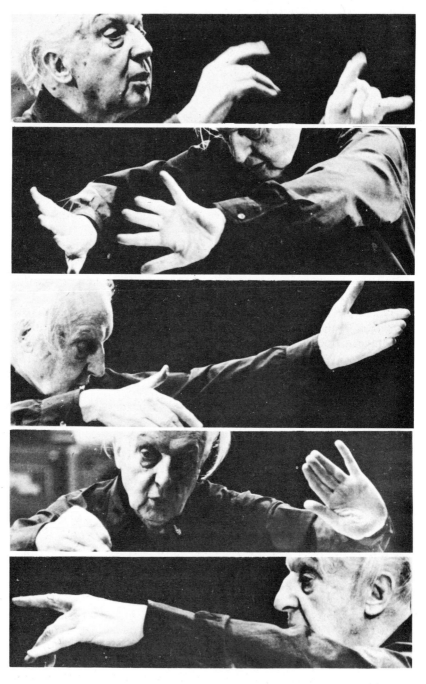

Glimpses of the famous profile and hands at the inauguration of Felt
Forum, New York, 1968. *Photo: Associated Press.*

premiére of this original composer's Fourth Symphony, about fifty years after completion of the work. Great difficulties had been overcome to make a performing edition, since the manuscript of the fourth movement had been scattered in many places, and had to be collected and deciphered before a performance could take place.

Music critics have been generous in their praise of the American Symphony Orchestra. John Ardoin, for instance, from *Musical America* several times hailed the new orchestra as one of the best in the USA, and after its first season there was honour and praise from the official side. President Kennedy sent his arts consultant, August Heckscher, with congratulations to Stokowski for his great achievements; and the cultural officer of New York City, Robert Dowling, presented him with the Handel Medal, conveying Mayor Wagner's thanks, appreciation and affection. The crowded hall gave the conductor a prolonged standing ovation, and when it died away, Stokowski thanked them for the honour bestowed upon him: 'When I ask the orchestra for a diminuendo or a pianissimo, I sometimes get it. You are more difficult.'

Stokowski had performed his old trick once again; in a short time and from fresh blood he had created a great symphony orchestra. But he had also succeeded in establishing a model training-programme for young musicians, and – which was very important to him – proved that such a programme can work anywhere, and help to supply first-class instrumentalists and conductors for the future.

In 1972, however, after the tenth anniversary of the orchestra, it seemed that Stokowski would not be able to continue as musical director any longer. He wrote to the Board of Directors, 'Because of the impossibility of recording in the United States, it is necessary for me now to record in Europe. For this reason I shall only be able to conduct the first pair of concerts for the 1972-3 season. Since I am leaving next week for Europe and will return only for those concerts, it is necessary for me to resign as Music Director.'

There is no doubt that the serious recording situation in USA was an important reason for Stokowski's decision; but age and failing strength were contributory factors. However, things turned out badly. Loss of subsidy from the Rubin Foundation made it impossible to raise enough money to obtain support from the Ford Foundation, and it became necessary to disband the orchestra. A glorious project was stopped abruptly at the height of its development; and the United States lost one of the greatest forces ever in its musical life.

But the orchestra refused to die. During the cancelled season many members tried to raise money for the next season. Former subscribers were invited to back up the young people who had taken over management of the orchestra, and made it a self-governing body. They

Stokowski tosses the ball in the annual softball match between the American Symphony and the New York Philharmonic, 19 May, 1970. *Photo: Associated Press.*

chose a musical-director themselves, voting for the brilliant young Japanese conductor Kazuyoshi Akiyama, who had earlier been a guest-conductor of the orchestra.

One great idea of Stokowski's never materialised; this was his aim of creating a permanent international youth orchestra organisation, of

Rehearsal with the International Youth Orchestra of 1973 at Morley College, London. *Photo: The Times.*

which the American Symphony Orchestra should be a part. This idea always haunted his mind from the days of the All American Youth Orchestra, and was revived on many different occasions, both before and after the formation of the American Symphony Orchestra – for instance in 1967, when he attempted to establish contacts with students at the Paris Conservatory, and in 1969 and 1973, when he trained and conducted the orchestras of the International Festival of Youth Orchestras in Switzerland and England respectively.

However, the world is not yet ready for such a project. Stokowski is still ahead of his time.

Chapter 15

Stokowski, the Musician

We have now investigated Stokowski's career from the early years in his native country until the time when he returned to England again as an old man. Not to retire as most people have by the age of ninety, but to find the right conditions for his continuing work, studies, concerts and recordings.

For more than sixty years he was at the head of major American orchestras, as conductor or creator, and from all sides acknowledged as one of the greatest conductors of our time. But sometimes his musical taste and judgement have been the object of controversy, not least owing to his radical attitude to his profession. With his restless intellect he was unlikely to take anything for granted, and all that could not stand objective examination was mercilessly changed, not least in his relations to the orchestra.

STOKOWSKI AND THE ORCHESTRA

Various stories have been told about Stokowski's attitude to his musicians. At times he is supposed to have been as cold as ice and unapproachable, at other times kind, and interested in their personal welfare. It has also been reported that once, after a year's absence from the Philadelphia Orchestra, he came onto the stage of the Academy of Music, and immediately started rehearsals without any greetings, or the least sign of pleasure at seeing the orchestra again. But a week later he suddenly began to assure his players how glad he was to see them and work together with them again. Other accounts have had him oscillate between periods when he lectured the orchestra for lacking humility towards the spiritual message of the music and times where he would take the lead in disrespectful jokes and ironic comments on the music. Another charge was that he did not even know the names of the players, and always referred to them by their instruments. In fact, he did often refer to instruments instead of players; but only to make his corrections short and clear. He knew the names of the players very well, and remembered them from far back in time.

All these legends have thrown doubt on Stokowski's sincerity, but they are wildly exaggerated. People who knew him well asssure us that they never observed such capriciousness; and the musicians whom he had worked with for years had great admiration for him. This is also true of European orchestras which he conducted as a guest. Here, for instance, is a statement by Hugh Maguire, former leader of the London Symphony Orchestra:

His first impact on an orchestra is most striking because he has got this fantastic reputation, going back many years, as being something of a dictator, as far as the musicians are concerned. When he first came to us, he was very charming, but he has in fact got more discipline in an orchestra than any other conductor I have ever met. He will not tolerate anybody slacking or anybody resting at all. He works in very short periods really – his rehearsals are generally a couple of hours – and during that time he expects everybody to co-operate to their utmost, with an inner discipline, which he has himself, and which he imparts to the rest of the men.

The strenuous work in itself is ordinarily sufficient for discipline; but sometimes he had to make comments. Generally he was mild and moderate, as in a rehearsal of the St Matthew Passion: 'Come on, chorus, letter E, come on, use your brains. You waste our time.' Or in Brahms' Second Symphony: 'You did it better yesterday. You are sleepy'. Occasionally ironic or irritated, as later on in the Brahms' Symphony: 'Come on, you, that lady, that one. Come on, play something! Yes, play! Do not talk! Talk with your violin! That is your instrument.' Or in Brahms' Fourth Symphony: 'Where are your souls? I do not understand you. You are good individual players, but you do not play intelligently. Pianissimo is pianissimo. You know what it means? Do it!'

On the other hand, Stokowski was not devoid of humour. On the contrary, he had a very keen sense of the humorous side of life, and he was swift to see it. For instance, after an exhausting attempt at the second movement of Shostakovitch's Tenth Symphony: 'That makes you warm after the snow, doesn't it?' Or in the second theme, third movement, of Brahms' Second Symphony: 'I am trying to make a crescendo there, but you resist me. Resist temptations, but not the conductor, please.'

Usually he would not tolerate musicians making jokes during work, suspecting it to be evidence of inattention; but if he was cheerful, he might accept it, asking someone to explain the humour of the situation. More often, he would take the initiative, but usually not until a rest period. Then he would talk to the orchestra like a grandfather to his little nephews or nieces. Thus, for instance, in an intermission after Debussy's *Six Epigraphes Antiques:* 'Now down here is a corridor, and at the end is a bar. Behind that wall is a tavern. After the intermission we have Brahms, so don't. After the concert, do!'

Generally rehearsals passed off in a calm and harmonious atmosphere, Stokowski's approach to the musicians always being polite and correct, never coarse or uncontrolled. For instance, in William Schuman's Seventh Symphony, first movement: 'Please, all subito piani, subito pianissimi. Please, do it. No. 30, please!' Or from Brahms' Second Symphony, third movement: 'There is a kind of natural crescendo there, and a natural diminuendo after it. Be kind enough to give it, will you please!'

At a first rehearsal there might sometimes be many stops, but generally speaking there were surprisingly few interruptions at his rehearsals. Often he went through a whole work or movement without any breaks and during the playing he would make small corrections with little exclamations. For balance of instruments: 'Solo, more solo!' – For antiphonal phrasing: 'Now celli. Bass. Contra. Bass. Celli!' – For dynamics: 'Take time, please. Fade it down, Now a little thick!' – Or, less often, with soft whistling or singing. No time was wasted on things that were already satisfactory, because 'One can rehearse too much, and then the spontaneity is lost.' But during the playing he would take elaborate notes on everything he wanted to correct, and afterwards gave an exact description of the details he wanted to improve. For instance, after No. 4 in Debussy's *Six Epigraphes Antiques:* 'Right. Just one spot. Please, violins, before letter C, three bars before. Phrase it more, will you. One-two! – More, more crescendo. One-two! – That's it. Fantastic.'

Stokowski demanded much from his musicians, but he knew how to get what he wanted. In Albeniz's *Iberia*, for instance: 'Harps only! – The lower tones less, the upper tones more. Always the upper tones more, please.' Or in *Götterdämmerung*: 'Dark tone. On the fingerboard, yes.' And: 'Heavy. Horns Gestopft.' There might also be an appeal to understand the music beyond the printed notes. For instance, in Shostakovitch's Tenth Symphony: 'Tenuto always, when it ends. Do not be literal!' But a moment after: 'Play correct notes!' Or in Brahms' Fourth Symphony, first movement: 'You see a rest in that bar. But do not look at it in that way. Play it through, longer there!'

On the other hand, he never pushed the musicians beyond the limit because he knew exactly the technical difficulties or physical strain each instrument presented. He knew when the time had come for new interest, and from his first years in Philadelphia introduced rest-periods. Examples: 'Contra, is it possible a little louder, that place?' – 'Horns, you are detached from four through five until six. Rest your lip! I wanted to keep you fresh to have a big passage there.'

He took a great interest in all the problems concerning musicians as a group; and he also valued and encouraged artistic skill in each of them. But he was rather aloof and impersonal to everyone. He distinguished strictly between human feeling and artistic justice, and he would never tolerate any mediocrity or resentment. If a musician was not able or ready to meet his demands, he would criticise him so harshly that he was not able to play a single correct note, and if the person did not retire on his own, he would be dismissed with a few polite, but icy words. Hot temper or invectives were unknown to Stokowski. Equally unknown to him were prejudices of any kind. He said:

Each player should be selected for mastery of his instrument – musical talent and understanding – imagination – love of music. No personal considerations or prejudices can be allowed. The player must be chosen on musical merit alone. There is in the minds of some men a prejudice against women in orchestras. My own experience has been that women give immense devotion to music and never-ending enthusiasm to the part they play in an orchestra. There really should be no question of whether instrumentalists in the orchestra are men or women.

Toscanini, in contrast, did not like women in the orchestra. He simply declared, 'If they are beautiful, they distract the men of the orchestra, and if they are not beautiful, they distract me.'

Stokowski always had a great admiration for Toscanini as a conductor. After attending his concerts in Berlin with the New York Philharmonic on its first European tour in 1930, he made an analysis of Toscanini's conducting, in which he brought out some of the essential points of his greatness:

His beat breaks every academic rule – yet is always clear and eloquent. But it is between the beats that something almost magical happens – one can always tell when he has reached the half-beat or quarter-beat or three-quarter beat, even when he does not divide his beats, and it is this certainty and clarity of beat which creates such a perfect ensemble when he conducts, so that the orchestra sounds like one giant instrument.

However, he did not identify himself with Toscanini's technique. It was the consistency and unity of his musicianship that so impressed him:

While I was observing the technical qualities of Toscanini's conducting I realised how relatively unimportant they are – it is the divine fire in him which elevates all he expresses.

With Toscanini, discipline was based upon tradition and uniformity. His technical directions in the orchestral parts were law for all the players. Stokowski's discipline was far less rigid, but at least as effective. He abandoned the uniform bowing and breathing-technique because he found that it restricts the musicians in their performance, whereas free bowing and breathing may agree with the inner nature of the music, calling for the creative power and artistic imagination of the musicians. A few examples illustrate this:

The fourth movement of Shostakovitch's Tenth Symphony: 'Bassoon, after 149, third bar, the second note should be tied to the third note, not struck again. And breathe perhaps before D, if you wish.' – A suggestion, not a command.

And in Brahms' Second Symphony, first movement: 'Strings, after E, where you begin on that G Sharp there, free bowing. Are there any bowing-marks in those parts? A long time ago, when I was more stupid than I am now, I insisted on those bowings. Ignore them, please. Bow freely!'

Or in No. 73 of the St Matthew Passion, encouraging the organ-player to explore his instrument: 'No, here is crescendo. Come on, crescendo – diminuendo. Is that all you have? It is not your fault. It is a very good organ in some ways, and very straight in others. Think what you can do with it there. Another thing you can do is, when you make the crescendo, you play two half-notes together in the pedal, so they clash, you know – Together! – Is that two together? All right. Go on, please!''

One of the results of this individual technique was the unrestrained development of the natural talents of the players, and often also the solution of technical problems. The musicians were not subdued, and felt a personal responsibility for the performance of the music, which their colleagues in a regimented orchestra were not likely to have. Another result was the matchless sound for which the Philadelphia

Orchestra become so famous, and which is an obvious hallmark of all the orchestras with which Stokowski has worked closely.

To increase the responsibility of the orchestra Stokowski cancelled experimentally for some years the position of leader, and instead let the players fill in turn the first chair of their group. About this he said:

In the modern orchestra, each individual should be responsible for his or her playing of the individual part. It is neither possible nor desirable for the head of a section to be watching each player in his section, because he is responsible for playing his own part, and in order to do that well must concentrate solely on the music, the rhythmic beat of the conductor, and the perfect control of tone production of his instrument. The traditional idea of passing the responsibility to the head of a section is weakening the musical morale of the orchestra. Each player must accept fully and completely the responsibility of his own part.

In his very first years as conductor Stokowski spent the summers in Europe, studying the instruments of the orchestra with some of the leading teachers. In this way he acquired a more thorough knowledge of all the possibilities and shortcomings of the instruments than most in his profession. This enabled him to improve the technique, intonation, tone and phrasing of many of his musicians. With his heavy demands, and the individual technique he encouraged, he often made his players the greatest instrumentalists in their field. This was true, for instance, of Marcel Tabuteau, for many years the solo oboist of the Philadelphia Orchestra. His playing was characterised by a distinct, subtle phrasing and a beautiful, rich tone, which can only come from an intimate knowledge of the instrument. Tabuteau was very particular about the reeds, and spent much time making and remaking his own reeds in order to adapt them to his technique. Other great instrumentalists were William Kincaid, the flautist, Walter Guetter, the bassoonist, Saul Caston, the trumpet-player, Samuel Mayes, the cellist and innumerable others. These players have been leading artists on their instruments, and became so because Stokowski forced them. He always had an uncanny instinct for talent, and often surprised professionals by selecting inexperienced musicians, who had hardly tried to play bigger classical works, for important positions in his orchestras; but he proved again and again that he selected the right people. Saul Caston was just such an inexperienced player, but Stokowski realised his talent and hired him, only seventeen years old, for the Philadelphia Orchestra. In 1923, after five years in the orchestra, Stokowski offered him the position of solo-trumpet. Caston felt that he was not able to fill that position, but Stokowski

Marcel Tabuteau practising backstage at the Academy of Music. *Photo: Philadelphia Orchestra.*

gave him important parts, for example the solo-introduction to Wagner's Rienzi Overture, and thus gave him the necessary self-confidence.

However, Stokowski's influence on orchestral playing in America is still more deep-rooted and far-reaching. Many of the excellent players he collected in his Philadelphia Orchestra have, as teachers at the Curtis Institute in Philadelphia or other important music schools, been responsible for the education of two or three generations of young musicians. These players today form the backbone of several American orchestras, and many orchestras have a playing-technique unmistakably akin to that of the Philadelphia Orchestra.

Stokowski was not satisfied with all our modern musical instruments. Some of them, especially the double-bass, are too weak in their low registers, and while he was in Houston he got the Allen Organ Company to construct an electronic keyboard-instrument to reinforce the double-basses. There were some problems with the musicians' union, but it came into use, for instance in the premiere and subsequent recording of Shostakovitch's Symphony No. 11.

He also found problems with the intonation of some of the wind instruments. The French horn, for instance, he considered very difficult to play, because it is necessary to produce many of the highest notes with lips only. Because of the harmonic series, the player cannot be sure to make them in tune. The trombone also has its shortcomings. Certainly it has a noble, pure sound; but the slide prevents a perfect legato, and rapid passages cannot be performed with a satisfactory intonation. Good valve-trombones might solve these problems.

Only by surmounting the shortcomings of our present instruments, and making better types, shall we be able to concentrate more fully on the inner qualities of music. Stokowski believed that new inventions will revolutionise the performance of music. Particularly, he expected much from instruments with electronic sound-production and amplification. About this he said:

Today we are on the verge of one of the greatest steps in the evolution of musical instruments that perhaps can ever take place – that is, the invention and development of musical instruments in which the tone is produced electrically, but is played and controlled through musicians' feeling, technical skill, and intuitive understanding. Some of these electrical instruments already exist, but are at present in a primitive stage. There are many ways of producing tone electrically, just as there are many ways of producing tone from strings, wooden tubes, metal tubes, and metal plates in the present-day orchestra. Possibly all these ways of producing tone electrically will finally be used, but the greatest variation will be in the manner of controlling the tone and playing of the instrument. It is probable that some electrical instruments will be played by keyboards, like the piano and present-day celeste, because instruments of this type will make it possible to play rapidly a series of tones with great precision and certainty. But some types of melodies, where one tone glides to another with a curved motion, will possibly be played on a wire somewhat like a cello string, or by electrical instruments similar to those invented by the Russian Theremin or the French musician Martenot.

There are those who fear the development of electrical instruments because they think they will make music mechanical. Exactly the opposite will take place. When the electrical instruments are relatively perfect, they will free musicians from our present constant preoccupation with the imperfections and technical difficulties of instruments. We shall be able to give all our feeling and thought to the inner essence of the music, because the instruments will respond with extreme sensitivity to every slight difference of feeling in the player and the music.

Also he considered the tempered scale as only a temporary solution of the problem of harmonic modulation. It represented considerable progress towards new means of expression, but meant a loss of pure intonation. He looked forward to the time when music would return to the untempered scale through the employment of electric instruments, and still be able to modulate into any other key.

The normal seating of the modern symphony orchestra is not the result of scientific investigation or acoustic experiments. It is mainly dictated by the historical development of the orchestra in the 16th and 17th centuries. It began with the string instruments, grouped round the conducting harpsichord player. Later, when new instruments were added, such as flutes, oboes, trumpets, horns and kettle-drums, they were merely placed behind the original ones; and this practice has continued since without anybody questioning it – except Stokowski. To him no tradition was good, unless it had purpose; but the traditional seating of the orchestra has no meaning any more, and does not give the best total sound of an orchestra. Therefore, he made detailed investigations of all the instruments, as to their best relative position, the best use of their directional tone-production, and the best balance of sound between the different groups.

The first visible result of these investigations was the seating of the second violins next to the first violins, and the removal of the cellos and violas to the front-right of the conductor. The motivation was lack of balance between the two sections, because the first violins turn their sound-holes to the auditorium, whereas the second violins turn them the opposite way, with a difference of sound-volume in consequence. Another advantage of the close proximity of the first and second violins was a better contrast between the high and low instruments of the orchestra, and between woodwinds and strings, in antiphonal playing. This seating plan was carried out in Philadelphia in 1921, and when proved to work, became permanent, and many other orchestras in America and Europe took up the practice.

Of a less permanent character was Stokowski's sensational experiment with the upside-down orchestra, which he introduced at his concerts in Philadelphia in November 1939. All the woodwinds were moved to the front of the stage; then followed all the high strings, flanked to the left by the trumpets and to the right by the horns. At the back the double-basses were spread out in one line on risers, with the heavy brass to the left, and the percussion to the right. Behind this new seating was an entirely novel acoustic reflector; the purpose was, in Stokowski's own words, 'to enrich the sound of the music and to blend and balance the tone of the entire orchestra.'

The arrangement got a mixed review in the daily press, one critic declaring it to be a glamorous flop. But others acknowledged the improved results. The *Philadelphia Bulletin* stated:

'There can hardly be any doubt that this new arrangement is acoustically logical. Those instruments which stand most in need of reflective reinforcement get it, and those that need it least are out in front where the powers of reflection are less intense.

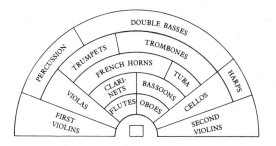

The traditional seating of an orchestra.

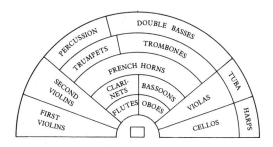

Stokowski's revised seating, from 1921.

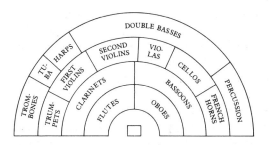

'The upside-down orchestra', from 1939.

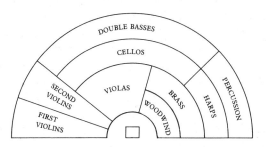

Stokowski's later seating arrangement.

The new plan had its most elaborate workout in the performance of Bach's Passacaglia and Fugue in C Minor. The way the double-basses carrying the ground-bass in the early variations came through the orchestral web was extremely effective, and a passage in a later variation where the horns are heard against the violins was certainly more striking than it would have been in the old seating-order. The separation of the horns from the trumpets and trombones seemed to be a very important development, and the colour of tone in the woodwinds was notably better than under ordinary circumstances.'

The acoustic reflector was Stokowski's own idea. It consisted of heavy plywood, supported by a firm framework, and with its carefully-calculated shape, wide at the front and narrow at the back – almost like a huge gramophone horn – it gave a rich, blended sound and fine separation of the instrumental groups in all parts of the auditorium. He also used such a reflector in other places where he conducted, and took a portable model on his tours to South and North America with the All American Youth Orchestra.

Later the acoustic reflector came into use with several other American orchestras, for instance with the Minneapolis Orchestra. Here, however, it was taken down again on the request of David Hall, former music director of Mercury Records. Mr Hall did not agree

The upside-down orchestra. Academy of Music, 1939. *Photo: Philadelphia Orchestra.*

with Stokowski on the usefulness of a reflector for recording. He was of the opinion that it is mainly the vertical sound effect of the orchestra which is essential in recording. Certainly, the Mercury recordings from the 1950s are realistic and clear; but their sound is also sharp and naked, without the special atmosphere a better utilisation of the auditorium might have given.

When Stokowski had finished a three-week period in Philadelphia with his new seating-plan, Ormandy returned to the podium, and at once reversed the orchestra to its usual seating. However, he made a diplomatic statement to the effect that there was no disagreement between him and Stokowski about the seating; it was just a matter of individual taste.

During his guest appearances in Philadelphia in 1960, Stokowski surprised and enchanted his old audience once more with another new seating of the orchestra. He placed the deep strings at the back, and moved all the woodwinds to the right, in front of the harps and the percussion. This seating gave more emphasis to the woodwind, and a fine balance between strings and wind instruments, a balance to which Stokowski attached much importance, because a great deal of music is composed or orchestrated on the basis of antiphonal alternation between strings and woodwinds.

Stokowski did not consider the seating of the orchestra fixed and unchangeable. Every concert hall has is own acoustical qualities, dependent on materials, form and size, and the best results can only be achieved through an individual seating arrangement. Seating that is good for concerts need not be good for radio-broadcast or recording; and different kinds of music often demand different seatings. Therefore, he used quite different seating for every single purpose, and his great knowledge about these problems usually gave the best possible results.

Related to the question of balance of orchestral sound are the relations between soloists or chorus and the orchestra. Stokowski worked more carefully to achieve this balance than any other conductor. He never drowned a soloist in orchestral sound, and even if a composer failed to pay attention to this question, he tried to create a balance between tutti parts and accompanying parts, not according to the written score, but according to the intentions the composer may have had.

We can study this side of his conducting talent in some of the recordings he has made with soloists or chorus. The recording of Ernest Bloch's *Schelomo*, for instance, with Emmanuel Feuermann (Victor 17336-38) is an example not only of fine playing, but also of balance; that is undoubtedly one of the reasons why it has never been surpassed. There are three different levels of orchestral playing – one with moderate use of accompanying parts for a few groups of instruments, giving full prominence to the soloist; another with equally-balanced orchestral accompaniment; and finally a shattering tutti by the orchestra only, making its comments on the action, almost like the chorus of ancient Greek drama.

The recording of Arnold Schoenberg's *Gurrelieder* from 1932 (Victor 7524-37) is another example of a well-balanced performance, giving the vocal parts their proper value against the sound of the strengthened orchestra; and the same is true of his reading of the 'Ride of the Valkyries' from *Die Walküre* in a stunning Wagner anthology on Victor LM/LSC 2555. He uses the original version with soloists, eight excellent young singers, whose performances are really made to sound what they are – eight individual parts, and not, as often heard, a chorus of screaming sirens.

Much has been said through the years about Stokowski's outward appearance as a conductor. Theatrical, spectacular and showmanlike are some of the adjectives used of him; mainly since the 1929-30 season, when he began to conduct without a baton – after he broke one by accident during a concert and realised how much freer he was to express himself with both hands. The next season he conducted the first American performance of Alban Berg's *Wozzeck* at the Broad Street Metropolitan Opera House, and this became front-page news, first because it was a remarkable achievement, but also for the impressive shadows his hands cast on the walls and ceiling during the performance. Whether this was intended or not remains an unanswered question, but I believe it was not. On the whole, baton-less conducting alone cannot account for the enormous public interest in Stokowski's person, as several other conductors did not use a baton, for example Safonov, Ormandy (in his younger days), and Mitropoulos. But, like all musicians, Stokowski was very particular about his hands, not out of vanity, but necessity. He nearly always wore gloves, and Mrs Hilda Galloway, of the Godson family, remembers that if ever a cut-glass bowl was handed to him at the table in their house he would almost drop it, saying, 'Never let such a thing touch my hands'. Stokowski's hands were not in fact unusual in any way, but what made them so elegant was the suppleness with which he visualised the music for his players in graphically clear movements. Nor did he attach any importance to the appearance of the conductor to the audience:

As music is for the ear and not for the eye, the visual part of conducting is relatively unimportant. The only visual part essential is for the players to be able to see clearly the notes they are reading, and at the same time to be able to see easily the conductor's beat and his eyes.

Portrait by Vandamm, New York, from the early 1930s. Such studio portraits often focused upon the famous hands.

The abandonment of the baton was no expression of originality, but in conformity with Stokowski's aversion against mere tradition, without any musical reason or necessity. Whether a conductor uses a baton or not is exclusively a question of personal character, he asserted. The only essential thing is the music. Besides, he did not altogether exclude the use of a baton. If the occasion made it natural, he preferred to use it in bigger works for the stage with large background choruses, from where it may otherwise be difficult to see the conductor's beat.

Among Stokowski's colleagues there are quite different opinions about batonless conducting, ranging from open-mindedness to rigid antagonism against the idea. This may be seen in an interesting article on the subject in *Musical America*, February 1955, on the occasion of the fiftieth anniversary of the introduction of batonless conducting in the USA. The most essential statement is this remark by Fritz Reiner, 'Baton or no baton? I question the importance of the subject raised. In the last analysis only the musical results mean something.'

In the same article Stokowski said, 'I have conducted a variety of orchestras, yet I have never found one either in America or Europe that had difficulty following me because I did not use a baton. The basic truth regarding the relation of players to conductor, and the achievement of a perfect ensemble, is the co-operation of everyone concerned in a willing and friendly spirit.' This is the point, and American orchestras certainly had no difficulty in following him. Not all European musicians agree that they have not had any difficulty in following him without a baton. Hugh Maguire made the following statement:

I know that a lot of musicians in the orchestra wish that he would use a baton, particularly the men who sit in the suburbs. They sometimes cannot catch what he is doing. I am, of course, sitting right under his nose, and I see every little gesture that he makes, but I think as a conductor he needs great attention from the orchestra because of his particular technique of conducting. In fact, some of his gestures are tiny, but nevertheless, he is extraordinarily clear if you watch him very closely and, of course, we are not accustomed, in this country and in Europe generally, as are the American orchestras, to Stokowski. They are accustomed to a conductor without a baton, we are not.

STOKOWSKI AND MUSIC

It has sometimes been alleged that Stokowski does not sufficiently respect the original intentions of the great composers, and that he sets orchestral effect above the inner context of the music. This charge is both true and untrue. He may change an instrumentation, exaggerate a phrasing, or accentuate a single part more than prescribed in the score, to satisfy his own musical taste, but more frequently to create a better balance of sound or harmony. It is also questionable if tradition, in the form of the original manuscripts of the composers, handed down to posterity, should always be the supreme law in the performance of music; or if it can be left to the performer to work out how the music was intended. Many people insist on the former; but the further back we go in time, the less sufficient is the musical notation; and without the insight of our great artists many of the wonderful masterpieces from past centuries might be next to impossible to perform.

Often there are also omissions or obvious errors in the musical notation. Stokowski has found many examples of such errors, especially imbalance of sound or harmony; and he felt that if they were not corrected the result would not be as the composer intended. Not even Toscanini, usually considered the most ardent advocate of the literal and uncompromising performance of the written notes, can be cited as an authority against it. He, too, has occasionally taken liberties with the scores; for instance in the orchestration of Schumann's *Rhenish Symphony* and Moussorgsky's *Pictures at an Exhibition*, to say nothing of the furious tempi in which he rushes through the minuets of Haydn and Mozart, depriving them of any resemblance to the original classical dance-movement.

At times Stokowski's departures from the written scores may be more extensive. In the Third Movement of Brahms' C Minor Symphony, he always omits the repetition of the second theme, but the result is an obvious improvement, because the dynamic and dramatic culmination of the theme motivates a direct transition to the repetition of the first theme. Still, his digressions do not always seem so well motivated, and are not even consistent. You have only to compare his older and his more recent recordings of Sibelius' *Finlandia* (Victor 7412 and Capitol (S)P 8399), of Tschaikovsky's Fifth Symphony (Victor 8589-94 and LM 1780), and of the suite from *The Firebird* by Stravinsky (Victor 8926-28, Columbia 11522-24D, Victor LM 9029, and Capitol (S)PAO 8407) to find examples. In the older recording of *Finlandia* there is a cut of three bars in the coda; in the new Capitol recording there is no cut. Likewise in the Fourth Movement of the Tschaikovsky Symphony, there is in the older version a cut of bars No. 468-71 and 473, but in the more recent version only a cut of bar No. 473. Finally, in the two first-mentioned recordings of *The Firebird* he omits the big variation in the Finale, whereas he makes no omissions in the more recent ones. It is difficult to see the necessity of tampering with these works, and with advancing age Stokowski clearly displayed greater faithfulness to the written notes. But cuts or no cuts, all the above-mentioned interpretations are excellent, they are only different, as at times were even his own

Stokowski at his work table in his New York apartment in the mid 1960s. *Photo: RCA.*

transcriptions. In the three Victor recordings of his condensed version of Strauss's *Tales from the Vienna Woods*, for instance, the introduction is performed respectively on a cello, a violin and an electronically-amplified zither.

Is there any explanation of these peculiarities in Stokowski, the musician? Yes, perhaps his insatiable striving towards perfect beauty, and his conception of music not as a fixed, unchangeable form, but as a living art in continuous development. Nevertheless, despite occasional digressions, he was one of the most gifted conductors, and his performances are unsurpassed for melodic beauty, dramatic power, definition and balance of sound.

If Stokowski had never made anything else, he would have become world-famous for his orchestral transcriptions of the music of Bach. Nobody has remained unaffected by them, and their detractors have even asserted that they were not Stokowski's own work, but were made by Sir Henry Wood (under the assumed name of Klenovski) or by the former clarinetist of the Philadelphia Orchestra, Lucien Caillet. Of course, this is entirely unfounded, and on several occasions firmly disavowed by Caillet, who was copyist of the orchestra in the 1920s and 1930s, and often wrote out the orchestral parts of the scores Stokowski brought to him. About the origin of the Bach transcriptions Stokowski said:

I used to play the organ, and I always loved the music of Bach, but when I became a conductor I did not get much opportunity to play that music. Then I orchestrated the Passacaglia and Fugue in C Minor, and I wished to play it in rehearsal, just for the fun of hearing it. We never played it in public, but one day the players said to me, "Why don't we play that in public? We enjoy it, perhaps the public will enjoy it." So we did play it, and to our surprise and satisfaction the public did like it.

In this way Stokowski set out upon his life-long practice of orchestral transcription, and it has contributed immensely to the great Bach renaissance of our century, also helped by the development of gramophone recording. However, the transcriptions also have musical qualities of their own, and since Stokowski authorised Broude Brothers, New York, to publish most of them, they have now become a permanent part of the repertoire of the modern symphony orchestra.

In Bach's time the instruments of the orchestra – and the orchestra itself – were still very undeveloped, and he wrote much of his music for the organ or other solo-instruments. This has limited the knowledge of it among the public. The orchestral works he wrote mainly for strings, with a few solo parts for flute, trumpet or oboe. There are many examples of unison passages for violins and wind instruments, and it is rare that wind instruments are used as contrasting groups to the strings within the orchestral texture. His imagination and creative power unfold quite differently at the organ, the harpsichord and with the violin; but if he had known the modern symphony orchestra, he would undoubtedly have taken advantage of its wide range of expression, just as Stokowski has done in many of his works.

It would be beyond the framework of this book to make a complete analysis of all the Bach transcriptions. Let it suffice to say that the great organ works have a true greatness in Stokowski's settings; much unnoticed beauty and religious mysticism is revealed in his transcriptions of the Schemelli songs; and the chorale preludes and solo works have been brought to new life by the modern symphony orchestra. It is remarkable that no two transcriptions are alike, and there are no mannerisms and no clichés. Every work has been transcribed according to its inner nature. The means range from the simplest, almost ascetic use of timbres, for example in Komm', süsser Tod (Schemelli no. 42), to the most stupendous display of every sound

The last page of Stokowski's transcription of Bach's Toccata and Fugue in D Minor. *Copyright: Broude Brothers, New York.*

register of the orchestra, in the climaxes of the Toccata and Fugue in D Minor. Quite unique is the Chaconne from Partita no. 2 in D Minor, which has in its rather free transcription become a quite independent work of art, beyond time and space in its strange and mystic beauty.

Stokowski cherished no illusions about the appreciation of his Bach transcriptions. But those who have flatly declared them to be sheer vandalism, out of an arrogant notion that they have an authorised opinion on music, can learn a great deal from his own modesty about them:

Those who do not like these orchestral transcriptions have a perfect right to their opinion, as we all have. They do not like them – it is very simple, then they should not listen to them. Those who do like them, they have also a right to their opinion, and if they listen to them and find pleasure in them, or if they make the music clearer to them, then that is perfectly all right. You see, I think there is a great misunderstanding about Bach, because the music of Bach that we found after his death has no marks of expression. Some persons think there should be no expression, but as Bach was a very warm-blooded man – in fact, he had twenty children. Cold-blooded men do not have twenty children – in fact, I do not know in the whole history of art any musician, or any painter, or any kind of an artist who had twenty children, but Bach had them, so evidently he was a warm-blooded man and was expressive. We know that he loved his children very much, he took great trouble for their education, so I think that Bach should be played expressively, but those who think the opposite have the same right to their opinion.

Another kind of transcription is his series of symphonic syntheses from some of Wagner's great music dramas. The term 'synthesis', by the way, is not Stokowski's, but Charles O'Connell's. Orchestral music may seem far from opera; but since many of Wagner's operas are more symphonic than dramatic, there is much justification for them.

The syntheses contain complete musical sequences, but Stokowski has not made it his task to follow the action of the drama in his arrangements. In some the scenes are only loosely connected if at all, but there are also a few in which he has succeeded in making a quite new musical coherence with no perceptible transition from one scene to another. Examples of the former are the syntheses from *Die Walküre*, *Siegfried*, and *Götterdämmerung*; whereas those of *Tristan and Isolde* and Act 3 from *Parsifal* are examples of the latter. In the synthesis from 'Parsifal' he has concentrated upon the figure of Parsifal. About this he said:

I have tried to follow the development from the time when Parsifal receives enlightenment and initiation from Gurnemanz. From that moment, I have

TABLEAUX D'UNE EXPOSITION

MOUSSORGSKY

Symphonic transcription by LEOPOLD STOKOWSKI

Orchestra: 4 Fl. (2 Picc.) (Alto Fl.), 4 Ob. (1 C. Ing.), 4 Cl. (1 E♭, 1 Bass, 1 E♭ Alto Sax.),
4 Fag. (1 C. Fag.), 8 Cor. (F) (5 at least), 4 (or 3) Tr. (C), 4 (or 3) Trb., Tuba
(Euph.), Timp., Perc. (4 Players) (T. Mil., T. Basc., Trgl., Piatti, G. C.,
Tam-Tam (Gong), Marimbaphone (or Xylo.), Vibraphone (or Glock.), Campane),
Organ (optional), Celesta, 2 (or 1) Arpe, Archi.

Duration: 27'44"

I. PROMENADE

The first page of Stokowski's transcription of 'Pictures at an Exhibition'.
Copyright: Peters Edition.

138

tried to continue this idea of more and more complete and profound perception on Parsifal's part of the mysteries of which the Grail is a symbol, and of which the outward and active manifestations are, first, Parsifal's initiation, and then his acceptance by the Knights, and finally their acknowledgement of him as their leader.

The instrumentation used for the syntheses are mainly Wagner's own, and where Stokowski has made slight rearrangements, they are generally intended to make the musical texture or the symphonic ideas clearer.

Besides the above-mentioned transcriptions, Stokowski also made a series of orchestrations of works of both older and newer composers. Among the works by newer composers are orchestrations of Albeniz's *Féte dieu a Seville* from *Iberia,* Moussorgsky's *Pictures at an Exhibition,* and Shostakovitch's Prelude no. 14, from opus 34. These transcriptions are evidence of his faculties as a musician, and give grandiose visions of the possibilities of expression of which the modern symphony orchestra is capable.

Creative musicians leave at their death a series of compositions, which will, under favourable conditions, continue to exist for centuries, whereas the performing artist usually leaves nothing lasting, except perhaps a couple of books and some gramophone recordings.

Several conductors have become dissatisfied with their art and devoted more of their time to composition. Examples of these composer-conductors are Bernstein, Dorati and Furtwängler. Other conductors have given themselves entirely to the performance of music, and carried this to the utmost perfection.

Stokowski is decidedly an example of the latter, but it is not commonly known that even he tried his hand at composition, mostly during his early years. As far as I know, his production comprises the following:

> *Benedicite Omnia Opera* for Chorus and Organ
> *Dithyrambe* for Flute, Harp and Cello
> *Gypsy Rhapsody*
> *Negro Rhapsody*
> *Pianissimo Amen* for Mixed Chorus
> *Reverie*
> *When Christ Was Born* for Mixed Chorus

Stokowski was always very discreet about his compositions, but in March 1972, at a concert in Town Hall, New York, he offered his *Reverie* as an encore. He introduced it this way to the audience:

'A very long time ago, many, many years, I composed something. I was just a student – Are you in a very critical mood?' – Applause. – 'That means yes. Then we won't play it.' – New applause. – 'We will try.'

After his death it was revealed that Stokowski also left an almost complete symphony in his library, which was inherited by the Curtis Institute. The curator, Edwin E. Heilakka, informs me that all the orchestral parts are there except the first flute part, and strangely enough the complete score has not yet been found, but I hope – and Mr Heilakka estimates it is possible – that this symphony may be completed for performance and recording at the centenary of Stokowski's birth in 1982.

Chapter 16

Stokowski, the Man

There has always been great interest in Stokowski the man. The amount of paper which has been used for writing about his enigmatic personality has far exceeded what has been applied to a serious evaluation of his contribution to music. In addition, the descriptions of his person are so contradictory that we do not know much more about him than without them. Nor was he ever willing to disclose any details himself; and his own silence has of course left ample room for the imagination to make his life far more sensational than it really was. Still, it cannot be denied that he was a character; yet since he was neither immoral nor unsocial nor in any way reprehensible, he had the right to live his life according to his own nature.

Physically Stokowski was something next to a miracle, and apart from the last few years, his tall, slender figure hardly changed during most of his career. Only his white hair became thinner and his features aged, while his expressive blue eyes remained the same to his very last day. He was conscious of this youthfulness himself, as is apparent from a concert he gave in Miami in the 1950s, where he entered into a violent dispute with the announcer about his age in front of the microphone. The announcer told listeners that the conductor was born in 1882, which, as we know, is correct; but Stokowski interrupted him, wanting to know who had told him such nonsense. 'I was born in 1887,' he asserted. Of course, the announcer was quite right, but got very embarrassed, and the producer had the broadcast interrupted.

Some years later Oliver Daniel, former Vice-President of Broadcast Music, Incorporated, New York, and one of Stokowski's few friends who could be quite frank with him, reverted to this episode again. He said, 'I think that was one of the meanest things you ever did,' but Stokowski just smiled and shrugged his shoulders. 'You know,' he answered, 'I didn't like the chap to bring up all that private stuff.'

Stokowski had practically speaking no illness; and his first serious illness can hardly be described as such, even though at the time it was the cause of much anxiety. After Christmas in 1960 he was playing ball with his two little sons in his Manhattan apartment, and suddenly had a bad fall in which he broke his right hip. He was immediately taken to hospital for careful examination, and surgical treatment proved necessary.

Naturally the accident gave rise to much anxiety about his future career, and the new production of Puccini's *Turandot* now seemed doomed. But every apprehension was falsified. A friend who visited him in hospital when he was still lying in a good deal of pain, caught sight of a large book beside him and asked curiously, 'What is that you have got on the bed-table?' He said, 'That is the score of *Turandot*. Don't you know that I am going to conduct that on 24 February?' The answer was clear evidence of Stokowski's never-failing devotion to music and of his enormous self-discipline, qualities that account for the fact that he very rarely failed to keep an appointment.

He did keep this appointment. No more than seven weeks after the accident, he limped on crutches into the orchestra pit of the Metropolitan Opera and led the first of a series of performances of *Turandot*. And he not only conducted it, but gave it a matchless reading. His greatest achievement, nevertheless, was undoubtedly his own presence, about which Robert Sabin wrote in *Musical America*:

'The hero of the evening was Mr Stokowski, and the audience recognised that fact by giving him a standing ovation at his first entrance and a series of salvos later on. It was deeply moving to see the silvery-haired maestro still on crutches conducting like a lad of twenty.'

Considerably more serious was what seemed to be a heart-attack, which he suffered in the summer of 1971, while he was fulfilling engagements in England. He complained to the staff at his hotel of ill-health and was immediately taken to hospital for careful examination and treatment. On the doctor's advice, all his engagements were cancelled, and he was ordered complete rest for one month. This period he spent in Switzerland, together with one of his daughters and her family; but in October he seemed to have recovered, and he went back to New York to open the new season of the American Symphony Orchestra, and there was no more talk of heart-ailments. What had looked like a heart-attack was later on ascribed to low blood-pressure, possibly because he had overworked himself.

On 18 April the following year more than one hundred people who had contributed to the support of the American Symphony Orchestra, and a crowd of notabilities from the musical and political world, gathered at the ballroom of the Plaza Hotel in New York. Among them were Leonard Bernstein, Pierre Boulez, Dorothy Maynor, Rudolf Serkin, Alan Hovhaness, August Heckscher, John B. Ford II, Nelson A. Rockefeller and many others. They had come to celebrate Stokowski's ninetieth birthday at a great party, but true to his nature the Nonagenarian did not care much about his age ('Just another birthday'), so he made it into an ordinary working-day. In the morning he rehearsed his orchestra as usual, in the afternoon he studied some scores, and in the evening he went on to the birthday party looking not the least exhausted. To be sure, ninety years is an awesome age, but music and the responsibility of family seem to keep a man alive. Stokowski had sworn that he would live at least until all his children had come of age, and with his determination it is not surprising that he did that by several years.

In June, Stokowski went to Europe as usual for his summer holidays, and also for the sixtieth anniversary of his debut with the

Rehearsal for the sixtieth anniversary concert with the London Symphony Orchestra in June 1972. *Photo: Press Association, London.*

London Symphony Orchestra. Of course it was evident that he had aged considerably. He looked fragile, he walked with difficulty, and off-stage he relied on a thick cane. But from a musical aspect he was unquestionably still at the height of his power.

That year Stokowski was also able to realise a plan he had long been nourishing, to retire to a place of his own. For a long time he had been looking for a peaceful country house surrounded by unspoiled nature; and such a place he found at Nether Wallop, Hampshire, in his native England.

After a concert in Paris in September he went to Prague for another engagement with the Czech Philharmonic Orchestra, but unfortunately he had a fall on the train and sprained a ligament. Nevertheless, devoted to duty, he fulfilled his engagement in Prague on crutches, but afterwards had to rest in England. He did not return to the USA again, nor commit himself to any other engagements abroad. Stokowski had come home.

In this connection, I would like to let the former vicar of St Andrew's Church, Nether Wallop, the Reverend M. G. M. Pitt, tell about Stokowski's last years. In a letter in 1978 Mr Pitt wrote:

'Stokowski lived in Nether Wallop for about six years at Place Farm House and had a house-keeper to look after him. He was away for many months of the year, but when at home he took an active part in our village concerns – like coming to our Danebury Singers on occasion, of which society he was the president.

Though not an Anglican, he came occasionally to our church and gave generously towards its upkeep, and in his last year I had the privilege of giving him his Easter Communion.

He was well liked and much admired by all music-lovers in our village – always friendly and very humble – a true gentleman.'

SOME MORE FEATURES

His childhood and most of his early years Stokowski spent in England, and his speech at that time is said to have been pure and fluent English; but the language he made use of the rest of his life was actually neither English nor American.

His vocabulary often had an international, and rather inconsistent structure, and in a short time he might change between English and foreign words for the same thing. For instance, in rehearsing part of *Götterdämmerung*: 'More deutlich, more impressive, heavier.' In Brahms' Second Symphony: 'Heroico, heroically, please.' About the

Stokowski arrives at the Royal Festival Hall for a rehearsal, June 1972.

harpsichord in Bach's time: 'The original was for violin, and he made it for klavier.' Or about watercolour technique: 'With aquarelle you can make just the faintest colours.' Sometimes he even pretended to have forgotten a certain English word: 'Piano, impertinent, kech! I do not—what is the English for it? Kech, kech! What is good? Impertinent?'

Another characteristic feature was his frequent omission of the definite and the indefinite articles, and a weakening of the diphthongs, which leaned towards the Slavonic languages. For instance, in rehearsing the Passion According to St Matthew: 'Can you hear organ where you are?' And from the same rehearsal: 'How is balance between organ and stage?' Sometimes he even omitted the subject of a sentence: 'It is one person spoils it all. Concentrate with your mind, or go away!'

It is questionable if these peculiarities were due to the Slavonic origin of his family on the paternal side, or to anything else in particular. In fact, his speech had no resemblance to any existing language. There is no explanation of these or other peculiarities, nor that after more than sixty years in the USA his speech had not the slightest American accent. However, Maestro Stokowski did not owe an explanation to anybody. It is sufficient that his speech was beautiful, clear and well-articulated, both imaginative and highly-cultivated. If you wish to judge for yourself, listen to the introduction he gives to Arnold Schoenberg's music in the Victor recording of *Gurrelieder* (Victor 7524), or to the comments on Beethoven's music in the last recording of the *Pastoral Symphony* (Victor LM 1830). They were made with an interval of more than twenty years between them and give the impression that his speech remained consistent through the years.

In some other respects too Stokowski was a man of paradoxes. He was one of the most frequently-photographed artists in our century, and yet few other persons have ever given so much trouble to the press as he did with his avoidance of publicity. Thus on a visit to Germany in 1951 he could only be persuaded to conduct a concert in Munich on condition that no pictures were taken while he was in the city. The German officials conscientiously ensured that the ban was observed, but nevertheless a female photographer succeeded in snapping his famous hands during the concert. With a display of unusually violent temperament, Stokowski snatched the camera from her and destroyed the film.

The whole episode was all the more incomprehensible as we know how frequently and willingly he posed before the camera; and most people were inclined to explain his behaviour as an indirect attempt to make publicity. This is entirely wrong. He always avoided sensation

A photo episode in Munich in 1951. *Photo: Nordisk Pressefoto.*

and preferred to be a mystic; but he never shrunk from publicity when it proved useful to music. Typical are some of his early electric recordings for which he made spoken introductions, for instance to Brahms' First Symphony (on Victor 6657), and concluded them with what sounded like commercial recommendation of the Victor products.

However, it seems that over the years Stokowski became more patient with press photographers. During one of the rehearsals at the Edinburgh Festival 1961, for instance, the photographers kept flashing for a very long time, without any objections on his part. It was not until it became distracting that he asked them kindly to withdraw from the organ-gallery.

It is reported that in his early years Stokowski was very aloof, but that he became more gentle with age. I cannot tell if that is true since I did not meet him until 1960. To me personally he was usually kind and forthcoming; but generally speaking he was reserved with strangers, such as reporters, autograph-hunters, snobs and others, who found it useful to follow in his wake. However, though he seemed very open to those who wanted to discuss music with him, they never really got to know him closely. He might readily state his opinion on a subject, but he would always deftly avoid revealing his own person or feelings. He was often joking, but even the jokes were part of the shield with which he covered himself; and if there was someone he did not want to speak to, he would say that he did not know of anybody by that name. He even met some of his own musicians in the street without showing the least signs of recognition.

Of course, all this is a clear indication that he wanted to be completely free and independent; but unfortunately that was not what happened during the last years, when he was dependent on assistance from others. In this situation he was practically cut off from contact with his friends by a group of more or less self-appointed followers, who jealously watched over their idol and their own positions around him.

Quite contradictory accounts have been given of Stokowski's habits. He has alternatively been described as a fanatical vegetarian and abstainer from tobacco and spirits – actually, he was a vegetarian in the middle of the 1930s, but only for a short experimental period – or as a devotee of the pleasures of the table. As a matter of fact, he was neither. He smoked and drank moderately, and had a predilection for exotic and highly-seasoned dishes and wines. Similar was his love of colours, which manifested itself in his own dress and houses. For that matter, he was not particular about his appearance, and once had the questionable honour of being listed among the worse dressed celebrities on the American scene.

His interests outside music were extraordinarily wide and included radio-broadcasting, recording-techniques, literature, architecture, art, philosophy and religion, and on his journeys in Europe, Africa, Asia, and South America he acquired a thorough knowledge of the culture and folk-music of many countries. His personal cultivation was very useful to him as an artist, but sometimes it threw doubt on the sincerity of his love of music. For instance, when Sibelius was once asked about his opinion of Stokowski, he gave the following answer, 'Stokowski is unquestionably a very great and most fascinating person. He is interested in everything – except perhaps music.'

Stokowski was baptised a Roman Catholic, but he has in turn been interested in Buddhism, Quakerism and ancient Christianity. In his philosophy, music was the greatest manifestation of the divine creative power, and he had unlimited respect for the human being and his natural and innate right to think, to believe, and to feel about music whatever he considers right, without any external influence. This tolerance he also extended to his colleagues about whom he was never heard to say a disparaging word. Unfortunately, the same is not true of them. Koussevitzky, for instance, had a great opinion of few others apart from himself; and Toscanini, on innumerable occasions, heaped invective on conductors whose ideas about music were not based on the same literal consistency as his own.

Stokowski's dynamic personality was the object all his life of great attention and many women felt attracted by him. He was the darling of the female inhabitants of Philadelphia when he was there, young as well as old. He also appreciated the company of women, particularly beautiful women, but only if they were interesting. He married three times, and each marriage ended with a divorce. In 1911 he married Olga Samaroff, the pianist. The marriage was no doubt happy, and the young couple were very popular and highly esteemed by the musical circles in Cincinnati and Philadelphia. The Women's Committees for the Philadelphia Orchestra demonstrated their affection on several occasions, among others at the tenth anniversary of Stokowski's tenure, and at their daughter, Sonia Maria's baptism. In 1923, however, they had grown apart, and the marriage was brought to an end.

In 1926 he married Evangeline Brewster Johnson, the daughter of a noted New Jersey business family. To this marriage were born two girls, Lyuba and Sadja. Stokowski took a great interest in their birth, as he did in all processes of nature. In 1937, however, he met Greta Garbo, the famous actress. They first saw each other at a party on the occasion of Deanna Durbin's appearance in 'A Hundred Men and a Girl, and with Stokowski's taste for interesting women, their meeting turned out distastrously for his marriage. Mrs Stokowski demanded a divorce, and after that Garbo and Stokowski were much seen together, particularly on his European tours, when they spent several weeks together in a villa in Ravello, besieged by scores of newspaper reporters. However, no marriage resulted from this alliance. It is said Stokowski gave his children preference to his feelings; but Greta Garbo claimed she never meant to enter into marriage.

In the meantime, Stokowski advanced in age to a point that nobody thought of connecting his name with women. Therefore, it was a sensation when in 1945 at the age of 63 he married the young heiress, Gloria Vanderbilt. In some cases, advanced age may be an obstacle to happy marriage; but with the immense vitality of a Stokowski it was not. A testimony to this was the birth of two children, Stanislau (born in 1950) and Christopher (born in 1952).

After a lonely and loveless childhood amongst aristocrats with no

Stokowski and Garbo in Rome, 1938. *Photo: World Wide Photo.*

Stokowski and his two boys, Chris and Stan, in Untermeyer Park, New York, 1957. *Photo: Oliver Daniel.*

time for children, Gloria had thrown herself into the arms of an Italian actor to whom she had been introduced at her social debut in Hollywood in 1941. The marriage became a disappointment, as the security and happiness she sought did not appear, perhaps because the war separated them, and in 1945 she got a divorce. Shortly after that she met Stokowski, in whom she saw both a mature husband and the father she had never really had. From Stokowski she learned everything about the arts, and now became absorbed in the theatre. But there did not seem to be room for Gloria's activities in the marriage, and they gradually drifted away from each other. In 1954 they parted without bitterness, but when a few years later it came to the question of custody for their two sons, the matter had to be settled in court. Stokowski wanted an extension of his custody of the children, but Gloria pleaded that while they were so young, only she could give them the love she had missed as a child. After settling the case, the Justice of the New York Supreme Court said, 'It is sad that an entire month of the court's time has been devoted almost exclusively to the resolution of problems which mature, intelligent parents should be able to work out themselves.'

In his later years Stokowski remained single, and watched his private life very strictly. 'I never talk about that side,' he said to me in Philadelphia in 1960. The achievements of the great artists naturally always become the property of the public, but their private life belongs to themselves.

Gloria Vanderbilt Stokowski arrives with her two attorneys to testify in the custody case against Stokowski in 1959. *Photo: United Press International.*

Chapter 17

Stokowski and the Gramophone

A history of the gramophone without Stokowski's name in it is unthinkable, and a history of the recording of classical music that does not deal with his achievements will be meaningless. But so far I have not seen any which does justice to his pioneering work.

Stokowski's recorded repertoire is not only one of the largest that exists, but he has also set a standard of orchestral playing and quality which most conductors have rarely achieved. Furtwängler, for instance, despaired when he compared his own poor recordings for Polydor with Stokowski's rich-sounding ones with the Philadelphia Orchestra and tried to switch to EMI, at that time also representing Victor in Europe; but he was very disappointed when he found no basic improvement in his new recordings. This was not surprising since Stokowski studied recording techniques and was active in developing new methods to improve the reproduction of music; so he understood the medium and its possibilities and limitations perfectly. But firstly, his work was in the field of music, and he did not attach more than limited importance to technique. He found that it was only important in so far as it served music.

Very early Stokowski realised that the seating of an orchestra which is best for concerts does not necessarily give the best results in recording, where the microphones call for different location of the instruments. He made countless experiments in this field, but the result was far from standard, because different kinds of music and different halls make many varying demands.

Charles O'Connell. *Photo: RCA.*

With his great knowledge of recording technique, Stokowski also knew the limits which the technical standards set to the dynamic range of the recordings. Therefore, in the 1930s he was able to obtain better results than others by adjusting the playing of the orchestra to the capacity of the recording equipment instead of having the engineers making constant alteration to the music at their control-boards. This special technique was developed in close co-operation with RCA Victor's former music-director, the late Charles O'Connell, and the chief engineer, Albert Pulley, to such perfection that they would often run a whole recording session without a single adjustment to the equipment. This is also one of the explanations for the realistic sound which has always been a hallmark of his recordings with the Philadelphia Orchestra.

But nowadays conditions are quite different. With modern tape recording, it is possible, without manipulation of the orchestra or the equipment, to record the entire audible frequency-range of the music, with a volume of thirty to sixty decibels, which is sufficient for most purposes.

Arthur C. Keller with some of the experimental recordings with the Philadelphia Orchestra from 1931-2. *Photo: Bell Laboratories.*

For many years after the invention of electric recording, it was not possible to reproduce the music with a larger frequency-range than 60-5,000 hz. Of course, Stokowski was not satisfied with this, and with Dr Harvey Fletcher from the Bell Laboratories he undertook experiments to discover the audible frequency-range. They found that the human ear can hear sounds with frequencies of up to about 13,000 hz. Therefore Stokowski urged RCA Victor's engineers to make experiments with an extension of the frequency-range, and in the middle of the 1930s they succeeded in producing recordings with up to 10,000 hz. This, however, only held true of the original masters. When they had gone through the usual manufacturing, there were rarely more than 8,000 hz left in the final products; but even this was a remarkable achievement.

With his untiring work to improve recordings Stokowski was also one of the pioneers of modern high fidelity technique. Together with Albert Pulley he was co-responsible for the New Orthophonic Recording System which RCA Victor applied to all its recordings of classical music from the early 1950s. The term 'orthophonic' had been used since the first electric recordings, but it was only now that it meant a full range of volume and frequencies, combined with a new cutting-process securing the quality of the finished product in transferring the tape to record. The recordings cover the whole audible frequency-range of 20-20,000 hz, and have a pre-amplification of up to 17 decibels for frequencies higher than 700 hz. But Stokowski found it necessary to include still higher frequencies in recording, even up to 25,000 hz, in order to add to the overall brilliance of recorded sound.

With the introduction of stereophonic sound-reproduction the record entered upon the fourth stage of its development. This was, however, nothing new for Stokowski. When the Bell Lab experiments took place in Philadelphia in the early 1930s, some of the recordings were made in stereo. Chief engineers Arthur C. Keller and Irad S. Rafuse developed a method of separating the high and low frequencies into two channels, and recording them on double-groove records. But this halved playing-time, and the equipment needed for play-back was so complicated and expensive that the method was never used commercially.

In 1938 the two engineers took out a patent on an improved method of cutting the two channels in the same groove of the master-disc, the modern 45/45-system, but it was not until after the Second World War and the invention of the long-playing record and tape-recording that the idea of applying it began to mature. First, however, a battle had to be fought between three competing systems, but on 25 March, 1958, the Record Industry Association of America settled the matter and approved the 45/45-system as standard. At the end of that year Stokowski's first stereophonic album saw the light of the day, when Capitol Records released his recording of Shostakovitch's Eleventh Symphony, made a few months earlier.

Stokowski is the only artist who has lived long enough to take part in all the phases of recording from the acoustic to the binaural stage. The first experiments with quadraphonic techniques were made by Vanguard in the late 1960s, using four-track stereo-machines both in recording and in play-back; but no records resulted from these first modern attempts in quadraphony. The problem of standardization of systems was – and still is – unsolved.

It was the small English label Unicorn that made the best coup on the threshold of the age of quadraphony. In May 1970 Stokowski gave the world-premiere of Andrzej Panufnik's masterpiece, *Universal Prayer*, in the Cathedral of St John the Divine in New York, in close co-operation with the composer. The Polish emigrant had come across the text of Alexander Pope while seaching for a prayer to the God of all religions; and Stokowski found his composition one of the most original and important of the twentieth century. Consequently he performed the work twice in the same programme to 4,000 listeners, and later that year gave several other performances, both in the USA and Britain.

The Managing Director of Unicorn, John Goldsmith, became interested in the work, and he approached the composer and Stokowski for a possible recording with British artists. Luckily Stokowski was in Europe most of the summer, and the recording took place in September in Westminster Cathedral, London, in two

Stokowski and Panufnik (right) at the world-premiere of 'Universal Prayer' in New York. *Photo: A. Hansen, New York.*

evening sessions. All the possibilities of quadrophonic use of the cathedral were turned to account, but paradoxically the recording was not released in quadraphony.

But let us go back to Stokowski's first recording, which took place on 22 October, 1917. With the Philadelphia Orchestra he spent a whole day in Victor's studios in Camden, and the result was two single-sided records with Brahms' Hungarian Dances Nos. 5 and 6 (Victor 64752 and 64753). Later there followed single-sided recordings of other short orchestral pieces, or condensed versions of larger works like the Overture to *Rienzi* (Victor 75602-03). In the early 1920s Victor succeeded in producing double-sided pressings, but for some time they confined themselves to re-publishing the old single-sided recordings in double sided editions, for example Brahms's Hungarian Dances (Victor 797) and Wagner's *Rienzi* Overture (Victor 6239). Later there followed some new publications, but still mostly shorter works, among them Debussy's *Prelude a l'apres-midi d'un faune* (Victor 6481), the Waltz from Gounod's *Faust* (Victor 944), and Prelude to Act 1 of Wagner's *Lohengrin* (Victor 6490). Therefore, it was a real sensation when, with Schubert's Unfinished Symphony, recorded in April 1924, Victor issued its first complete recording of a whole symphony (Victor 6459-61). This album, however, was followed by only a few others. That was not because the recordings were poor – indeed, they were among the best that had been made – but, as will be seen later, simply because the era of acoustic recordings was over.

Technically Stokowski's acoustic recordings compare extremely well with those of other conductors, and from an artistic point of view they are very fine, as far as we are able to tell from the imperfect reproduction. As in all acoustic recordings, the orchestration is adapted with brass and woodwind instruments substituting or doubling some of the parts for the lower strings; but the adaptations are deftly made and give convincing and effective results.

Stokowski himself was not satisfied with his first recordings. On the whole, he was never satisfied with any of them, as he was of opinion that in music and its reproduction there are no limits. This dissatisfaction made him one of the greatest forces in the art and science of recording. His dissatisfaction with the first acoustic recordings was so great that he was on the point of entirely giving up making records. The adapted orchestras and the distorted sound seemed so hopeless that he could not see any future for the phonographic industry. Later he realised that this was a foolish attitude, and that he should go on making records, and himself contribute to their improvement. When at length an entirely new recording method came into use, he felt that progress was on its way.

This was in 1925, and by then the record industry had gone into decline. The public was getting tired of imperfect, harsh-sounding acoustic recordings, and sales had decreased alarmingly. Victor's response was the introduction of electric recording, which for the first time made it possible to distinguish the instruments clearly from each other. In July came Saint-Saëns's *Dance macabre* (Victor 6505), and in October Tschaikovsky's *Marche slave* (Victor 6513). These recordings were not announced as electric, but the improved reproduction made it clear to the public that a new technique had been adopted.

In 1926 the improvements became still more obvious. The dynamic range was increased considerably, the adaptation of the orchestration ceased, and last – but not least – recordings were now made in the Academy of Music, where most recordings with Stokowski and the Philadelphia Orchestra have since taken place. From the beginning of this epoch originate the short versions of the two Strauss waltzes *On the Beautiful Blue Danube* and *Tales from the Vienna Woods* (Victor 6584) and Liszt's Hungarian Rhapsody no. 2 (Victor 6652); and in

The short versions of the Strauss waltzes remained bestsellers through the 1950s. When a new 45 rpm single version passed 1,000,000 pressings, Stokowski received a golden copy from Emmanuel Sachs, Vice President of RCA. *Photo: Leo Friedman, New York.*

1927 came the world-famous transcription of Bach's Toccata and Fugue in D Minor (Victor 6751). These three recordings became best-sellers with millions of pressings, usually only achieved by 'pop' music. Containing unabridged classical works they were also technical miracles for the music-lovers of those days, and even compared with present day techniques there is a surprisingly large amount of music preserved in their grooves.

From the period until 1930 I would single out the transcription of Albeniz's *Fete dieu a Seville* (Victor 7158), Rachmaninov's Piano Concerto no. 2 with the composer as soloist (Victor 8148-52), and Stravinsky's *Le Sacre du Printemps* (Victor 7227-30). The Albeniz composition was unanimously hailed as one of Stokowski's finest recordings, and as he did not make a new recording of it until 1976, it soon became a precious rarity in the collector's library. The technical quality of Rachmaninov's Second Piano Concerto recording was never very good. The piano is rather prominent, and the orchestra too much in the background; but although more than thirty recordings have been made since then, most of them with modern high fidelity technique, none of them have approached Stokowski's and the composer's magical interpretation, with its deep Russian melancholy and passion, essential qualities of the work itself.

The recording of Stravinsky's *Sacre* was a landmark in the history of the gramophone. With its excellent technique and musical brilliance it remained quite unchallenged for a decade. Then Stravinsky, with his obsessive wish to make the definitive performances of all his music, recorded it for Columbia, but without convincing us that the composer is the best interpreter of his own works. Stokowski's *Sacre* recording was a unique achievement in other respects. In fact, the record companies were uninterested in music by non-popular composers and mainly exploited the wishes of the public. Victor refused to let Stokowski record *Sacre*, and suggested a recording of some Sousa marches instead; but he was not so easy to dismiss. He declared himself willing to record the Sousa marches if he got his *Sacre*. So he did, and in this way both Sousa and Stravinsky were made available to the public in excellent performances.

From 1931, on account of increasing economic difficulties, the recording sessions were again transferred to the studios in Camden, and with the help of a large number of microphones a reduced orchestra of about seventy players was made to sound like the full Philadelphia Orchestra. Typical examples from this period are the first recording of Sibelius's Fourth Symphony (Victor 7683-86) and Scriabin's *Poeme d'Extase* and *Prometheus* (Victor 7515-18). They are both good performances, but poor recordings, and because of the studio conditions completely dead acoustically and lacking in atmosphere. An exception was made with the first American performance of Arnold Schoenberg's *Gurrelieder*, which took place at the Broad Street Metropolitan Opera House, and was recorded during the public performance on 8 April, 1932 (Victor 7524-37). For its time this was a gorgeous recording and several reissues of it held an honoured position in the RCA Victor catalogue up to the late 1950s.

Generally speaking, this was a gloomy period for the record industry. The great Depression made sales decrease alarmingly, and Victor had to reduce the number of classical releases. At the same time great hopes were put on an interesting experiment of increasing the playing-time on each side of a record. An attempt to do so by making the grooves narrower was a failure, but by reducing the velocity to 33 rpm. Stokowski and the Victor engineers managed to raise it to about 15 minutes per side. On 15 July, 1931, the new technique was tested at a recording session in the Academy of Music, Stokowski leading the Philadelphia Orchestra in a performance of Beethoven's Fifth Symphony. The whole work was cut on two masters, and after having been pressed on record in a new plastic material called vitrolac, it was demonstrated to an invited audience in the Savoy-Plaza Hotel in New York on 17 September. The enthusiasm was great, particularly at the entirely new feature of being able to play whole movements of a symphony without interruptions every four minutes.

On 1 October the recording was released (Victor L 7001), and faith in it was so great that some of the recordings on 78's were also offered in the new technique, for instance Rimsky-Korsakov's *Russian Easter* Overture (Victor L 7002) and Shostakovitch's First Symphony (Victor 11744-46). But hopes had been pitched too high, and when the first enthusiasm was over, it had to be admitted that the experiment was a failure. The technical quality was much inferior to that of ordinary records, and Victor did not succeed in producing record-players and pick-ups that were good enough to turn the new technique to advantage; so after a couple of years the production of long-playing records stopped. But as a pioneer work, the experiment had been valuable in preparing the way for present-day techniques.

From 1933 the record industry was making progress again, and techniques improved gradually without any really new inventions. In those years Stokowski experimented with overlapping and fading the music in works lasting for several records. From a musical standpoint, this technique was a considerable step onward. Until then it had been necessary to make recordings in series of short sessions, according to the number of record-sides; but now it became possible, by means of two sets of cutting machines, to make uninterrupted recordings, and the musicians were able to get a certain continuity in their performance. But the new technique was in the first place intended for a continuous playing on two record-players; so for discophiles with only one player it was irritating and superfluous, and given up after two years.

Today with modern tape-recording and long-playing techniques, this problem has got its solution, and Stokowski was in favour of uninterrupted takes of complete works or movements. Usually the recordings had been preceded by concerts, and he began a session without rehearsing. After two or three takes the producer had enough material for the final master-tape. But even without any preceding concert, Stokowski would often follow the same procedure; and as recently as August 1975 he made a version of Rachmaninov's *Vocalise* which was so flawless that it was decided to use it without any editing.

Contributing to these marvellous results were Stokowski's many years' experience in the recording studio, and also the unusually relaxed atmosphere he was able to create at the sessions. Typical was a session in Chicago with the Suite from Shostakovitch's *The Age of Gold* in 1968. Over the intercom was heard the solemn voice of the producer, 'Age of Gold, Take One'; but immediately Stokowski said from the podium, 'Don't be so formal', and all the tension among the players and the technicians was dispelled.

Recording session with the Chicago Symphony Orchestra in Medinah Temple 1968. *Photo: RCA*

Returning to the years 1933-35, from this period originated some of Stokowski's most famous recordings. Among them were the second version of Bach's Toccata and Fugue in D Minor (Victor 8697), the Chaconne from Partita no. 2 in D Minor (Victor 8492-94), Dvorak's Ninth Symphony (Victor 8737-41), Rimsky-Korsakov's *Scheherazade* (Victor 8698-8703), Tschaikovsky's *Nutcracker* Suite (Victor 8662-64), Music from Wagner's *Die Walküre* (Victor 8542-45), and Rachmaninov's *Rhapsody on a Theme by Paganini* (Victor 8553-55). The Rachmaninov work was dedicated to the Philadelphia Orchestra, and the session, which followed shortly after the world premiere in Baltimore, 7 November, 1934, was the last time the two friends were united in the recording studio.

In 1936 the first recordings with extended frequency range ('extended range recording') began to appear. The first album contained the suite from Stravinsky's *Firebird* and Shostakovitch's Prelude in E Flat Minor, op. 34, nr. 14 (Victor 8926-28). In these records the music was reproduced with a new realism, and it was clear that a new technique had been taken into use. Only a few people could take advantage of it, since not many people at that time were in possession of record-players that could reproduce higher frequencies than 5,000 hz; but played on modern equipment these records still compare surprisingly well with most modern recordings.

Stokowski together with Rheinhold Gliere (left) and Aram Khachaturian in Russia. *Photo: Decca Records.*

After the *Firebird*, and until Stokowski left the Philadelphia Orchestra in 1941, there followed an endless series of recordings, which, with their high technical and musical qualities, rise as landmarks in the history of recordings. Let me single out the Bach transcriptions (Victor 14580-83 and 11-8576-78), Saint-Saëns's *Dance macabre* (Victor 14162), Moussorgsky's *A Night on the Bare Mountain* in the excellent Stokowski version from the film *Fantasia* (Victor 17900), the symphonic synthesis from *Boris Godunov,* based upon Moussorgsky's original score (Victor 14546-48), *Pictures at an Exhibition* in his own orchestration (Victor 17414-17), Gliere's Third Symphony (*Ilya Mourometz*) in a version Stokowski edited, together with Gliere, from the original, far too protracted, score (Victor 18262-67), the beautiful and expressive reading of Brahm's C Minor Symphony (Victor 8971-75), Shostakovitch's Symphonies no. 5 (Victor 15737-42) and 6 (Victor 18391-95), music from Act 1 and 3 of Wagner's *Tannhäuser* (Victor 15310-14), and Mozart's Sinfonia Concertante in E Flat Major, K. 297 b (Victor 17732-35). The latter is one of Stokowski's very few Mozart recordings, and his only one with the Philadelphia Orchestra.

Stokowski's work with the Philadelphia Orchestra is one of the peaks in the performance of music and one of the great chapters in the history of recording. Together, his recordings with this orchestra are nothing less than an historical document. On several occasions it has been pointed out, not least by David Hall, now head of the Rodgers and Hammerstein Archives, what a cultural obligation we have to perpetuate it in long-playing form. Until now, RCA Victor has not lived up to this responsibility. It is true that they reissued some of the recordings on the Camden label in the 1950s, but the idea was to make a low-priced series of popular classics, and since the recordings did not represent modern technique they were issued under a pretended name (Warwick Symphony Orchestra) and without naming the conductor. That was scandalous and a serious devaluation of great performances like Brahms's First Symphony (CAL 105) and Mozart's Sinfonia Concertante (CAL 213). But still worse was an attempt to 'improve' the sound by adding an ugly artificial reverberation to some of them, such as Tschaikovsky's *Nutcracker* Suite and Saint-Saëns's *Carnival of the Animals* (CAL 100). A more dignified attempt to revive the great performances was the reissue on Collectors' Items label, but very few discs were produced in this series. Most important among them were the famous Rachmaninov recordings (LCT 6123) and the historic premiere of Arnold Schoenberg's *Gurrelieder* (LCT 6012).

Both of these series have been discontinued for many years, and since then little has been done. On RCA only a commemoration of the sixtieth anniversary of Stokowski's debut with the Philadelphia

Orchestra (VCM 7101), and on the Victrola label merely another reissue of the *Gurrelieder* (AVM 2-2017).

In the summers of 1940 and 1941 there was an interlude in Stokowski's connections with RCA Victor when he recorded with the All American Youth Orchestra for American Columbia. Of course, these young musicians did not have the same experience as their older colleagues; but it is amazing how they approach the Philadelphia Orchestra both in performance and technique. This is particularly evident where the same works have been recorded with both orchestras, for instance Bach's Toccata and Fugue in D Minor (Amr. Col. 11757-58D), Dvorak's Ninth Symphony (Amr. Col. 11349-54SD), and Stravinsky's *Firebird* Suite (Amr. Col. 11522-24D). In my opinion, the Dvorak-recording with the All American Youth Orchestra is even better than the last one with the Philadelphia Orchestra (Victor 8737-41), and perhaps the most vital ever made. Interesting too are the recordings of contemporary American music, which Stokowski insisted on making, especially the exacting *Tales of Our Countryside* by Henry Cowell (Amr. Col. 11964-65D).

Technically the recordings with the Youth Orchestra are not entirely successful. Most of them were made in different studios in North and South America, many with rather dead acoustics and little spatial effect. Besides, most of these recordings bear the stamp of wartime, the shortage of proper pressing-materials, and careless manufacturing.

From 1942 Stokowski worked with RCA Victor again, this time in recordings with the NBC Symphony Orchestra. Unfortunately they amount to few because of the previously-mentioned ban on recording issued the same year because of disagreement between the Musicians' Union and the American Symphony Orchestra League. The NBC recordings are individualistic and electrifying at the same time; but the technical quality ranges from fair to poor. Among the best are a suite from Prokofiev's opera *Love for Three Oranges* (Victor 18497) and Rimsky-Korsakov's *Russian Easter Overture* (Victor 11-8426-27). In the latter Stokowski took the theme for solo trombone in the middle section and wrote, on the basis of Russian Orthodox liturgy, a beautiful chant to be sung by a bass-singer. This was not the original intention of the composer, but it sounds authentic and impressive.

When the recording ban ended, Stokowski's contract with the NBC Symphony Orchestra had finished, and then there followed a few recordings with the New York City Symphony Orchestra. The strings sound quite impressive, and one can hear that the young wind players have been trained to give the same intonation and beautiful phrasing that we have grown accustomed to from the Philadelphia Orchestra. The best recording from this period is Beethoven's *Pastoral*

Symphony. Presence and reverberation are combined in a harmonious blending, and the performance is both good Beethoven and good Stokowski (Victor 11-9011-15).

A more experienced group of players was the Hollywood Bowl Symphony Orchestra, represented by some exceptionally well-sounding recordings. I single out De Falla's *El Amor Brujo*, which is unsurpassed in musical eloquence and vitality (Victor 11-9393-95); and Virgil Thomson's film score *The Plow That Broke the Plains*, which won a Grand Prix as the best orchestral recording in 1946 (Victor 11-9520-21). Three of the Hollywood Bowl recordings have been transferred to long-playing records, namely *El Amor Brujo* (Victor LM 1054), Brahms' First Symphony (Victor LM 1070), and Tschaikovsky's Sixth Symphony (Camden CAL 152); but they were discontinued again several years ago, just like the Philadelphia recordings.

In the years 1947-9 Stokowski undertook a new series of recordings for American Columbia, because the New York Philharmonic Orchestra, to which he was attached at that time, had an exclusive contract with this company. Some critics, who had had reservations concerning the lack of musical judgement and artistic consistency in Stokowski's musicianship in the early 1940s, discovered with satisfaction that his work with the Philharmonic was close to that with the Philadelphia Orchestra. His recordings with the orchestra confirm this view. Tschaikovsky's *Francesca da Rimini* possesses a rare musical intensity and almost hair-raising dramatic power (Amr. Col. 12938-40D) and Vaughan Williams's Sixth Symphony, which he gave its American premiere, is perpetuated in an almost definitive performance (Amr. Col. 12977-80D). The recordings with the New York Philharmonic have also been documented in long-playing form, and their reproduction compares quite well even with present-day technique. They are not available for the time being, but it is to be hoped that they will be reissued.

Apart from some of its pre-orthophonic recordings, Stokowski's Symphony Orchestra for RCA Victor is only represented on long-playing records. With this orchestra a great part of the old Philadelphia repertoire was re-recorded, and although there is an interval of about twenty years between the two recording periods, RCA Victor succeeded fairly well. The first of these recordings are of an uneven technical quality, ranging from excellent (Tschaikovsky's *Sleeping Beauty* – LM 1010 and the two Bach-programmes – LM 1133 and LM 1176) to fair (Haydn's Symphony no. 53 – LM 1073) and poor (Dvoraks Ninth Symphony – LM 1013).

After the introduction of the New Orthophonic Recording System, technical quality improved enormously. But most of the Leopold

Stokowski visiting Vaughan Williams in England 1958. *Photo: Decca Records.*

Stokowski Symphony Orchestra recordings were made earlier, so there are only a few with the modern technique. Among these I prefer, as representing him at his best, 'Russian Music' (LM 1816), Romanian Rhapsodies no. 1 and 2 by Enesco (LM 1878), Roger Goeb's Third Symphony and Bartok's Sonata for 2 Pianos and Percussion (LM 1727), and Lou Harrison's Suite for Violin, Piano, and Orchestra and Ben Weber's Symphony on Poems by William Blake (LM 1785). The last two are among the few recordings RCA Victor made of contemporary music with Stokowski in the 1940's and the 1950's.

When Toscanini retired from public appearances at the beginning of 1954, RCA decided to disband the NBC Symphony Orchestra, but before this happened Stokowski assembled the orchestra for a series of recording sessions, the results of which rank among the best recordings he made for RCA Victor. This to some extent made up for the lack of documentation of his work with this orchestra in the early 1940s, but more recordings, especially of contemporary music, might have been desired. Beethoven's *Pastoral Symphony* gets an unusually euphonic performance. 'Scene at the Brook' is a miracle of phrasing, and the 'Thunder Storm' is unique for musical realism and sound

Stokowski checking a recording for RCA. *Photo: RCA.*

balance (LM 1830). There is also a poetic, monumental performance of Sibelius's Second Symphony. The interpretation has a grandiose atmosphere of Finnish heroism, nature and desolation, which is set off by the depth of the recording (LM 1854). The only work of contemporary music from this session is a suite from Gian-Carlo Menotti's ballet *Sebastian*. Recording and performance are unquestionably excellent, but the work in itself is not very interesting and not a Stokowski speciality which it would seem worth the trouble to record (LM 1858).

Stokowski has sometimes made several recordings of the same work. Of Stravinsky's Firebird Suite, for instance, there exist no less than seven different recordings. There are at least two good reasons for this. First, different recording companies often want to record the same work with a certain artist and, secondly, an artist will frequently re-record a certain work when former issues are deleted. This maintenance of the repertoire has preserved many Stokowski specialities for us in the record catalogues. But it seems incomprehensible that he made six recordings of Liszt's Hungarian Rhapsody no. 2, five recordings of Tschaikovsky's *Humoreske*, and five recordings of the same composer's *Solitude*. His valuable musical knowledge might have been better applied in recording greater works, which are somewhat more sparse in number in his recording list.

In 1956-9 there was complete deadlock between Stokowski and RCA Victor. Some supposed that they had broken off the relations, which might not have been surprising, since RCA Victor had for several years carried on a conservative policy. The company had concentrated mainly on new recordings of classical war-horses with the Boston and Chicago Orchestras, and besides that been busily occupied with issues on record of taped broadcasts of Toscanini concerts from the archives of the old NBC Symphony Orchestra.

In 1960 recordings were resumed, and the orchestra for two of them was handpicked, but now named RCA Victor Symphony Orchestra. However, it bears the unmistakable personal stamp of its conductor, so it ought to have been named Leopold Stokowski Symphony Orchestra. One of these recordings was to have been with the great Swedish soprano Birgit Nilsson in the final scenes of *Salome* and *Götterdämmerung*, but as she was suddenly indisposed, other music was brought in at the last minute. In that way we got music by Enesco, Liszt and Smetana (Victor LM/LSC 2471), all fine performances, but as a Stokowski novelty, of little interest. More important is a coupling of Handel's *Royal Fireworks Music* and the Suite from the *Water Music* (LM/LSC 2612). Both are transcribed by Stokowski, but unlike Hamilton Harty's arrangements for modern orchestra, he is much closer to the Handelian ideal of an orchestra. Stokowski's orchestra is somewhat larger than Handel's own (with its 125 musicians it represents one of the largest orchestras ever assembled for recording)

A recording session with RCA in Manhattan Center, New York, 1955. The orchestra is separated into groups for spaciousness and clarity of sound. *Photo: RCA.*

but the augmentation of the orchestra in the woodwind and strings is not for the sake of dynamics, but for tonal texture and clarity. There is an authenticity and festivity in these performances which may make purists turn up their noses, but non-purists will have a strong experience of Handel's music.

Of great interest too is the last recording Stokowski made with Symphony of the Air, of scenes from Wagner's Rheingold, *Tannhäuser, Tristan und Isolde,* and *Die Walküre* (LM/LSC 2555). Stokowski was always an ardent Wagner conductor, and through his syntheses gave us the essence of Wagner's dramas. This is also true of this recording, which gives sonorous samples of Wagner and Stokowski.

From 1962 his connections with RCA Victor were once again infrequent, mostly for reasons of policy, and shortly after he had made some excellent recordings with the Chicago Symphony Orchestra of works by Rimsky-Korsakov, Khachaturian, and Shostakovitch, RCA gave up that orchestra too to concentrate exclusively on the Philadelphia Orchestra.

In 1956 Stokowski entered into co-operation with Capitol Records. Within the field of classical music Capitol was rather a new label, but it has achieved very good results in 'Full Dimensional Sound', a recording method characterised by effect-free realism and absolute faithfulness to the recorded performances. The pressings, however, are not always flawless, and sometimes surface-hiss is somewhat high, which is particularly irritating in recordings made at a moderate volume level. But these objections are not serious, and generally speaking Stokowski's Capitol recordings are most satisfying.

Let me mention *Music for Strings* ((S) PAO 8415) and *The Orchestra* ((S) SAL 8385), which are showpiece records. They give pictures of the orchestra and its possibilities, and are at the same time examples of the orchestral playing technique which gave Stokowski his fame as a musician. With the Houston Symphony Orchestra he recorded Gliere's Third Symphony ((S) P 8402) and Shostakovitch's Symphony no. 11, the latter in connection with its American premiere in Houston on 7 April, 1958 ((S) PBR 8448). With these recordings the Houston Orchestra appeared on record for the first time, and it did so on the level of the greatest American orchestras.

From Stokowski's guest appearances in Europe there were a few discs, among them the Orchestre National de la Radiodiffusion Francaise in a programme of French music ((S) P 8463) and one with the Berlin Philharmonic Orchestra in Suites from *The Firebird* and *Petrouchka* by Stravinsky ((S) PAO 8407). These recordings are, of course, stamped with the characteristic Stokowskian playing technique, but he has made no attempt to change the European orchestras into mere copies of the great American orchestras. He himself gave the reason for this:

All orchestras have different sound, and I think it is wonderful that we have these differences. They are an evidence that we have not become like machines, and not lost our individuality.

In 1958 and 1959 Stokowski also made some recordings on the new Everest label. This company was also interested in modern music, and its splendid recording technique secured perfect reproduction. This was partly due to the fact that Everest made the recordings on 35 mm magnetic film, while most other companies made them on half-inch magnetic tape. Magnetic film gave not only a complete frequency response within the range of 20-20,000 hz, but also the lowest intermodulation obtained until then. The thick material eliminated magnetic print-through, and with its sprocket-holes ensured against any tendency to wow or flutter.

Stokowski's recordings for Everest were made with the Houston Symphony Orchestra and the New York Stadium Orchestra. With the Houston Orchestra he made an eminent performance of Brahms's Third Symphony characterised by beautiful melodic phrasing and harmonic balance. In the first and fourth movements he sets somewhat brisker tempi than we are accustomed to, and the music is less heroic than usual; but in the second and third movements there is a sublime peaceful mood which makes for a sterling performance (LPBR 6030/SDBR 3030). With the same orchestra there is a recording of Fikret Amirov's suite *Azerbaijan Mugam*, a folkloristic work on Azerbaijan modes and melodies; not ultra modern, but well-written Russian music. The recording is coupled with Scriabin's singular, impressionistic, and more revolutionary work *Poeme d'Extase*, which gets a very fine and fascinating performance (LPBR 6032/SDBR 3032). The recordings with the New York Stadium Orchestra are also of a very high quality, both artistically and technically, and it is difficult to single out any of these recordings. On the whole Stokowski's recordings for Everest contribute substantially to the documentation of his art in the late 1950s.

In 1958 he also made a series of recordings with Symphony of the Air for United Artists. This label is not distinguished for any extraordinary technical qualities, but its recordings with Stokowski contain some of the most superb performances he made. The repertoire ranges from pre-classical to modern, with more of the latter. Beethoven's Seventh Symphony has both monumentality and vitality, and unfolds all its bacchic life and elegiac beauty. Very effective too are the marked tempi with the rather slow funeral-like allegretto, which can also be heard in the excellent old Philadelphia recording (UAL 7003/UAS 8003). Quite unmatched is the recording of Respighi's colourful symphonic poem *The Pines of Rome*. Visions of this work have never been more clearly realised: the gay and noisy play of the children at Villa Borghese, the gloomy mourning-song from the Catacombs, the lyric impressionism of the summer night under the pines on Gianiculum, and the fantastic, triumphal procession of the Roman legionaries along Via Appia on their way to the Capitol. For several years it has been the fashion to turn up the nose at the contents and external splendours of that sort of music, but in this recording there is such expressiveness and architectural beauty that even the most persistent adversaries of programme-music cannot remain unaffected (UAL 7001/UAS 8001). Finally no less remarkable is a recording of Shostakovitch's First Symphony, which Stokowski gave its first American performance in 1928. For many years a 1933 recording with the Philadelphia Orchestra remained a landmark among recordings of modern music, a fact recognised by later reissues of it. The new recording for United Artists sounds definitive. It has gorgeous technique, and orchestral playing, and is a gorgeous performance (UAL 7004/UAS 8004). And the entire series of recordings was a real feat, considering that most of them were made at nightly sessions in Carnegie Hall in less than one week.

In October 1961 one of the most remarkable records of the past twenty years was published. American Columbia issued the first recording with Stokowski and the Philadelphia Orchestra after their reunion, introducing De Falla's *El Amor Brujo* and his own synthesis of Love Music from Act 2 and 3 of Wagner's *Tristan and Isolde* (ML 5479/MS 6147). When listening to them one can only despair at the thought of what we might have had if all the old Philadelphia Orchestra recordings had been made with modern techniques. Of course, all those recordings were advanced for their time, but compared with the present day techniques they give only a remote picture of the orchestral sound that was put down in wax.

The record is a wonderful proof that the many years of close co-operation between Stokowski and the Philadelphia Orchestra were not fruitless. All the characteristic qualities he drew from the orchestra are revived in a musically perfect and electrifying *El Amor*, and in an incandescent but restrained and calculated *Tristan*, perhaps the best he gave us. I would also like to mention the soloist in *El Amor Brujo*, the young mezzo-soprano Shirley Verrett-Carter. Not only because she has a beautiful, rich voice and a technique which makes her well-fitted for the particular Spanish *cante hondo* necessary for the work, but also because she is typical of Stokowski's faculty to select the right

Stokowski discussing De Falla's 'El Amor Brujo' with Shirley Verrett-Carter before recording it. *Photo: Columbia Records.*

soloist for each kind of music; not always big names, just as often young and unknown artists, but always artists with talent and personality.

Another release, originating from Stokowski's 1960 appearances, was works of Bach (ML 5713/MS 6313). On this we have an excellent example of a contemporary authentic conception of the Fifth Brandenburg Concerto, which not only keeps the original instrumentation, but also exploits the modern instruments in the best manner. The fillers are three of Stokowski's famous transcriptions of Bach's chorale preludes in their first modern versions since the 1930s.

In 1962 *Musical America* announced a new recording of Arnold Schoenberg's *Gurrelieder*, supposed to have been made in connection with four performances Stokowski gave in Philadelphia and New York in March 1961, but it was never released, and Columbia has always given evasive answers to inquiries about it. Complete silence was also maintained about more new recordings with Stokowski and the Philadelphia Orchestra, even though countless opportunities offered themselves to make them from the vast repertoire he performed at his guest-appearances in Philadelphia during most of the 1960s, the last on 13 February, 1969. In this way the last opportunity to revive one of the most unique combinations in the history of orchestral music was almost lost for ever.

Attention should also be directed to the single recording Stokowski made for American Decca in 1961 with Symphony of the Air. The work is Brahms's Serenade No. 1 in D Major for Orchestra, a composition which has perhaps been undeservedly neglected. In fact, it is well-written and pleasant, anticipating the later Brahms in both harmony, orchestration and taste. The performance is, true to the character of the music, straight and unpretentious, but notwithstanding it brings out every note of the score with the utmost clarity and beauty. It is indeed one of the gems in the repertoire of recorded music (DL 10031/710031), but it is also a sad reminder of the discontinuation of a great orchestra that never got a chance to show what it could have developed into with regular support and permanent, foresighted leadership.

Still more remarkable is the fact that American Decca was the first company to introduce the American Symphony Orchestra on the record market, featuring William Dawson's *Negro Folk Symphony* (DL 10077/710077). The importance of this recording is perhaps not the choice of repertoire – though it is a noble work, containing moments of great music, and also one of Stokowski's remarkable first performances in the 1930s – but its documentation of Stokowski's pioneering work in expanding musical activity in the USA. This documentation is a cultural obligation of the recording companies.

Earlier in this book is mentioned the world-premiere of Charles Ives's Fourth Symphony. The event was made possible only by a grant from the Samuel Rubin Foundation, and who else but Stokowski

From the recording of Charles Ives's Fourth Symphony in Manhattan Center, 1965. *Photo: Columbia Records.*

could also have solicited a subsidy for recording the work. The result is overwhelming. All the sublimity of the double-fugue in the third movement is there, and the complexities in tonality and rhythm in the second and fourth movements are brought out with perfection and clarity with the assistance of the co-conductors, David Katz and José Serebrier (Amr. Col. ML 6175/MS 6775).

Equally interesting are the recordings Stokowski made for European Decca in a series termed Phase Four Stereo. This process of recording, representing some of the most advanced techniques, made use of a twenty-channel console mixer through which any signal from the music could be placed with any desired degree of presence and any desired location on the horizontal plane on the four-track master tape on which it was registered.

To begin with the new technique was tried only on popular music, but since it turned out successful, it was decided early in 1964 to use it for the recording of serious music too. And who should be the first conductor for the project but Stokowski. He had always been the pioneer of so many new methods in recording, so why not in Phase Four Stereo for serious music. An official from Decca approached him, and he was so intrigued that it was not difficult to persuade him to undertake a new *Scheherazade,* on condition that he could supervise all phases of the recording, from the first preparations to the finished mastertape.

The result is amazing. The London Symphony Orchestra is playing wonderfully, and the sound is glorious and substantial, not concert-hall realism, which Stokowski was not sure provides the best way of listening to music, but an ideal super-realism which can never be achieved in the concert-hall. There was some scepticism as to how the new technique could be used in playing ducks and drakes with a score, but this was unfounded, because Stokowski was too discerning a musician to let such a thing happen, and his supervision of the process was a sufficient guarantee against it (LK 4658/PFS 4062).

The next issue in Phase Four Stereo came in 1965 with Stokowski's own orchestration of Moussorgsky's *Pictures at an Exhibition.* It is not an improvement of Ravel's version, but an independent realisation of the original work, omitting Promenade No. 3, the Tuilleries, and the Market at Limoges, which have been added in later editions of the score. The orchestra is the New Philharmonia Orchestra, which plays superbly, and the performance and recording are stupefying and cannot leave anybody unaffected (LK 4766/PFS 4095).

Until 1973 a long series of well-known classics was recorded, most with the London Symphony Orchestra. In the meantime a serious crisis harassed the majority of the American recording-industry, so that these records constitute the most important documentation of

Stokowski's conductorship in the late 1960s and early 1970s. Most spectacular among them is a recording of the first European performance of Charles Ives's Orchestral Set No. 2 coupled with Messiaen's *L'Ascension* (PFS 4203). Ives's strange polyphony was difficult for the London players in rehearsal, but the recording leaves no doubt that they master it as well as any American orchestra.

A complete, detailed analysis of Stokowski's recordings would fill a whole book, but I cannot avoid including his recordings for the Vanguard Recording Association. In 1960 this company entered co-operation with West Projects Inc. to make a series of recordings of American music. The start was made in the summer of 1960 with the

Stokowski tests the Dolby-technique for his recording of Stravinsky's 'L'Histoire du Soldat'. *Photo: Vanguard Records.*

first recording of Ernest Bloch's prize-winning work *America* from 1928. Stokowski himself was one of the five judges who awarded the prize on behalf of *Musical America*, and also gave the first performance of the work in Philadelphia in December the same year; but since then the composition has, quite unjustly, seldom been performed. In this revival with Symphony of the Air Stokowski gives, with his sense of detail and architecture, a beautiful, clear account of the throng of musical ideas, and out of them the 'America'-hymn gradually develops and rises into a grandiose and logical conclusion to the work (VRS 1056/VSD 2065). Another recording in this series is the symphonic suites from Virgil Thomson's two well-known film-scores *The River* and *The Plow That Broke the Plains*, both inspired by American folk music, and splendidly performed (VRS 1071/VSD 2095).

In 1966 Stokowski once again pioneered, in making the first recording with the new Dolby system, for better elimination of tape hiss. The music chosen for the event was Stravinsky's *L'Histoire du soldat*, a work that had been in his repertoire since the early 1920s, but never before recorded with him. The performance is excellent, dry and rhythmic, 'like a clenched fist', as Stokowski remarked at a playback; and the dubbed narrations by French actors are impressive, both in the French and in the English versions (VSD 71165/66).

Recording session at Walthamstow Town Hall, London, with RCA in 1973. To the left, producer Richard Mohr. *Photo: Anthony Crickmay, London.*

The Recording of Rachmaninov's Third Symphony at West Ham Central Mission, London. To the right Sidney Sax, leader of the National Philharmonic Orchestra. *Photo: David G. Francis.*

The last Vanguard release with Stokowski was one of the first quadraphonic recordings, featuring the American Symphony Orchestra in Tschaikovsky's Fourth Symphony and a transcription of Scriabin's Etude in C Sharp Minor, op. 2, no. 1 (VSQ 30001). The recording is fine, the playing gorgeous, and the performance breathtaking. Regarding the symphony, however, the reading is highly individualistic, with strange, uncalled for ritardandi; but whether one likes it or not, one cannot help being captured by the orchestra's enormous skill and Stokowski's formidable musical imagination.

In 1973 the rich flow of recordings from European Decca began to dry up, only a few remaining to be released. It appears that one reason was that Decca did not want to invest in the very insecure market of quadraphony, and with his never-dying appetite for new techniques, Stokowski was tempted to sign a contract with RCA Victor for ten records. The company eventually presented a programme composed of both retakes of some older recordings like Dvorak's Symphony no. 5 (9) (CRL 2-0334) and new works in his recorded repertoire, not least a gorgeous reading of Mahler's Second Symphony, incredibly his first official Mahler symphony on records (ARL 2-0852). Strangely enough, the two recordings were not released in quadraphony, whereas the others, a Beethoven symphony (ARD 1-0600), a

Tschaikovsky symphony (ARD 1-0426), and a new volume of Bach transcriptions (ARD 1-0880) were; but all are performed with the intensity and serenity of a fulfilled man. They are true documents of the art of the old Leopold Stokowski.

In 1974 Stokowski decided to give his last public concert (New Philharmonia Orchestra, 14 May), apart from an invitation to conduct the Royal Philharmonic Orchestra on his 100th birthday, and concentrated his activity on recordings. In the spring of 1975 he completed his contract with RCA Victor, recording for the fifth time Rimsky-Korsakov's *Scheherazade*, and then a small new American company, by the name of Desmar, entered the scene and made a scoop by persuading Stokowski to make his first recording of Rachmaninov's Third Symphony, which he had given its world premiere in Philadelphia on 6 November, 1936. As he had retired from public conducting, a special orchestra had to be assembled, and the choice fell upon the National Philharmonic Orchestra, a virtuoso studio orchestra otherwise used for film- and tv-productions, and composed of the best first-desk players of the established orchestras, and free-lance musicians of the highest quality. The result was a magnificent performance, and the conducting like that of a man in his fifties. When asked his opinion of the orchestra, Stokowski, now having some difficulty in recognising persons and places, answered, 'I am always happy with this orchestra' (Desmar DSM 1007).

Play-back of the recording of Rachmaninov's Third Symphony. With Stokowski, producer Anthony Hodgson. *Photo: David G. Francis.*

179

Stokowski's last recording session at the EMI studios, London, in June 1977. *Photo: Timothy Good.*

Now, after a lapse of eight years, American Columbia returned and got an exclusive six-year contract covering the time up to Stokowski's 100th birthday, with an option on both sides to prolong it by another six years. The first sessions for Columbia, again with the National Philharmonic Orchestra, took place in May 1976, and resulted in a complete take of Tschaikovsky's *Aurora's Wedding*. Plans were also made for some of the following sessions, among others new recordings of Sibelius's First Symphony and Brahms's Second Symphony, but none of the larger works or contemporary compositions still missing from his recording repertoire, because, as it was stated, he had trouble with his eyesight and was no longer able to memorise new works.

It is deplorable that the big record companies were so slow to make a representative recording schedule with Stokowski before it was too late. In the event only the first year of the contract with Columbia was fulfilled. During the first week of June 1977 Stokowski completed two sessions with Bizet's C Major Symphony and Mendelssohn's Italian Symphony, and then the summer holiday intervened. It was arranged to start the next season on 19 September with a recording of Rachmaninov's Symphony no. 2, but shortly before that he caught a virus-infection, and on 13 September died in his sleep after what is thought to have been a heart-attack.

POST RECORD

Stokowski left an enormous and valuable legacy of recordings to posterity, but the record-companies have left an equally large debt. This consists of all the recordings they never made of most of the great performances he gave of contemporary music, of many of the major eighteenth and nineteenth century works, and of his occasional productions for the opera houses.

Why didn't we get, for instance, a Mahler Eighth Symphony, a Prokofiev *Alexander Nevsky* Cantata, Schoenberg's orchestral works, Sibelius's Fifth, Sixth and Seventh Symphonies, Vaughan Williams's Eighth and Ninth Symphonies, a new *Gurrelieder* and a new *Sacre*.

Headstone on Stokowski's grave at Marylebone Cemetery, East Finchley England.

Why didn't we get a Bach St Matthew Passion, a Brahms Requiem, some Mozart and Haydn symphonies; and why were his performances of Monteverdi's *Orfeo*, Dalla-Piccola's *The Prisoner* and Puccini's *Turandot* not recorded?

This negligence is next to impossible to repair, but with goodwill from musical organisations and the combined efforts of music-loving people, it should be possible to remedy some of the worst sins. This is exactly what has been arranged now.

In the spring of 1979 a group of dedicated people, mostly English, met in London on the initiative of Stephen G. Smith of Southampton to form a Leopold Stokowski Society. I was present at the inaugural meeting, and here was the right Stokowskian spirit. Strikingly, the majority present were younger men, just born when Stokowski's tenure in Philadelphia ended – in fact, I was one of the oldest – and their devotion to him just as great as that of the youth among his audiences in times past. Mr. Smith was elected editor of the bulletin of the society, the *Toccata*; and a long-time admirer and friend of Stokowski's, Edward Johnson – also a younger man – was elected chairman of the committee.

Of particular interest, among the principal aims of the Leopold Stokowski Society, are plans to reissue on LP some of the legendary old Philadelphia Orchestra recordings, under the supervision of the excellent American producer Ward Marston; and to provide issues of some of the memorable performances which still exist in archives all over the world. The society has already got far with these plans. Releases are made both under their own label and in collaboration with some of the record-companies.

Chapter 18

Epilogue

With the death of Leopold Stokowski the musical-world lost one of its greatest and most colourful figures, and a giant among its conductors.

An estimate of Stokowski as an artist can be made on the basis of his musical creed, expressed in his inspiring and unpretentious book, *'Music for All of Us'*. To him music was not isolated, but an organic part of nature and life. Music is the highest expression of divine creative power, and the great composers are those human beings who are responsive to its mighty inspiration. It is the privilege and responsibility of the musician to convey this inspiration from the composer to the listener. The way in which Stokowski experienced music himself gives us the key to a deeper understanding of some of his spectacular qualities as a musician:

Music is dynamic – ever evolving – flowing like a river – never static. True music is inspired – it must be played and sung with inspiration. Uninspired music is stiff and dull and dead – not really music but mechanical sound. Real music is alive – it has the impulsive heartbeat and surge of life – never sounds twice alike – never become hard and inflexible and stagnant – but is always breathing and pulsating.

Stokowski himself was dynamic, his performances inspired, always living and pulsating. His entire musical career was one long task of developing music to yet greater perfection, work which he thought would never end. He was often accused of searching for self-assertion and sensation. This is entirely wrong. His opinions on music were modest; he considered tolerance indispensable to all true art. Attempts to decide what is good or bad, right or wrong in music is a tyranny worse than dictatorship, and quite disastrous to joy and sincerity.

The physical and psychical effect of music on man is unquestionable, but not yet sufficiently explored. Stokowski was of opinion that music can have a very strong influence upon the human mind, and therefore he considered it to be a civic affair to investigate this problem and to establish civic centres – great parks with stadiums, cinemas, theatres, museums, schools and auditoriums for performances of concert, opera and ballet. In this way art will become a natural part of daily life, and great music the property of everybody. Even while he was in Philadelphia, Stokowski outlined plans for such a recreation centre, with the Philadelphia Orchestra as its backbone; but the time was not yet ripe for such great, foresighted ideas.

Without Stokowski the music of the twentieth century would have been much poorer. We have had several great conductors, but most have first of all been identified as great interpreters, and often in rather limited fields of music. At their best they have given us grand artistic experiences, but at their deaths they generally leave nothing lasting behind them. Quite different was Stokowski. His relationship with music was universal; and he never consciously made himself a specialist in one limited domain. As the great orchestra-builder of our time, he has had a far-reaching influence on playing-technique, sound, intonation, phrasing and acoustics, and his untiring work with the reproduction of music in radio, on record, and on film have given valuable, lasting results. But imperishable and inspiring is the elementary idea which was the motive of all his activities: Music is for all of us. He was himself an artist for all of us.

Literature

Edward Adrian: Bach, Beethoven, and Bureaucracy
University of Alabama Press, 1971)

Abram Chasins: Leopold Stokowski – A Profile
(Hawthorn Books, New York, 1979)

David Ewen: Dictators of the Baton
(Ziff Davis Publishing Company, New York, 1948)

Roland Gelatt: The Fabulous Phonograph
(J. B. Lippincott Company, New York, 1955)

David Hall: The Disc Book
(Long Player Publications, New York, 1955)

David Hall: The Record Book
(The Citadel Press, New York, 1948)

Philip Hart: Orpheus in the New World
(Norton and Company, New York, 1973)

Edward Johnson: Stokowski
(Triad Press, London, 1973)

Irving Kolodin: The Metropolitan Opera
(Alfred A. Knopff, New York, 1968)

Herbert Kupferberg: Those Fabulous Philadelphians
(Charles Scribner's Sons, New York, 1969)

Leonard Maltin: The Disney Films
(Bonanza Books, New York)

John H. Mueller: The American Symphony Orchestra
(Indiana University Press, Bloomington, 1951)

Charles O'Connell: The Other Side of the Record
(Alfred A. Knopff, New York, 1947)

Maurice Pearton: The LSO at 70
(Victor Gollancz, London, 1974)

Clair R. Reis: Composers, Conductors and Critics
(Oxford University Press, New York, 1955)

Paul Robinson: Stokowski
(Lester and Orpen, Canada, 1977)

Hubert Roussel: The Houston Symphony Orchestra, 1913-71
(University of Texas Press, Austin, 1972)

Olga Samaroff: An American Musician's Story
(Norton and Company, New York, 1939)

Harold C. Schoenberg: The Great Conductors
(Victor Gollancz, London, 1968)

Howard Shanet: Philharmonic
(Doubleday, New York, 1975)

Leopold Stokowski: Music for All of Us
(Simon and Schuster, New York, 1943)

Deems Taylor: Fantasia
(Simon and Schuster, New York, 1940)

Robert Walker. Rachmaninov, His Life and Times
(Midas Books, England, 1980)

Francis A. Wister: 25 Years of the Philadelphia Orchestra
(Women's Committees for the Philadelphia Orchestra, 1925)

David Wooldridge: Conductor's World
(Barrie and Rockliff, London, 1970)

Discography

Abbreviations

AC . . . . American Columbia (Division of CBS)
Ace . . . . Ace of Diamonds (Division of European Decca)
AD . . . . . . American Decca
AVE . . . . . . Audio-Visual Enterprises (Geneva)
Bach . . . . . . Bach Guild (Division of Vanguard)
Cam . . . . . . Camden (Division of RCA)
Cap . . . . Capitol
CBS . . . . American Columbia (European Division)
CC . . . . Cameo Classics
CRI . . . . Composers' Records Inc.
Disney . . . . . Disneyland (Record Division of Disney Productions Inc.)
EC . . . . European Columbia
ED . . . . European Decca
EE . . . . EMI Electrola
Ev . . . . Everest
HMV . . . . . His Master's Voice
IPA . . . . International Piano Archives
L . . . . London
LSS . . . . Leopold Stokowski Society
O . . . . Odyssey (Division of American Columbia)
OR . . . . Opus Records
OTA . . . . . . Off the Air Record Club
P . . . . Philips

Pa . . . . Parnassus
Q . . . . Quintessence (Various sources)
S . . . . Seraphim (Division of Capitol)
U . . . . Unicorn
UA . . . . United Artists
UISMCRS . University of Illinois School of Music Custom Recording
          Series
V . . . . RCA Victor
Va . . . . Victrola (Division of RCA)
Van . . . . Vanguard
VS . . . . Varese Sarabande

(ac). . . . . Automatic coupling
(t). . . . . Transcription for orchestra by Stokowski
(19—) . . . . Year of recording
(Composer and/or work)
 . . . . Coupling

Orchestras
AAYO . . . . . All American Youth Orchestra
ASO . . . . . . American Symphony Orchestra
BPO . . . . . . Berlin Philharmonic Orchestra
CPO . . . . . . Czech Philharmonic Orchestra
CSO . . . . . . Chicago Symphony Orchestra
HBSO . . . . . Hollywood Bowl Symphony Orchestra
HRO . . . . . . Hungarian Radio Orchestra
HRPO . . . . . Hilversum Radio Philharmonic Orchestra
HSO . . . . . . Houston Symphony Orchestra
LAPO . . . . . Los Angeles Philharmonic Orchestra
LPO . . . . . . London Philharmonic Orchestra
LSO . . . . . . London Symphony Orchestra
LSSO . . . . . Leopold Stokowski Symphony Orchestra
NaPO . . . . . National Philharmonic Orchestra
NBCSO . . . NBC Symphony Orchestra
NPO . . . . . . New Philharmonia Orchestra
NSOL . . . . . The New Symphony Orchestra of London
NYCSO . . . New York City Symphony Orchestra
NYPO . . . . . New York Philharmonic Orchestra
NYSO . . . . . New York Stadium Orchestra
ONRF . . . . . L'Orchestre National de la Radiodiffusion Francaise
OSR . . . . . . L'Orchestre de la Suisse Romande
PhO . . . . Philharmonia Orchestra

PO . . . . The Philadelphia Orchestra
RCAVSO . . RCA Victor Symphony Orchestra
RPO . . . . . . Royal Philharmonic Orchestra
SA . . . . Symphony of the Air
SFSO . . . . . San Francisco Symphony Orchestra
USSRSO . . . The Russian State Orchestra

Amateur Orchestras
IFYO . . . . . International Festival Youth Orchestra
UISO . . . . . University of Illinois Symphony Orchestra

Record and Tape Numbers

Ace of Diamonds
SDD 100 . . . . 33 rpm record	12 inches	stereo

American Columbia
11000D-12999D . . . . . 78 rpm record	12 inches	electric
17000D-19999D . . . . . 78 rpm record	10 inches	electric
BM . . . . 33 rpm record	12 inches	mono
CL . . . . 33 rpm record	12 inches	mono
D3S 600 . . . . 33 rpm records	12 inches	stereo
M 30000 . . . . 33 rpm record	12 inches	stereo
M4 30000 . . . . 33 rpm records	12 inches	stereo
MA 30000 . . . . cartridge	8 tracks	stereo
MAQ 30000 . . . . cartridge	8 tracks	quadra
MGP . . . . 33 rpm records	12 inches	stereo
ML 2000 . . . . 33 rpm record	10 inches	mono
ML 4000 . . . . 33 rpm record	12 inches	mono
MQ 30000 . . . . 33 rpm record	12 inches	quadra
MS 6000 . . . . 33 rpm record	12 inches	stereo
MT 30000 . . . . cassette	4 tracks	stereo

American Decca
DCM 3200 . . . . 33 rpm record	12 inches	mono
DL 10000 . . . . 33 rpm record	12 inches	mono
DL 710000 . . . . 33 rpm record	12 inches	stereo

Artia
MK 1500 . . . . 33 rpm record	12 inches	mono

Audio-Visual Enterprises
AVE 30000 . . . . 33 rpm record	12 inches	stereo

Bach Guild
BGS 70000 . . . . 33 rpm record	12 inches	stereo

Bruno
BR 14000 . . . . 33 rpm record	12 inches	mono

Brunswick

AXA 4500	33 rpm record	12 inches	mono
SXA 4500	33 rpm record	12 inches	stereo

Buena Vista

BVS 101	33 rpm records	12 inches	stereo
101 VC	cassettes	4 tracks	stereo
101 VT	cartridges	8 tracks	stereo

Camden

CAE 100	45 rpm record	7 inches	mono
CAL 100	33 rpm record	12 inches	mono

Cameo Classics

GOCLP 9000	33 rpm record	12 inches	mono or stereo

Capitol

L, P, PAO, SAL	33 rpm record	12 inches	mono
PBR	33 rpm records	12 inches	mono
SL, SP, SPAO	33 rpm record	12 inches	stereo
SPBO, SPBR	33 rpm records	12 inches	stereo
SSAL, STK	33 rpm record	12 inches	stereo

CBS

73000	33 rpm record	12 inches	stereo
40-73000	cassette	4 tracks	stereo
BRG 60000	33 rpm record	12 inches	mono
SBRG 60000	33 rpm record	12 inches	stereo

CBS Classics

M 61000	33 rpm record	12 inches	mono

CBS Harmony

30000	33 rpm record	12 inches	stereo
40-30000	cassette	4 tracks	stereo

Composers' Records Inc.

100	33 rpm record	12 inches	mono
SD 100	33 rpm record	12 inches	stereo

Desmar

DSM 1000	33 rpm record	12 inches	stereo
E 1000	cassette	4 tracks	stereo

Disneyland

STER 101	33 rpm records	12 inches	stereo
WDL 4101	33 rpm record	12 inches	mono
WDL S 4101	33 rpm record	12 inches	stereo
WDX 101	33 rpm records	12 inches	mono

EMI Electrola

C 063-29000	33 rpm record	12 inches	stereo

European Columbia

33 C 1000	33 rpm record	10 inches	mono
33 CX 1000	33 rpm record	12 inches	mono

European Decca

D94D2	33 rpm records	12 inches	stereo
DPA 500	33 rpm record	12 inches	stereo
EPFC 4000	cartridge	8 tracks	stereo
K94K2	cassettes	4 tracks	stereo
KCSP 100	cassette	4 tracks	stereo
KDPC 500	cassette	4 tracks	stereo
KPFC 3-4	cassettes	4 tracks	stereo
KPFC 4000	cassette	4 tracks	stereo
LK 4000	33 rpm record	12 inches	mono
OPFS 3-4	33 rpm records	12 inches	stereo
PFS 4000	33 rpm record	12 inches	stereo
SPA 100	33 rpm record	12 inches	stereo

Everest

LPBR 6000	33 rpm record	12 inches	mono
SDBR 3000	33 rpm record	12 inches	stereo

His Master's Voice

2-100	78 rpm record	10 inches	acoustic (single)
3-0100	78 rpm record	12 inches	acoustic (single)
7ER 5000	45 rpm record	7 inches	mono
7R 100	45 rpm record	7 inches	mono
ALP 1000	33 rpm record	12 inches	mono
BLP 1000	33 rpm record	10 inches	mono
D 1000	78 rpm record	12 inches	electric
DA 100-999	78 rpm record	10 inches	acoustic
DA 1000	78 rpm record	10 inches	electric
DB 100-999	78 rpm record	12 inches	acoustic
DB 1000	78 rpm record	12 inches	electric
E 500	78 rpm record	10 inches	electric

HMV Concert Classics

SXL P 30000	33 rpm record	12 inches	stereo
TC SXL P 30000	cassette	4 tracks	stereo

International Piano Archives

IPA 100	33 rpm record	12 inches	mono
MJA 1000	33 rpm record	12 inches	mono

Leopold Stokowski Society

LS 1	33 rpm record	12 inches	mono or stereo

London

M 521000	cassette	4 tracks	stereo
M 821000	cartridge	8 tracks	stereo
M 94000	cassette	4 tracks	stereo
M 95000	cartridge	8 tracks	stereo
PM 55000	33 rpm record	12 inches	mono
SPC 21000	33 rpm record	12 inches	stereo

Odyssey

Y 30000	33 rpm record	12 inches	stereo

Y4 30000 . . . . 33 rpm records	12 inches	stereo
YT 30000 . . . . cassette	4 tracks	stereo
YT4 30000 . . . . cassettes	4 tracks	stereo

Opus Records

MGL . . . . 33 rpm record	12 inches	mono

OTA

Set 6 . . . . 33 rpm records	12 inches	mono

Parnassus

1 . . . . 33 rpm record	12 inches	mono

Pensanze

PR 1 . . . . 33 rpm record(s)	12 inches	mono

Philips

6500 100 . . . . 33 rpm record	12 inches	stereo
7300 100 . . . . cassette	4 tracks	stereo

Pye Nixa

PCNH 1 . . . . 33 rpm record	12 inches	quadra
PCNHX 1 . . . . 33 rpm record	12 inches	quadra
ZCPHG 1 . . . . cassette	4 tracks	stereo
ZCPNH 1 . . . . cassette	4 tracks	stereo

Quintessence

PMC 7000 . . . . 33 rpm record	12 inches	mono or stereo
P4C 7000 . . . . cassette	4 tracks	mono or stereo

RCA Victor

10-1000 . . . . 78 rpm record	10 inches	electric
11-8000 . . . . 78 rpm record	12 inches	electric
12-0000 . . . . 78 rpm record	12 inches	electric
18-0000 . . . . 78 rpm record	12 inches	electric
49-0000 . . . . 45 rpm record	7 inches	mono
500-1199 . . . . 78 rpm record	10 inches	acoustic
1200-2499 . . . . 78 rpm record	10 inches	electric
6000-6499 . . . . 78 rpm record	12 inches	acoustic
6500-8999 . . . . 78 rpm record	12 inches	electric
14000 . . . . 78 rpm record	12 inches	electric
64000 . . . . 78 rpm record	10 inches	acoustic (single)
74000 . . . . 78 rpm record	12 inches	acoustic (single)
AGK 1-0000 . . . . cassette	4 tracks	stereo
AGL 1-0000 . . . . 33 rpm record	12 inches	stereo
ANL 1-2000E . . . . 33 rpm record	12 inches	stereo
ANS 1-2000E . . . . cartridge	8 tracks	stereo
ARD 1-0000 . . . . 33 rpm record	12 inches	quadra
ARD 2-0000 . . . . 33 rpm records	12 inches	quadra
ARK 1-0000 . . . . cassette	4 tracks	stereo
ARL 1-0000 . . . . 33 rpm record	12 inches	stereo
ARL 2-0000 . . . . 33 rpm records	12 inches	stereo
ARM 1-0000 . . . . 33 rpm record	12 inches	mono

ARM 3-0000	33 rpm records	12 inches	mono
ARS 1-0000	cartridge	8 tracks	stereo
ART 1-0000	cartridge	8 tracks	quadra
CRL 1-0000	33 rpm record	12 inches	stereo
ERA	45 rpm record	7 inches	mono
ERB	45 rpm records	7 inches	mono
L 1000	33 rpm record	10 inches	electric
L 7000	33 rpm record	12 inches	electric
L 11000	33 rpm record	12 inches	electric
LCT 1-999	33 rpm record	10 inches	mono
LCT 1000	33 rpm record	12 inches	mono
LCT 6000	33 rpm records	12 inches	mono
LM 1-999	33 rpm record	10 inches	mono
LM 1000	33 rpm record	12 inches	mono
LM 6000	33 rpm records	12 inches	mono
LM 9000	33 rpm record	12 inches	mono
LRM 7000	33 rpm record	10 inches	mono
LSC 2000	33 rpm record	12 inches	stereo
MCK 500	cassette	4 tracks	stereo
R8S 1000	cartridge	8 tracks	stereo
R8S 5000	cartridges	8 tracks	stereo
RK 1000	cassette	4 tracks	stereo
RK 5000	cassettes	4 tracks	stereo
SRS 3000	33 rpm records	12 inches	stereo
VCM 7000	33 rpm records	12 inches	mono
VCS 7000	33 rpm records	12 inches	stereo
WCT	45 rpm records	7 inches	mono
WDM 1000	45 rpm records	7 inches	mono
WEPR	45 rpm records	7 inches	mono

RCA Victor First Edition

DMM 4-0000	33 rpm records	12 inches	mono
DPM 4-0000	33 rpm records	12 inches	mono

Regal

SREG 2000	33 rpm record	12 inches	stereo

Seraphim

S 60000	33 rpm record	12 inches	stereo
SIB 6000	33 rpm records	12 inches	stereo
4XG 60000	cassette	4 tracks	stereo
4X2G 6000	cassettes	4 tracks	stereo

UISMCRS

CRS	33 rpm record	12 inches	mono

Unicorn

RHS 300	33 rpm record	12 inches	stereo

United Artists

UAL 7000	33 rpm record	12 inches	mono
UAS 8000	33 rpm record	12 inches	stereo

Vanguard

7175-30001H	.... cartridge	8 tracks	quadra
S	.... 33 rpm record	12 inches	stereo
VCS	.... 33 rpm record	12 inches	stereo
VRS	.... 33 rpm record	12 inches	mono
VSD	.... 33 rpm record	12 inches	stereo
VSQ	.... 33 rpm record	12 inches	quadra
ZCVB	.... cassette	4 tracks	stereo

Varese Sarabande

VC 81000	.... 33 rpm record	12 inches	stereo

Victrola

AVM 1-1000	.... 33 rpm record	12 inches	mono
AVM 2-2000	.... 33 rpm records	12 inches	mono
VIC 1000	.... 33 rpm record	12 inches	mono
VICS 1000	.... 33 rpm record	12 inches	stereo

Adolphe Adam
Selections from 'Giselle'
(Collections)

LSSO – V 12-1208-12(ac)(1950)
V WDM 1394
V LM 1083
HMV ALP 1133
Va VIC 1020

Isaac Albeniz
'Fête dieu à Seville'
from 'Iberia' (t)
(Collections)

PO – V 7158(1928)
HMV D 1888
NaPO – AC M 34543(1976)
AC MT 34543
AC MA 34543
CBS 73589
CBS 40-73589

Fikret Amirov
Azerbaijan Mugam
(Scriabin: 'Poeme d'Extase')

HSO – Ev LPBR 6032(1959)
Ev SDBR 3032

Anonymous
'Deep River'
(Collections)
With the Norman Luboff Choir

NSOL – V LM 2593(1961)
V LSC 2593

'Etenraku' (Ritual Japanese Music)
(Eichheim: 'Bali')

PO – V 14142(1935)

'Praise God from Whom All Blessings
Flow'
(Collections)
With the Norman Luboff Choir

NSOL – V LM 2593(1961)
V LSC 2593

Russian Christmas Music (t)
(Bach: Chorale 'Ein feste Burg')
(Handel: Sinfonia from 'Messiah')

PO – V 1692(1934)

LSSO – V 11-9837(1947)
V 49-0974
V ERA 119

Two Ancient Liturgical Melodies (t)   PO – V 1789(1935)
                                        HMV DA 1551

J. S. Bach
Brandenburg Concerto no. 2 in F Major   PO – V 7087-89(1928)
('Wir glauben all' an einen Gott')   V 17246-50(ac)
                                            HMV D 1708-10
                                            HMV D 7420-22(ac)
Brandenburg Concerto no. 5 in D Major   PO – AC ML 5713(1960)
(Chorale Preludes)   AC MS 6313
                                            CBS 30061
                                            CBS 40-30061
                                            O Y 33228

Chorale from Cantata no. 4 (t)   PO – V 14583(1937)
(Sarabande from Partita no. 1)   HMV DB 3366
(Collections)   LSSO – V WDM 1569(1950)
                                            HMV 7ER 5004
                                            V LM 1176
(Collections)   CPO – L SPC 21096(1972)
                                            L M 521096
                                            L M 821096
                                            ED PFS 4278

Chorale from Cantata no. 147 (t)   LSSO – V 12-3159(1950)
(Aria from Cantata no. 208)   V 49-3159
(Little Fugue in G Minor)   HMV DB 21570
                                            HMV 7R 170
(Collections)   V WDM 1569
                                            V ERA 89
                                            HMV 7ER 5004
                                            V LM 1176
(Collection)   V LM 1877
(Collections)   NSOL – V LM 2593(1961)
With the Norman Luboff Choir   V LSC 2593
                                            V VCS 7077
                                            V RK 5072
                                            V R8S 5072
(Collection)   V LSC 5004
                                            V RK 1196
                                            V R8S 1196
                                            Q PMC 7019
(Collections)   LSSO – Bach BGS 70696(1967)
                                            Van S 363
                                            Van VCS 707-08
                                            Van ZCVB 707-08
(Collection)   Van VCS 701-02
Sinfonia from Cantata no. 156 (t)   NBCSO – V 18498(1941)
                                            HMV DB 6150
(Collections)   LSO – V ARL 1-0880(1974)
                                            V ARK 1-0880
                                            V ARS 1-0880
                                            V ARD 1-0880
                                            V AGL 1-3656
                                            V AGK 1-3656

Aria from Cantata no. 208 (t)	LSSO – V 12-3159(1950)
(Chorale from Cantata no. 147)	V 49-3159
(Collections)	V WDM 1569
	V LM 1176
(Collection)	V LM 1877
(Collections)	NSOL – V LM 2593(1961)
With the Norman Luboff Choir	V LSC 2593
	V VCS 7077
	V RK 5072
	V R8S 5072
(Collection)	V LSC 5004
	V RK 1196
	V R8S 1196
	Q PMC 7019
(Collections)	LSSO – Bach BGS 70696(1967)
	Van S 363
	Van VCS 707-08
	Van ZCVB 707-08
(Collection)	Van VCS 701-02
Chorale 'Ein feste Burg' (t)	PO – V 1692(1934)
(Anonymous: Russian Christmas Music)	
(Chaconne from Partita no. 2)	HMV DB 2453
	HMV DB 7860(ac)
(Toccata and Fugue in D Minor)	AAYO – AC 11758D(1941)
	AC 11759D(ac)
(Shostakovitch: Prelude in E Flat	AC 12903D
Minor)	
(Collections)	LSSO – Cap P 8489(1958)
	Cap SP 8489
	Cap SPAO 8694
	S S 60235
	S 4XG 60235
(Collections)	LSO – V ARL 1-0880(1974)
	V ARK 1-0880
	V ARS 1-0880
	V ARD 1-0880
	V AGL 1-3656
	V AGK 1-3656
Chorale Prelude 'Aus der Tiefe	PO – V 7553(1930)
rufe ich' (t)	HMV DB 1789
Chorale Prelude 'Christ lag in	PO – V 7437(1931)
Todesbanden' (t)	HMV DB 1952
(Little Fugue in G Minor)	
Chorale Prelude 'Ich rufe zu dir' (t)	PO – V 6786(1927)
(Prelude no. 8 in E Flat Minor from	HMV D 1464
'Wohltemperiertes Klavier' I)	
(Collections)	V DMM 4-0341
(Prelude and Fugue in E Minor)	PO – V 11-8577(1939)
(Collections)	PO – AC ML 5713(1960)
	AC MS 6313
	O Y 33228

	CBS 30061
	CBS 40-30061
(Collection)	AC MGP 17
Chorale Prelude 'Nut kommt der	PO – V 8494(1934)
Heiden Heiland' (t)	V 8495(ac)
(Chaconne from Partita no. 2)	
('Komm', süsser Tod')	HMV DB 2274
(Collections)	PO – AC ML 5713(1960)
	AC MS 6313
	O Y 33228
	CBS 30061
	CBS 40-30061
(Collection)	AC MGP 17
Chorale Prelude 'Wachet auf' (t)	LSO – V ARL 1-0880(1974)
(Collections)	V ARK 1-0880
	V ARS 1-0880
	V ARD 1-0880
	V AGL 1-3656
	V AGK 1-3656
Chorale Prelude 'Wir glauben all' an	PO – V 7089(1929)
einen Gott' (t)	V 17246(ac)
(Brandenburg Concerto no. 2 in F Major)	HMV D 1710
	HMV D 7420(ac)
(Collections)	LSSO – V WDM 1569(1950)
	V ERA 89
	HMV 7ER 5004
	V LM 1176
(Collections)	PO – AC ML 5713(1960)
	AC MS 6313
	O Y 33228
	CBS 30061
	CBS 40-30061
(Collection)	AC MGP 17
(Collections)	CPO – L SPC 21096(1972)
	L M 521096
	L M 821096
	ED PFS 4278
Sinfonia from Christmas Oratorio	PO – V 7142(1929)
	HMV D 1741
(Collections)	LSSO – Cap P 8489(1958)
	Cap SP 8489
	S S 60235
	S 4XG 60235
(Collections)	LSSO – Bach BGS 70696(1967)
	Van S 363
Second Movement from Concerto no. 5	AAYO – AC 11976D(1941)
in F Minor for Piano and Orchestra (t)	AC 11979-81D(ac)
Bourrée from English Suite no. 2	PO – HMV DA 1639(1936)
in A Minor (t)	
(Chopin: Prelude no. 24 in D Minor)	

(Collections)	V DMM 4-0341
(Collections)	LSSO – V DM 1512(1950)
	V ERA 89
	V LM 1133
(Collections)	LSSO – Cap P 8489(1958)
	Cap SP 8489
Sarabande from English Suite no. 3 in G Minor (t) ('Komm', süsser Tod')	PO – V 8496(1934)
(Siciliano from Sonata no. 4 in C Minor)	HMV DB 2275
Great Fugue in G Minor (t)	PO – V 1728(1934)
'Komm', süsser Tod' (t)	PO – V 8432(1933)
(Beethoven: Symphony no. 9 in D Minor)	V 8433(ac)
(Sarabande from English Suite no. 3)	V 8496
('Nun kommt der Heiden Heiland')	HMV DB 2274
	AAYO-AC 11773D(1941)
(Air from Suite no. 3 in D Major)	AC 11775-76D(ac)
(Purcell: Aria from 'Dido and Aeneas')	LSSO – V 12-3087(1950)
	V 49-3087
(Collections)	V WDM 1569
	V LM 1176
	V ERB 7033
	V LRM 7033
	HMV BLP 1074
(Collections)	LSSO – Cap P 8489(1958)
	Cap SP 8489
	S S 60235
	S 4XG 60235
(Collections)	LSO – V ARL 1-0880(1974)
	V ARK 1-0880
	V ARS 1-0880
	V ARD 1-0880
	V AGL 1-3656
	V AGK 1-3656
Little Fugue in G Minor (t)	PO – V 7457(1931)
('Christ lag in Todesbanden')	HMV DB 1952
(Beethoven: Symphony no. 5 in C Minor)	AAYO – AC 11547D(1940)
	AC 11548D(ac)
(Still: Scherzo from Afro-American Symphony)	AC 11992D
(Collections)	LSSO – V WDM 1569(1950)
	V LM 1176
	V ERA 89
	HMV 7ER 5004
(Chorale from Cantata no. 147)	HMV DB 21570
	HMV 7R 170
(Collections)	LSSO – Cap P 8489(1958)
	Cap SP 8489
	Cap SP 8673
	S S 60235
	S 4XG 60235

(Collections)	LSO – V ARL 1-0880(1974)
	V ARK 1-0880
	V ARS 1-0880
	V ARD 1-0880
	V AGL 1-3656
	V AGK 1-3656

'Mein Jesus, was für Seelenweh' (t)	PO – V 14582(1936)
(Chorale from Passion According to	HMV DB 3405
St Matthew)	AAYO – AC 19004D(1941)
(Collections)	LSSO – V DM 1512(1950)
	V LM 1133
(Collection)	V ERB 52
(Collections)	V LM 1875
	HMV ALP 1387
(Collections)	LSSO – Cap PAO 8415(1957)
	Cap SPAO 8415
	S SIB 6094
	S 4X2G 6094
(Collections)	CPO – L SPC 21096(1972)
	L M 521096
	L M 821096
	ED PFS 4278

Sarabande from Partita no. 1 in	PO – V 14583(1936)
B Minor (t)	HMV DB 3366
(Chorale from Cantata no. 4)	
(Collections)	LSSO – Cap P 8489(1958)
	Cap SP 8489
	S S 60235
	S 4XG 60235

Chaconne from Partita no. 2 in	PO – V 8492-94(1934)
D Minor (t)	V 8495-97(ac)
('Nun kommt der Heiden Heiland')	
('Ein feste Burg' and Fugue no. 2	HMV DB 2451-53
in C Minor from 'Wohltemperiertes	HMV DB 7860-62(ac)
Klavier' I)	
(Collections)	LSSO – V DM 1512(1950)
	V LM 1133
(Collections)	LSO – V ARL 1-0880(1974)
	V ARK 1-0880
	V ARS 1-0880
	V ARD 1-0880
	V AGL 1-3656
	V AGK 1-3656

Prelude from Partita no. 3 in E Major (t)	AAYO – AC 11983D(1941)
(Mendelssohn: Scherzo from 'A Mid-	
summer Night's Dream')	
(Collections)	LSSO – Cap PAO 8415(1957)
	Cap SPAO 8415
	Cap P 8650
	Cap SP 8650
	S S 60278
	S 4XG 60278

(Collections)	LSO – V ARL 1-0880(1974)
	V ARK 1-0880
	V ARS 1-0880
	V ARD 1-0880
	V AGL 1-3656
	V AGK 1-3656
Passacaglia and Fugue in C Minor (t)	PO – V 7090-91(1929)
(Brandenburg Concerto no. 2 in F	V 17246-50(ac)
Major)	HMV D 1702-03
(Collections)	V VCM 7101
	PO – V 14580-81(1936)
	HMV DB 3252-53
	AAYO – AC 11714-15D(1941)
	AC 11716-17D(ac)
(Collections)	LSSO – V DM 1512(1950)
	V LM 1133
	V ERB 7033
	V LRM 7033
	HMV BLP 1074
(Collections)	LSSO – Cap P 8489(1958)
	Cap SP 8489
	S S 60235
	S 4XG 60235
(W. A. Mozart: Concerto no. 20 in	IFYO-AVE 30696(1969)
D Minor for Piano and Orchestra)	
(Collections)	CPO – L SPC 21096(1972)
	L M 521096
	L M 821096
	ED PFS 4278
'Es ist vollbracht' from Passion	PO – V 8764(1934)
According to St John (t)	HMV DB 2762
	PO – V 11-8578(1940)
	HMV DB 6181
Chorale from Passion According to	PO – V 14582(1936)
St Matthew (t)	HMV DB 3405
('Mein Jesus, was für Seelenweh')	
Prelude and Fugue in E Minor (t)	PO – V 11-8577(1937)
('Ich rufe zu dir')	
(Bloch: 'Schelomo')	V 17338
	V 17342(ac)
	V WCT 69
Andante from Solo Sonata no. 2 in	AAYO – AC 11978D(1941)
A Minor (t)	AC 11979-81D(ac)
Siciliano from Sonata no. 4 in	PO – V 8495(1933)
C Minor (t)	
(Adagio from Toccata, Adagio, and Fugue	
in C Major)	
(Sarabande from English Suite no. 3)	HMV DB 2275
(Collections)	LSSO – V DM 1512(1950)
	V ERA 244
	V ERB 52

	V LM 1133
	V LM 1875
	HMV ALP 1387
Suite no. 2 in B Minor for Orchestra	LSSO – V WDM 1569(1950)
(Collections)	V LM 1176
Sarabande only	V ERA 244
(Collections)	V ERB 52
	V LM 1875
	HMV ALP 1387
Air from Suite no. 3 in D Major for	PO – V 1843(1936)
Orchestra (t)	HMV DA 1605
	AAYO – AC 11774D(1941)
('Komm', süsser Tod')	AC 11775-76D(ac)
(Collections)	LSSO – Cap P 8458(1958)
	Cap SP 8458
	Cap L 9216
	Cap SL 9216
	Cap P 8650
	Cap SP 8650
	S S 60278
	S 4XG 60278
(Collections)	LSO – V ARL 1-0880(1974)
	V ARK 1-0880
	V ARS 1-0880
	V ARD 1-0880
	V AGL 1-3656
	V AGK 1-3656
Adagio from Toccata, Adagio, and Fugue	PO – V 8495(1933)
in C Major (t)	
(Siciliano from Sonata no. 4 in C Minor)	
(Beethoven: Symphony no. 9 in D Minor)	HMV DB 2335
	HMV DB 7745(ac)
Toccata and Fugue in D Minor (t)	PO – V 6751(1927)
	HMV D 1428
(Collections)	V VCM 7101
	V DMM 4-0341
	PO – V 8697(1934)
	HMV DB 2572
(Stravinsky: 'Le Sacre du Printemps')	PO – Disney WDL 4101A(1939)
	Disney WDL S 4101A
(Collections)	Disney WDX 101
	Disney STER 101
	Buena Vista BVS 101
	Buena Vista 101 VC
	Buena Vista 101 VT
(Chorale 'Ein feste Burg')	AAYO – AC 11757-58D(1941)
	AC 11759-60D(ac)
	LSSO – V 11-9653(1947)
	V 49-0263
(Collections)	V ERB 7033
	V LRM 7033
	HMV BLP 1074
	V LM 2042

(Collections)	LSSO – Cap P 8399(1956)
	Cap SP 8399
	Cap SPAO 8694
	S S 60235
	S 4XG 60235
	S SIB 6094
	S 4X2G 6094
(Collections)	CPO – L SPC 21096(1972)
	L M 521096
	L M 821096
	ED PFS 4278
	ED D94D2
	ED K94K2
First Movement from Trio Sonata no. 1	PO – V 11-8576(1939)
in E Flat Major (t)	HMV DB 6260
(Palestrina: 'Adoramus te Christe')	
Fugue no. 2 in C Minor from	PO – V 1985(1934)
'Wohltemperiertes Klavier' I (t)	
(Frescobaldi: Gagliarda)	
(Chaconne from Partita no. 2 in D Minor)	HMV DB 2453
	HMV DB 7860(ac)
(Collections)	Cam CAL 120
Prelude no. 8 in E Flat Minor from	PO – V 6786(1927)
'Wohltemperiertes Klavier' I (t)	HMV D 1464
('Ich rufe zu dir')	
	AAYO – AC 11977D(1941)
	AC 11979-81D(ac)
(Collections)	CPO – L SPC 21096(1972)
	L M 521096
	L M 821096
	ED PFS 4278
Prelude no. 24 in B Minor from	PO – V 7316(1929)
'Wohltemperiertes Klavier' I (t)	HMV D 1938
(Handel: Sinfonia from 'Messiah')	
(Haydn: Serenade from Quartet in	HMV D 1995
F Major, op. 3, no. 5)	
(Collections)	LSSO – V LM 2042(1950)

Samuel Barber

Adagio for Strings	LSSO – Cap SAL 8385(1956)
(Collections)	Cap SSAL 8385
	Cap SP 8673
	S SIB 6094
	S 4X2G 6094

Bela Bartok

Concerto for Orchestra	HSO – Ev LPBR 6069(1960)
	Ev SDBR 3069
Music for Strings, Percussion, and	LSSO – Cap P 8507(1959)
Celeste	Cap SP 8507
(Martin: Petite Symphonie Concertante)	
Sonata for Two Pianos and Percussion	LSSO – V WDM 1727 (1952)
(Goeb: Symphony no. 3)	V LM 1727

Ludwig van Beethoven

Concerto no. 5 in E Flat Major	ASO – AC ML 6288(1966)
for Piano and Orchestra	AC MS 6888
Soloist: Glenn Gould	CBS BRG 72483
	CBS SBRG 72483
(Collection)	O Y4-34640
	O YT4-34640
Overture to 'Coriolanus'	LSO – V ARL 1-0600(1974)
(Symphony no. 3 in E Flat Major)	V ARD 1-0600
Overture to 'Egmont'	NPO – L SPC 21139(1973)
(Symphony no. 7 in A Major)	L M 521139
	ED PFS 4342
	ED KPFC 4342
(Collections)	ED D94D2
	ED K94K2
'Die Ehre Gottes aus der Natur', op. 48,	NSOL – V LM 2593(1961)
no. 4	V LSC 2593
(Collections)	
With the Norman Luboff Choir	
Leonore Overture no. 3	NaPO – Pye PCNHX 6(1976)
(Collections)	Pye ZCPNH 6
Turkish March from 'The Ruins of	LSSO – V LM 2042(1955)
Athens'	(NBCSO)
(Collections)	
Symphony no. 3 in E Flat Major	LSO – V ARL 1-0600(1974)
(Overture to Coriolanus')	V ARD 1-0600
Symphony no. 5 in C Minor	PO – V L 7001(1931)
(Collection)	V DPM 4-0210
(Bach: Little Fugue in G Minor)	AAYO – AC 11543-47D(1941)
	AC 11548-52D(ac)
(Schubert: Symphony no. 8 in B Minor)	LPO – L SPC 21042(1969)
	L M 94042
	LM 95042
	ED PFS 4197
Symphony no. 6 in F Major	PO – Disney WDL 4101C(1939)
(Moussorgsky: 'A Night on the Bare	Disney WDL S 4101C
Mountain' – Schubert: 'Ave Maria')	
(Collections)	Disney WDX 101
	Disney STER 101
	Buena Vista BVS 101
	Buena Vista 101 VC
	Buena Vista 101 VT
	NYCSO – V 11-9011-15(1945)
	V 11-9016-20(ac)
	Cam CAL 187
(Stokowski: Sounds of Nature)	NBCSO – V LM 1830(1954)
	HMV ALP 1268
Second movement only	V ERB 52
(Collections)	V LM 1875
	HMV ALP 1387

Symphony no. 7 in A Major	PO – V 6670-74(1927)
	V 7042-46(ac)
	HMV D 1639-43
	HMV D 7112-16(ac)
	Cam CAL 212
(Schubert: Symphony no. 8 in B Minor)	Pa 5
(Collections)	V DMM 4-0341
	SA – UA UAL 7003(1958)
	UA UAS 8003
(Collections)	Q PMC 7110E
	Q P4C 7110E
(Overture to 'Egmont')	NPO – L SPC 21139(1973)
	L M 521139
	ED PFS 4342
	ED KPFC 4342
Second Movement from Symphony no. 8	PO – V 74661(1920)
in F Major	HMV 3-0579
(Mozart: Third Movement from	V 6243
Symphony no. 40 in G Minor)	HMV DB 385
Symphony no. 9 in D Minor	PO – V 8424-32(1934)
(Bach: 'Komm', süsser Tod')	V 8433-41(ac)
Soloists: Agnes Davies, Ruth Cathcart,	
Robert Bett, and Eugene Lowenthal	
With the Philadelphia Orchestra Chorus	
(Bach: Adagio from Toccata, Adagio, and	HMV DB 2327-35
Fugue in C Major)	HMV DB 7745-53(ac)
Soloists: Heather Harper, Helen Watts,	LSO – L SPC 21043(1967)
Alexander Young, and Donald McIntyre	L M 94043
With the London Symphony Orchestra	L M 95043
Chorus	ED PFS 4183
	ED KPFC 4183
	ED EPFC 4183
Poul Ben-Haim	
'From Israel'	SA – UA UAL 7005(1959)
(Bloch: 'Schelomo')	UA UAS 8005
Theodore Berger	
Rondino giocoso	LSSO – Cap P 8458(1958)
(Collections)	Cap SP 8458
Irving Berlin	
'God Bless America'	AAYO – AC 17204D(1940)
(Stafford Smith: 'The Star-Spangled	
Banner')	
Hector Berlioz	
'Dance of the Sylphs' from	LSSO – V WDM 1628(1951)
'Damnation of Faust'	
(Ibert: 'Escales')	
(Collections)	
	V LM 151
	V LM 9029
(Collections)	LSO – L SPC 21059(1970)
	ED PFS 4220

	L SPC 21112
	L M 521112
	L M 821112
(Collection)	ED DPA 519-20
	ED KDPC 519-20
Hungarian March from 'Damnation of	PO – V 6823(1927)
Faust'	HMV D 1807
(Saint-Saëns: Bacchanal from 'Samson	
and Delilah')	
(Collections)	V VCM 7101
(Collections)	NaPO – Pye PCNH 4(1975)
	Pye ZCPHG 4
Roman Carnival Overture	NaPO – Pye PCNHX 6(1976)
(Collections)	Pye ZCPNH 6
Symphonie Fantastique	NPO – L SPC 21031(1968)
	L M 94031
	L M 95031
	ED PFS 4160
	ED KPFC 4160
	Ace SDD 495

George Bizet

Suite no. 1 from 'L'Arlesienne'	PO – V 7124-26(1929)
	V 7127-29(ac)
	HMV D 1801-03
	HMV D 7363-65(ac)
Suites no. 1 and 2 from 'L'Arlesienne'	LSSO – V ERB 24(1952)
(Symphony in C Major)	V WDM 1706
	V LM 1706
	HMV ALP 1181
	Va VIC 1008
(Suite from 'Carmen')	NaPO – AC M 34503(1976)
	AC MT 34503
	AC MA 34503
	CBS 76587
	CBS 40-76587
Adagietto from Suite no. 1	LSSO – V ERA 244(1952)
(Collections)	V ERB 52
	V LM 1875
	HMV ALP 1387
Spanish Dance from Suite no. 2	PO – V 1113(1922)
(Brahms: Hungarian Dance no. 1 in	
G Minor)	
Suite from 'Carmen'	PO – V L 1000 (V 1356 + V 6873
	+ V 6874)
	NYCSO – V 11-8795-98(1945)
	V 11-8799-8802(ac)
	HMV DB 9505-08(ac)
	V WDM 1002
	V LM 1069

(Suites no. 1 and 2 from 'L'Arlesienne')	NaPO – AC M 34503(1976)
	AC MT 34503
	AC MA 34503
	CBS 76587
	CBS 40-76587
Prelude to Act 1 of 'Carmen'	PO – V 64822(1919)
(Ippolitov-Ivanow: Procession from	V 796
'Caucasian Sketches')	
(Prelude to Act 4)	PO – V 1356(1927)
	HMV E 531
'Changing of the Guard' from Act 1	PO – V 66263(1923)
of 'Carmen'	
('March of the Smugglers' from Act 3)	V 1017
	HMV DA 612
('March of the Smugglers' from Act 3)	PO – V 6874(1927)
	HMV D 1618
Preludes to Act 2 and 3 of 'Carmen'	PO – V 6873(1927)
('Gypsy Dance' from Act 2)	HMV D 1816
'March of the Smugglers' from Act 3	PO – V 66264(1923)
of 'Carmen'	
('Changing of the Guard' from Act 1)	V 1017
	HMV DA 612
('Changing of the Guard' from Act 1)	PO – V 6874(1927)
	HMV D 1618
Prelude to Act 4 of 'Carmen'	PO – V 1356(1927)
(Prelude to Act 1)	HMV E 531
Symphony in C Major	LSSO – V WDM 1706(1952)
(Suites no. 1 and 2 from 'L'Arlesienne')	V LM 1706
	HMV ALP 1181
	Va VIC 1008
(Mendelssohn: Symphony no. 4 in	NaPO – AC M 34567(1977)
A Major)	AC MT 34567
	AC MA 34567
	CBS 76673
	CBS 40-76673

Ernest Bloch

'America'	SA – Van VRS 1056(1959)
(Bloch: About 'America')	Van VSD 2065
With the American Concert Choir	Van S 346
'Schelomo'	PO – V 17336-38(1940)
(Bach: Prelude and Fugue in E Minor)	V 17342-44(ac)
Soloist: Emmanuel Feuermann	V WCT 69
	HMV DB 5816-18S
	HMV DB 8862S-64(ac)
(Rimsky-Korsakov: Prelude to Act 3	HMV DB 6055-57
of 'Ivan the Terrible')	
	V LCT 14
(Collections)	Cam CAL 254
	V DMM 4-0341
(Ben-Haim: 'From Israel')	SA – UA UAL 7005(1959)

Soloist: George Neikrug   UA UAS 8005

Luigi Boccherini
Minuet from String Quintet in E Major,   PO – V 66058(1922)
op. 13, no. 5 (t)   HMV 2-947
(Tschaikovsky: 'Dance of the Flutes'   V 798
from 'The Nutcracker')
(Haydn: Serenade from Quartet in   PO – V 7256(1929)
F Major, op. 3, no. 5)   HMV D 1864
(Collections)   Cam CAL 120
(Collections)   LSSO – Cap P 8458(1958)
                                                        Cap SP 8458
                                                        Cap L 9216
                                                        Cap SL 9216
                                                        Cap P 8650
                                                        Cap SP 8650
                                                        S S 60278
                                                        S 4XG 60278

Alexander Borodin
'In the Steppes of Central Asia'   LSSO – V ERB 1816(1953)
(Collections)   V LM 1816
                                                        Q PMC 7026E
                                                        Q P4C 7026E
(Polovtsian Dances from 'Prince Igor')   V ERB 7056
                                                        V LRM 7056

Polovtsian Dances from 'Prince Igor'   PO – V 6514(1925)
(Ippolitov-Ivanov: 'In the Village'
from 'Caucasian Sketches')

                                                 PO – V 15169-70(1937)
                                                        HMV DB 3232-33
(Stravinsky: 'Petrouchka')   Cam CAL 203
(Collections)   V DMM 4-0341
With Women's Chorus   LSSO – V 12-1193-94(1950)
(De Falla: 'El Amor Brujo')   V LM 1054
                                                        Va Vic 1043
('In the Steppes of Central Asia')   V ERB 7056
                                                        V LRM 7056
Excerpts only   V 10-4242
                                                        HMV DA 2073
                                                        V 49-4242
With the John Alldis Choir and the   RPO – L SPC 21041(1969)
Welsh National Opera Chorus   L M 94041
(Collections)   L M 95041
                                                        ED PFS 4189
                                                        L SPC 21111
                                                        L M 521111
                                                        L M 821111
Nocturne from String Quartet no. 2   LSSO – Cap PAO 8415(1957)
in D Major   Cap SPAO 8415
(Collections)   Cap L 9216
                                                        Cap SL 9216
                                                        Cap P 8650
                                                        Cap SP 8650

```
                                    S S 60278
                                    S 4XG 60278
```

Johannes Brahms
Academic Festival Overture   NPO – V ARL 1-0719(1974)
(Symphony no. 4 in E Minor)   V ARK 1-0719
    V ARS 1-0719
    V ARD 1-0719
    V ART 1-0719

Hungarian Dance no. 1 in G Minor (t)   PO – V 1113(1920)
(Bizet: Spanish Dance of Suite no. 2
from 'L'Arlesienne')
(Gliere: 'Russian Sailors' Dance' from   PO – V 1675(1934)
'The Red Poppy')   HMV DA 1398
(Collections)   Cam CAL 123
    Cam CAE 192

(Dolan: 'A Message for Liza' from   HBSO – V 10-1302(1946)
'Lady in the Dark')   V 49-1293
(Collections)   NaPO-Pye PCNH 4(1975)
    Pye ZCPHG 4

Hungarian Dance no. 5 in F Sharp Minor   PO – V 64752(1917)
(Hungarian Dance no. 6 in D Flat Major)   V 797

Hungarian Dance no. 6 in D Flat Major   PO – V 64753(1917)
(Hungarian Dance no. 5 in F Sharp
Minor)   V 797

Serenade no. 1 in D Major, op. 11   SA – AD DL 10031(1960)
    AD DL 710031
    AD DCM 3205
    VS VC 81050

Minuet only   PO – V 1720(1935)
    HMV DA 1462

Symphony no. 1 in C Minor   PO – V 6657S-62(1927)
    HMV D 1499-1503
    HMV D 7671-75(ac)
    V L 11647-48

(Wagner: Overture to 'Rienzi')   CC GOCLP 9009H
    PO – V 8971-75(1935)
    V 16712-16(ac)
    HMV DB 2874-78
    Cam CAL 105
    HBSO – V 12-1223-27(1945)
    V 12-1228-32(ac)
    V 18-0020-24
    V 18-0025-29(ac)
    HMV DB 6860-64
    V WDM 1402
    V LM 1070

(Collections)   LSO – L SPC 21090-91(1972)
    ED OPFS 3-4
    ED KPFC 3-4

Symphony no. 1 only   L SPC 21131
    L M 521131

	L M 821131
	ED PFS 4305
	ED KPFC 4305
Symphony no. 2 in D Major	PO – V 7277-82(1929)
	V 7283-88(ac)
	HMV D 1877-82
	HMV D 7262-67(ac)
(Tragic Overture)	NaPO – AC M 35129(1977)
	AC MT 35129
	CBS 76667
	CBS 40-76667
Symphony no. 3 in F Major	PO – V 6962-66(1928)
	V 17258-62(ac)
	HMV D 1769-73
	HMV D 7225-29(ac)
	Cam CAL 164
(Weber: 'Invitation to the Dance')	LSS LS 1
	HSO – Ev LPBR 6030(1959)
	Ev SDBR 3030
Third Movement only	PO – V 74722(1921)
(Tschaikovsky: Third Movement from	V 6242
Symphony no. 6 in B Minor)	
Symphony no. 4 in E Minor	PO – V DPM 4-0210(1931)
(Collection)	
	PO – V 7825-29(1933)
	V 7830-34(ac)
	AAYO – AC 11553-58D(1941)
	AC 11559-64D(ac)
(Academic Festival Overture)	NPO – V ARL 1-0719(1974)
	V ARK 1-0719
	V ARS 1-0719
	V ARD 1-0719
	V ART 1-0719
Tragic Overture	NaPO – AC M 35129(1977)
(Symphony no. 2 in D Major)	AC MT 35129
	CBS 76667
	CBS 40-76667

William Byrd

Pavane and Gigue 'Earl of Salisbury' (t)	PO – V 1943(1937)
	HMV DA 1637
(Collections)	LSO – L SPC 21130(1972)
	ED PFS 4351
	ED KPFC 4351

Thomas Canning

Fantasy on a Hymn by Justin Morgan	HSO – Ev LPBR 6070(1960)
(Collections)	Ev SDBR 3070

Joseph Canteloube

'Songs of the Auvergne'	ASO – V LM 2795(1965)
(Collections)	V LSC 2795
Soloist: Anna Moffo	

Marc Antonio Cesti
'Tu mancavi a tormentarmi' (t)   LSSO – V WDM 1721(1952)
(Collections)   V LM 1721
   V ERB 52
   V LM 1875
   HMV ALP 1387
(Collections)   SA – UA UAL 7001(1958)
   UA UAS 8001

Emmanuel Chabrier
Espana Rhapsody   PO – V 74621(1919)
(Saint-Saëns: Bacchanal from 'Samson and   V 6241
Delilah')   HMV DB 384
(Collections)   NaPO – Pye PCNH 4(1975)
   Pye ZCPHG 4

Frederic Chopin
Mazurka no. 13 in A Minor, op. 17,   PO – V 1855(1937)
no. 4 (t)
(Collections)   HSO – Ev LPBR 6070(1960)
   Ev SDBR 3070
(Collections)   LSO – L SPC 21130(1972)
   ED PFS 4351
   ED KPFC 4351

Mazurka no. 25 in B Minor, op. 33,   PO – V 18267(1937)
no. 4 (t)   V 18268(ac)
(Gliere: Symphony no. 3 in B Minor)
(Collections)   NaPO – AC M 34543(1976)
   AC MT 34543
   AC MA 34543
   CBS 73589
   CBS 40-73589

Prelude no. 4 in E Minor, op. 28 (t)   PO – V 1111(1922)
(Tschaikovsky: Chant sans Paroles in
A Minor, op. 40, no. 6)
(Prelude no. 24 in D Minor)   LSSO – V 49-3855(1950)
(Collections)   V LM 1238
Prelude no. 24 in D Minor, op. 28 (t)   PO – V 1998(1937)
(Stravinsky: Pastorale)
(Bach: Bourrée from English Suite no. 2   HMV DA 1639
in A Minor)
(Prelude no. 4 in E Minor)   LSSO – V 49-3855(1950)
(Collections)   V LM 1238
(Collections)   HSO – Ev LPBR 6070(1960)
   Ev SDBR 3070
(Collections)   NaPO – AC M 34543(1976)
   AC MT 34543
   AC MA 34543
   CBS 73589
   CBS 40-73589

Selections from 'Les Sylphides'   LSSO – V 12-1208-12(ac)(1950)
(Collections)   V WDM 1394
   V LM 1083

	HMV ALP 1133
	Va VIC 1020
	V ERB 7022
	V LRM 7022
	HMV DB 21255
Waltz no. 7 in C Sharp Minor, op. 64, no. 2 (t) (Collections)	HSO – Ev LPBR 6070(1960) Ev SDBR 3070

Jeremiah Clarke
'A Trumpet Voluntary' (t)
(Haydn: Serenade from Quartet in
F Major, op. 3, no. 5)
(Collections)
(Collections)

	HBSO – V 11-9419(1946) HMV DB 6737
	Cam CAL 153
	LSO – L SPC 21130(1972)
	ED PFS 4351
	ED KPFC 4351

Aaron Copland
Selections from 'Billy the Kid'
(Griffes: 'The White Peacock')

NYPO – AC 19011D(1947)
AC ML 2167

Arcangelo Corelli
Concerto Grosso in G Minor, op. 6,
no. 8
(Collections)

LSSO – Bach BGS 70696(1967)
Van S 363

Henry Cowell
'Persian Set'
(Harrison: Suite for Violin, Piano, and
Orchestra)

LSSO – CRI 114(1957)

'Tales of Our Countryside'
Piano: Henry Cowell

AAYO – AC 11964-65D(1941)
AC 11966-67D(ac)

Paul Creston
Scherzo from Symphony, op. 20
(Gould: Guaracha from Latin-American
Symphonette)

AAYO – AC 11713D(1941)

William Dawson
Negro Folk Symphony

ASO – AD DL 10077(1963)
AD DL 710077
Brunswick AXA 4520
Brunswick SXA 4520
VS VC 81056

Claude Debussy
'Children's Corner'

LSSO – V 10-1488-90(1949)
V WDM 1327
V LM 9
V LM 9023

(Tschaikovsky: Suite from 'The Nutcracker')

V ANL 1-2604E
V ANS 1-2604E

No. 4 only
No. 5 only
No. 2, 5 and 6
(Collections)

V ERA 119
V ERA 244
NYSO – Ev LPBR 6108(1958)
Ev SDBR 3108

(Collection)	Ev SDBR 3327
'Dance sacré et Dance profane'	PO – V 7455-56(1931)
(Thomas: Gavotte from Act 2 of 'Mignon')	HMV DB 1642-43
Harp: Edna Phillips	
'Soirée dans Grenade' from	PO – V DMM 4-0341(1940)
'Estampes' (t)	
(Collections)	
(Collections)	NaPO – AC M 34543(1976)
	AC MT 34543
	AC MA 34543
	CBS 73589
	CBS 40-73589
'Iberia' (No. 2 of 'Images' III)	ONRF – Cap P 8463(1958)
(Collections)	Cap SP 8463
	S S 60102
	HMV CC SXL P 30263
	HMV CC TC SXL P 30263
'La Mer'	LSO – L SPC 21059(1970)
(Collections)	ED PFS 4220
	L SPC 21109
	L M 521109
	L M 821109
	Ace SDD 455
'Nocturnes'	PO – V 15814-16S + 2034(1937)
With Women's Chorus	HMV DB 3596 + DA 1742 +
	DB 3981-82S
(Moussorgsky: Symphonic Synthesis from	Cam CAL 140
'Boris Godunow')	
'Sirènes' only	HMV DB 5714-15S
(Collections)	LSSO – V WDM 1560(1950)
With the Robert Shaw Chorale	V LM 1154
'Fêtes' only	V ERA 47
('Clair de Lune' from 'Suite	HMV 7ER 5011
Bergamasque')	
(Ravel: Rapsodie Espagnole)	LSO – Cap P 8520(1959)
With the BBC Women's Chorus	Cap SP 8520
	S S 60104
'Fêtes' only	Cap SP 8673
(Collections)	
'Nuages' only	PO – V 7453(1929)
	HMV DB 1614
(Collections)	V DMM 4-0341
'Fêtes' only	PO – V 1309(1927)
	HMV E 507
(Collections)	V DMM 4-0341
'Prelude a l'apres-midi d'un faune'	PO – V 6481(1924)
	HMV DB 840
	PO – V 6696(1927)
	HMV D 1768
(Collections)	V DMM 4-0341
	PO – V 17700(1940)

	HMV DB 10117
	LSSO – V 12-1119(1949)
	HMV DB 21279
	V 49-0942
(Collections)	V WDM 1560
	V LM 1154
	V ERB 7024
	V LRM 7024
(Collections)	LSSO – Cap P 8399(1956)
	Cap SP 8399
	Cap SP 8673
	S SIB 6094
	S 4X2G 6094
(Collections)	LSO – L SPC 21090-91(1972)
	ED OPFS 3-4
	ED KPFC 3-4
	L SPC 21109
	L M 521109
	L M 821109
	Ace SDD 455
	ED D94D2
	ED K94K2
(Collection)	ED DPA 519-20
	ED KDPC 519-20
Prelude no. 10 I ('La Cathédrale engloutie') (t)	PO – V 7454(1930)
(Collections)	V DMM 4-0341
(Moussorgsky: 'Pictures at an Exhibition')	NPO – L PM 55004(1965)
	L SPC 21006
	L M 94006
	ED LK 4766
	ED PFS 4095
(Collections)	L SPC 21109
	L M 521109
	L M 821109
	Ace SDD 455
'Clair de Lune' from 'Suite Bergamasque' (t)	PO – V 1812(1937)
	HMV DA 1634
(Collections)	Cam CAE 188
	Cam CAL 123
	LSSO – V 10-1534(1948)
	V 49-1009
('Fêtes' from 'Nocturnes')	V ERA 47
	HMV 7ER 5011
(Collections)	V WDM 1560
	V LM 1154
(Collections)	LSSO – Cap P 8399(1956)
	Cap SP 8399
	Cap SPAO 8694
	S SIB 6094
	S 4X2G 6094
(Collections)	NaPO – AC M 34543(1976)

AC MT 34543
AC MA 34543
CBS 73589
CBS 40-73589

Leo Delibes
Selections from 'Sylvia'
(Collections)

LSSO – V 12-1208-12(ac)(1950)
V WDM 1394
V LM 1083
HMV ALP 1133
V ERB 7022
V LRM 7022
Va VIC 1020

Robert Dolan
'A Message for Liza' from 'Lady in the Dark'
(Brahms: Hungarian Dance no. 1)

HBSO – V 10-1302(1946)
V 49-1293

Arcady Dubensky
'The Raven'
Narrator: Benjamin de Loache

PO – V 2000-01(1933)
V L 1006

Paul Dukas
'L'Apprenti sorcier'
(Rimsky-Korsakov: Prelude to Act 3 of 'Ivan the Terrible')
(Sibelius: Berceuse from 'The Tempest')
(Collections)
(Other artistes)
(Collections)

PO – V 17501-02(1937)
HMV DB 6038-39

HMV DB 3533-34
Cam CAL 118
PO – Disney 3016(1939)
Disney WDX 101
Disney STER 101
Buena Vista BVS 101
Buena Vista 101 VC
Buena Vista 101 VT

Fanfare from 'La Péri'
(Collections)

LSSO – Cap SAL 8385(1956)
Cap SSAL 8385
Cap SP 8673
S SIB 6094
S 4X2G 6094

Henri Duparc
'Extase' (t)
(Collections)

LSO – L SPC 21130(1972)
ED PFS 4351
ED KPFC 4351

Antonin Dvorak
Serenade for Strings in E Major
(Collections)

RPO – Desmar DSM 1011(1975)
Desmar E 1047

Slavonic Dance in E Minor, op. 72, no. 2
(Collections)

CPO – L SPC 21117(1972)
L M 521117
ED PFS 4333
ED KPFC 4333
L SPC 21130
ED PFS 4351
ED KPFC 4351

Symphony no. 9 (5) in E Minor	PO – V 6565-69 + 6743(1927)
	V 7097-7101(ac)
	HMV D 1893-97
	HMV D 7291-95(ac)
(Collection)	V CRL 2-0334
Earlier recording	V 6565-69(1925)
	PO – V 8737-41(1934)
	V 8742-46(ac)
	HMV DB 2543-47
	HMV DB 7911-15(ac)
	Cam CAL 104
	AAYO – AC 11349-54SD(1940)
	AC 11355-60SD(ac)
	LSSO – V 12-0484-88(ac)(1947)
	V 18-0189-93(ac)
	V WDM 1248
	V LM 1013
(Collection)	NPO – V CRL 2-0334(1973)
	V MCK 580
Second Movement only	PO – V 74631(1919)
(Liszt: Hungarian Rhapsody no. 2)	V 6236

Henry Eichheim
'Bali'	PO – V 14141-42(1934)
(Anonymous: 'Etenraku')	
'Japanese Nocturne'	PO – V 7260(1929)
(Richard Strauss: 'Dance of the Seven	HMV D 1936
Veils' from 'Salome')	

Edward Elgar
Enigma Variations	CPO – L SPC 21136(1972)
(Collection)	L M 521136
	ED PFS 4338
(Collections)	ED D94D2
	ED K94K2
'Nimrod' only	L SPC 21130
(Collections)	ED PFS 4351
	ED KPFC 4351

George Enesco
Romanian Rhapsody no. 1	LSSO – V 12-0069(1947)
	HMV DB 6828
	V 49-0127
(Romanian Rhapsody no. 2)	LSSO – V ERB 7043(1953)
	V LRM 7043
(Romanian Rhapsody no. 2 + Liszt:	V LM 1878
Hungarian Rhapsodies no. 1, 2, and 3)	Q PMC 7023E
	Q P4C 7023E
(Collections)	RCAVSO – V LM 2471(1960)
	V LSC 2471
	V VCS 7077
	V RK 5072
	V R8S 5072
Romanian Rhapsody no. 2	LSSO – V ERB 7043(1953)

(Romanian Rhapsody no. 1)	V LRM 7043
(Romanian Rhapsody no. 1 + Liszt:	V LM 1878
Hungarian Rhapsodies no. 1, 2, and 3)	Q PMC 7023E
	Q P4C 7023E

Manuel de Falla

'El Amor Brujo'	HBSO – V 11-9393-95(1946)
Soloist: Nan Merriman	V 11-9396-98(ac)
	HMV DB 21039-41
(Borodin: Polovtsian Dances from 'Prince	V LM 1054
Igor')	Va VIC 1043
(Wagner: Love Music from Act 2 and 3	PO – AC ML 5479(1960)
of 'Tristan and Isolde')	AC MS 6147
Soloist: Shirley Verrett-Carter	CBS BRG 61288
	CBS SBRG 61288
	O Y 32368
Ritual Fire Dance only	AAYO – AC 11879D(1941)
(Novacek: 'Moto perpetuo')	
'Nights in the Gardens of Spain'	NYPO – OR MLG 71(1949)
(Other artistes)	
Soloist: William Kapell	
Dance no. 1 from 'La Vida Breve'	PO – V 6997(1928)
(Tschaikovsky: 'Romeo and Juliet')	V 6900(ac)
	HMV 1949

Harold Farberman

First Part of 'Evolution'	LSSO – Cap SAL 8385(1956)
(Collections)	Cap SSAL 8385

Cesar Franck

Andante from 'Grand Piece	PO – V 14947(1937)
Symphonique' (t)	
(Tschaikovsky: Solitude, op. 73, no. 6)	
'Panis Angelicus' from Messe Solennelle,	PO – V 8964(1936)
op. 12 (t)	V 16706(ac)
(Symphony in D Minor)	
(Sibelius: 'Valse triste' from	HMV DB 3318
'Kuolema')	
Symphony in D Minor	PO – V 6726-30(1927)
	V 7032-36(ac)
	HMV D 1404-08
	HMV D 7137-41(ac)
('Panis Angelicus')	PO – V 8959-64(1935)
	V 16706-11(ac)
	HMV DB 3226-31S
	HMV DB 8305S-10(ac)
(Ravel: Fanfare from 'L'Eventail de	HRPO – L SPC 21061(1970)
de Jeanne')	L M 94061
	ED PFS 4218

Girolamo Frescobaldi

Gagliarda (t)	PO – V 1985(1934)
(Bach: Fugue no. 2 in C Minor from	
'Wohltemperiertes Klavier' I)	

(Palestrina: 'Adoramus te Christe')	HMV DA 1606
(Collections)	LSSO – V WDM 1721(1952)
	V LM 1721
	V ERB 52
	V LM 1875
	HMV ALP 1387
(Collections)	SA – UA UAL 7001(1958)
	UA UAS 8001
	Q PMC 7110E
	Q P4C 7110E

Giovanni Gabrieli

Canzona quarti toni à 15	LSSO – V WDM 1721(1952)
(Collections)	V LM 1721
'In Ecclesiis Benidicite Domino' (t)	LSSO – V WDM 1721(1952)
(Collections)	V LM 1721
With Double Chorus	
Organ: Charles Courboin	
Sonata pian e forte	SA – UA UAL 7001(1958)
(Collections)	UA UAS 8001

Alexander Glazunow

Concerto in A Minor for Violin	LSO – L SPC 21090-91(1972)
and Orchestra	ED OPFS 3-4
(Collections)	ED KPFC 3-4
Soloist: Sylvia Marcovici	L SPC 21111
	L M 521111
	L M 821111
'Dance Orientale' from 'Scenes de Ballet'	PO – V 1335(1927)
(Ippolitov-Ivanow: Procession from	HMV E 521
'Caucasian Sketches')	

Rheinhold Gliere

'Russian Sailors' Dance' from 'The Red	PO – V 1675(1934)
Poppy'	HMV DA 1398
(Brahms: Hungarian Dance no. 1 in	
G Minor)	
(Collections)	V VCM 7101
(Collections)	LSSO – V ERB 1816(1953)
	V LM 1816
	Q PMC 7026E
	Q P4C 7026E
(Moussorgsky: 'A Night on the Bare	HMV 7ER 5060
Mountain')	
Symphony no. 3 in B Minor	PO – V 18262-67(1940)
(Chopin: Mazurka no. 25 in B Minor,	V 18268-73(ac)
op. 33, no. 4)	V WCT 1106
	V LCT 1106
	HSO – Cap P 8402(1956)
	Cap SP 8402
	S S 60089

Christoph Willibald Gluck

Lento from 'Armide'	LSSO – Cap PAO 8415(1957)

(Collections)	Cap SPAO 8415
	S S 60278
	S 4XG 60278
Sicilienne from 'Armide'	LSSO – Cap PAO 8415(1957)
(Collections)	Cap SPAO 8415
	S SIB 6094
	S 4X2G 6094
Lento from 'Ifigenia in Aulis'	LSSO – Cap PAO 8415(1957)
(Collections)	Cap SPAO 8415
	Cap P 8650
	Cap SP 8650
	S SIB 6094
	S 4X2G 6094
Ballet Music from 'Orpheus and	PO – V 74567(1917)
Euridice'	
(Mendelssohn: Scherzo from 'A Mid-	V 6238
summer Night's Dream')	
(Collections)	LSSO – Cap P 8458(1958)
	Cap SP 8458
	Cap P 8650
	Cap SP 8650
	S S 60278
	S 4XG 60278
'O Saviour, Hear Me' from 'Orpheus	NSOL – V LM 2593(1961)
and Euridice'	V LSC 2593
(Collections)	
With the Norman Luboff Choir	

Roger Goeb
Symphony no. 3	LSSO – V WDM 1727(1952)
(Bartok: Sonata for Two Pianos and	V LM 1727
Percussion)	
(Ben Weber: Symphony on Poems by	CRI 120
Wiliam Blake)	

Morton Gould
Dance Variations for Two Pianos and	SFSO – V LM 1858(1953)
Orchestra	
(Menotti: Suite from 'Sebastian')	
Soloists: Arthur Whittemore and	
Jack Lowe	
Guaracha from Latin-American	AAYO – AC 11713D(1941)
Symphonette	
(Creston: Scherzo from Symphony, op. 20)	

Charles Gounod
Waltz from Act 2 of 'Faust'	PO – V 66171(1923)
(Thomas: Gavotte from Act 2 of	V 944
'Mignon')	HMV DA 562

Percy Grainger
English and Irish Folk Tunes	LSSO – V WDM 1663(1950)
(Collections)	V LM 1238

Piano: Percy Grainger   V ARL 1-3059
Excerpts   V ERA 124
     HMV 7ER 5046

Enrique Granados
Intermezzo from 'Goyescas'   LSSO – V 12-0470(1947)
(Revueltas: 'Sensemaya')   HMV DB 6915
     V 49-0882
(Collections)   V LM 151
     V LM 9029

Edvard Grieg
'Anitra's Dance' from 'Peer Gynt'   PO – V 64768(1917)
(Schubert: Moment Musicale no. 3 in   V 799
F Minor)

Concerto in A Minor for Piano and   HBSO – IPA 508(1945)
Orchestra
(Collection)
Soloist: Percy Grainger

Charles Griffes
'The White Peacock'   NYPO – AC 19012D(1947)
(Copland: 'Billy the Kid')   AC ML 2167

George Frederic Handel
Tamburina from 'Alcina'   LSSO – Cap P 8458(1958)
(Collections)   Cap SP 8458

Selections from 'Messiah'   LSO – L PM 55012(1966)
Soloists: Sheila Armstrong,   L SPC 21014
Norma Proctor, Kenneth Bowen,   L M 94014
and John Cameron   L M 95014
Harpsichord: Charles Spinks   ED LK 4840
Organ: Philip Ledger   ED PFS 4113
With London Symphony Orchestra   ED SPA 284
Chorus

Sinfonia from 'Messiah'   PO – V 7316(1930)
(Bach: Prelude no. 24 in B Minor   HMV D 1938
from 'Wohltemperiertes Klavier' I)
(Collections)   Cam CAL 120
(Anonymous: Russian Christmas Music)   LSSO – V 11-9837(1947)
     V 49-0974
     V ERA 119

Overture in D Minor (t)   PO – V 1798(1935)
     HMV DA 1556

Royal Fireworks Music (t)   RCAVSO – V LM 2612(1961)
(Water Music Suite)   V LSC 2612
     V AGL 1-2704
     Va VICS 1513

Water Music Suite (t)   PO – V 8550-51(1934)
     HMV DB 2528-29
(Royal Fireworks Music)   RCAVSO – V LM 2612(1961)
     V LSC 2612
     V AGL 1-2704

(Collections)	VaVICS 1513
	V VCS 7077
	V RK 5072
	V R8S 5072
Largo from 'Xerxes'	NSOL – V LM 2593(1961)
(Collections)	V LSC 2593
	V VCS 7077
	V RK 5072
	V R8S 5072

Lou Harrison

Suite for Violin, Piano, and Orchestra	LSSO – V LM 1785(1952)
(Ben Weber: Symphony on Poems by	
William Blake)	
Soloists: Anahid and Maro Ajemian	
(Cowell: 'Persian Set')	CRI 114

Joseph Haydn

Serenade from Quartet in F Major, op. 3,	PO – V 7256(1929)
no. 5 (t)	HMV D 1864
(Boccherini: Minuet from String Quintet	
in E Major, op. 13, no. 5)	
(Bach: Prelude no. 24 in B Minor from	HMV D 1995
'Wohltemperiertes Klavier' I)	
(Collections)	Cam CAL 120
(Clarke: 'A Trumpet Voluntary')	HBSO – V 11-9419(1946)
	HMV DB 6747
(Collections)	NaPO – Pye PCNH 4(1975)
	Pye ZCPHG 4
Symphony no. 53 in D Major	LSSO – V 12-1088-89(1949)
	V WDM 1352
(Liszt: 'Les Preludes')	V LM 1073

Gustav Holst

'The Planets'	LAPO – Cap P 8389(1956)
With the Roger Wagner Chorale	Cap SP 8389
	S S 60175
	S 4XG 60175

Engelbert Humperdinck

Prelude to 'Hänsel and Gretel'	LSSO – V 12-1321(1949)
	HMV DB 21256
	V 49-1376
(Tschaikovsky: 'Waltz of the Flowers'	HMV 7ER 5016
from 'The Nutcracker')	
(Collections)	V LM 2042
'Evening Prayer' from 'Hänsel and Gretel'	NSOL – V LM 2593(1961)
(Collections)	V LSC 2593
With the Norman Luboff Choir	

Jacques Ibert

'Escales'	LSSO – V WDM 1628(1951)
(Berlioz: 'Dance of the Sylphs' from	
'Damnation of Faust')	
(Collections)	V LM 151

	V LM 9029
(Collections)	ONRF – Cap P 8463(1958)
	Cap SP 8463
	S S 60102
	HMV CC SXL P 30263
	HMV CC TC SXL P 30263

Michail Ippolitov-Ivanow
'In the Village' from 'Caucasian   PO – V 6514(1925)
Sketches'
(Borodin: Polovtsian Dances from 'Prince
Igor')
(Khachaturian: 'Masquerade' Suite)   NYPO – AC 12758D(1947)
                                          AC 12759D(ac)

'Procession' from 'Caucasian Sketches'   PO – V 66106(1922)
(Bizet: Prelude to Act 1 of 'Carmen')   V 796
(Glazunow: 'Dance orientale' from 'Scenes PO – V 1335(1927)
de Ballet')   HMV E 521
(Collections)   Cam CAL 123
                                          V VCM 7101
(Collections)   NaPO – Pye PCNH 4(1975)
                                          Pye ZCPHG 4

Charles Ives
Four Songs for Chorus and Orchestra   ASO – AC M4 32504(1967)
('Majority', 'They Are There', 'An
Election', and 'Lincoln, the Great
Commoner')
(Collection)
With the Gregg Smith Singers and the
Ithaca College Concert Choir

Orchestral Set no. 2   LSO – L SPC 21060(1970)
(Messiaen: 'L'Ascension')   L M 94060
With the London Symphony Orchestra   ED PFS 4203
Chorus

Robert Browning Overture   ASO – AC ML 6415(1966)
(Collection)   AC MS 7015
                                          CBS BRG 72646
                                          CBS SBRG 72646

Symphony no. 4   ASO – AC ML 6175(1965)
Assistant conductors: David Katz   AC MS 6775
and José Serebrier   CBS BRG 72403
With New York Schola Cantorum   CBS SBRG 72403
(Collection)   AC D3S 783

Werner Josten
Canzona Seria   ASO – CRI SD 267(1971)
('Jungle')

Concerto Sacro I and II   ASO – CRI 200 (1965)
Piano: David del Tredici   CRI SD 200

'Jungle'   ASO – CRI SD 267(1971)
(Canzona Seria)

Aram Khachaturian
'Masquerade' Suite   NYPO – AC 12756-58D(1947)
(Ippolitov-Ivanow: 'In the Village' from   AC 12759-61D(ac)
'Caucasian Sketches')
(Tschaikovsky: 'Francesca da Rimini')   AC ML 4071

Symphony no. 2   SA – UA UAL 7002(1958)
                                   UA UAS 8002

Symphony no. 3   CSO – V LSC 3067(1968)
(Rimsky-Korsakov: Russian Easter   V R8S 1122
Overture)

Zoltan Kodaly
Suite from 'Hary Janos'   HRO – LSS LS 2(1967)
(Stravinsky: Suite from 'Petrouchka')

Kurt Leimer
Concerto no. 4 for Piano and Orchestra   SA – EE C 063-29030(1959)
Soloist: Kurt Leimer

Anatol Liadov
'Dance of the Amazon', op. 65   PO – V 1112(1924)
(Stravinsky: 'Fireworks', op. 4)

Eight Russian Folk Dances   PO – V 8491 + 1681(1934)
                                   HMV DB 2443 + DA 1415
                                   V L 11752
                                   Cam CAE 256

Franz Liszt
Hungarian Rhapsodies no. 1, 2, and 3   NBCSO – V LM 1878(1955)
(Enesco: Romanian Rhapsodies no. 1   Q PMC 7023E
and 2)   Q P4C 7023E

Hungarian Rhapsody no. 2   PO – V 74647(1920)
(Dvorak: Second Movement from   V 6236
Symphony no. 5 (9) in E Minor)

                                PO – V 6652(1926)
                                   HMV D 1296
(Collections)   V VCM 7101
                                PO – V 14422(1936)
                                   HMV DB 3086
                                   AAYO – AC 11646D(1941)
Hungarian Rhapsody no. 1   NBCSO – V LM 1878(1955)
(Hungarian Rhapsodies no. 2 and 3   Q PMC 7023E
Ernesco: Romanian Rhapsodies no. 1 and 2) QP4C 7023E
(Collections)   RCAVSO – V LM 2471(1960)
                                   V LSC 2471
                                 V VCS 7077
                                 V RK 5072
                                 V R8S 5072

Hungarian Rhapsody no. 3   NBCSO – V LM 1878(1955)
(Hungarian Rhapsodies no. 1 and 2   Q PMC 7023E
+ Enesco: Romanian Rhapsodies no. 1   Q P4C 7023E
and 2)

'Les Preludes'   LSSO – V 12-0677-78(1947)
                                V 12-0679-80(ac)
                                V WDM 1277

(Haydn: Symphony no. 53 in D Major)   V LM 1073

Charles Martin Loeffler
'A Pagan Poem'   LSSO – Cap PAO 8433(1957)
(Schoenberg: 'Verklärte Nacht')   Cap SPAO 8433
     S S 60080

Jean Baptiste Lully
Prelude to 'Alceste'   PO – V 7424(1930)
(March from 'Thésée' and Nocturne   HMV DB 1587
from 'Le Triomphe de L'Amour')
March from 'Thésée'   PO – V 7424(1930)
Prelude to 'Alceste' and Nocturne   HMV DB 1587
from 'Le Triomphe de L'Amour')
(Collections)   LSSO – V WDM 1971(1052)
     V LM 1721

Nocturne from 'Le Triomphe de   PO – V 7424(1930)
L'Amour'   HMV DB 1587
(Prelude to 'Alceste' and March from
'Thésée')
(Collections)   LSSO – V WDM 1721(1952)
     V LM 1721
     V ERB 52
     V LM 1875
     HMV ALP 1387

Gustav Mahler
Symphony no. 2 in C Minor   LSO – Pensanze PR19(1963)
(Symphony no. 8 in E Flat Major)
Soloists: Rae Woodland and Janet Baker
With the BBC Chorus and Choral Society

Soloists: Brigitte Fassbaender and   LSO – V ARL 2-0852(1974)
Margaret Price   V ARD 2-0852
With the London Symphony Orchestra
Chorus

Symphony no. 8 in E Flat Major   NYPO – OTA Set 6(1950)
Soloists: Francis Yeend, Uta Graf,
Camilla Williams, Martha Lipton,
Louise Bernhardt, Eugene Conley, Carlos
Alexander, and George London
With the Westminster Choir and Schola
Cantorum
(Symphony no. 2 in C Minor)   Pensanze PR 19

Frank Martin
Petite Symphonie Concertante for Harp,   LSSO – Cap P 8507(1959)
Harpsichord, Piano, and Two String   Cap SP 8507
Orchestras
(Bartok: Music for Strings, Percussion,
and Celeste)

Harl McDonald
'The Arkansas Traveler'   PO – V 18069(1940)
(Novacek: 'Moto perpetuo')   HMV DB 5966
(Shostakovitch: Symphony no. 6)   V 18395
     V 18396(ac)

(Collection)	Cam CAL 238
Concerto for Two Pianos and Orchestra Soloists: Alexander Kelberine and Jeannie Behrend	PO – V 15410-12(1937) V 15413-15(ac) HMV DB 5700-02
'Dance of the Workers' from 'Festival of Workers' (Rhumba from Symphony no. 2)	PO – V 8919(1935) HMV DB 2913
Rhumba from Symphony no. 2 ('Dance of the Workers' from 'Festival of Workers')	PO – V8919(1935) HMV DB 2913
(Collection)	Cam CAL 238

Felix Mendelssohn

Scherzo from "A Midsummer Night's Dream' (Gluck: Ballet Music from 'Orpheus and Euridice') (Bach: Prelude from Partita no, 3 in E Major)	PO – V 74560(1917) V 6238 AAYO – AC 11983D(1941)
Symphony no. 4 in A Major (Bizet: Symphony in C Major)	NaPO – AC M 34567 (1977) AC MT 34567 AC MA 34567 CBS 76673 CBS 40-76673

Gian Carlo Menotti

Suite from 'Sebastian' (Gould: Dance Variations for Two Pianos and Orchestra) (Prokofiev: Suite from 'Romeo and Juliet')	NBCSO – V LM 1858(1954) V ARL 1-2715 V ARK 1-2715 V ARS 1-2715

Olivier Messiaen

'L'Ascension' (Vaughan Williams: Symphony no. 6 in E Minor) (Ives: Orchestral Set no. 2)	NYPO – AC 13061-63D(ac)(1947 + 1949) AC ML 4214 LSO – L SPC 21060(1970) L M 94060 ED PFS 4203

Claudio Monteverdi

Vespro Della Beata Vergine Soloists: Miriam Stewart, Dorothy Clark, William Miller, and Bruce Foote Organ: Paul Pettinga With University of Illinois Oratorio Society	UISO – UISMCRS CRS 1(1951)

Modeste Moussorgsky

Scenes from 'Boris Godunov' Soloists: Nicola Rossi-Lemeni, Lawrence Mason, and Raymond Cauwet Chorus Master: Kurt Herbert Adler	SFSO – V WDM 1764(1952) V LM 1764
Symphonic Synthesis from 'Boris Godunov' (t)	PO – V 14546-48(1936) V 16542-44(ac)

	HMV DB 3244-46
(Debussy: 'Nocturnes')	Cam CAL 140
	AAYO – AC 11848-50D(1941)
	AC 11851-53D(ac)
(Tschaikovsky: 'Romeo and Juliet')	OSR – L SPC 21032(1968)
	L M 94032
	L M 95032
	ED PFS 4181
(Collections)	L SPC 21110
	L M 521110
	L M 821110
	Ace SDD 456
Suite from 'Khovantchina'	LSSO – V ERB 1816(1953)
(Collections)	V LM 1816
	Q PMC 7026E
	Q P4C 7026E
Prelude to Act 4 of 'Khovantchina' (t)	PO – V 74803(1922)
(Sibelius: 'Finlandia')	V 6366
	HMV DB 599
(Stravinsky: Suite from 'The Firebird')	PO – V 6775(1927)
	V 7047(ac)
(Stravinsky: Dance from 'The Firebird')	HMV D 1427
(Collections)	NaPO – Pye PCNH 4 (1975)
	Pye ZCPHG 4
'A Night on the Bare Mountain' (t)	PO – V 17900(1940)
	HMV DB 5900
	V 49-0722
(Collections)	Cam CAL 118
	V VCM 7101
Together with Schubert's 'Ave Maria'	PO – Disney WDL 4101C(1939)
(Beethoven: Symphony no. 6 in F Major)	Disney WDL S 4101C
(Collections)	Disney WDX 101
	Disney STER 101
	Buena Vista BVS 101
	Buena Vista 101 VC
	Buena Vista 101 VT
(Collections)	LSSO – V ERB 1816(1953)
	V LM 1816
	Q PMC 7026E
	Q P4C 7026E
(Gliere: 'Russian Sailors' Dance'	HMV 7ER 5060
from 'The Red Poppy')	
(Collections)	LSO – L SPC 21026(1967)
	L M 94026
	ED LK 4927
	ED PFS 4139
	L SPC 21110
	L M 521110
	L M 821110
	Ace SDD 456
(Collection)	ED DPA 519-20
	ED KDPC 519-20

'Pictures at an Exhibition' (t)	PO – V 17414-17(1939)
	V 17422-25(ac)
	HMV DB 5827-30
	HMV DB 8914-17(ac)
	AAYO – AC 11805-08D(1941)
	AC 11809-12D(ac)
(Debussy: Prelude no. 10 I)	NPO – L PM 55004(1965)
	L SPC 21006
	L M 94006
	ED LK 4766
	ED PFS 4095
(Collections)	L SPC 21110
	L M 521110
	L M 821110
	Ace SDD 456
Last Two Movements only (Ravel)	LSSO – Cap SAL 8385(1956)
(Collections)	Cap SSAL 8385
	Cap SPAO 8694
	S SIB 6094
	S 4X2G 6094
Last Two Movements only (t)	NPO – ED SPA 159(1965)
(Collections)	ED KCSP 159

W. A. Mozart

Concerto no. 20 in D Minor for Piano and Orchestra, K.466 (Bach: Passacaglia and Fugue in C Minor) Soloist: Maria Isabella de Carli	IFYO – AVE 30696(1969)
Concerto no. 21 in C Major for Piano and Orchestra, K.467 Soloist: Myra Hess	NYPO – IPA MJA 1967(1949)
Overture to 'Don Giovanni' (Collections)	NaPO – Pye PCNHX 6 (1976) Pye ZCPNH 6
German Dances, K.605, no. 3 (Tschaikovsky: 'Dance of the Sugar Plum Fairy' from 'The Nutcracker') (Collections)	LSSO – V 10-1487(1948) V 49-0553 V ERA 119 V LM 1238
Serenade no. 10 in B Flat Major, K.361	ASO – Van VRS 1158(1966) Van VSD 71158
Excerpts only (Collections)	Van VCS 707-08 Van ZCVB 707-08
Sinfonia Concertante in E Flat Major, K.297b Soloists: Marcel Tabuteau (oboe), Bernard Portnoy (clarinet), Sol Schoenbach (bassoon), and Mason Jones (horn)	PO – V 17732-35(1940) V 17740-43(ac) HMV DB 20023-26 HMV DB 10118-21(ac)
(Other artistes)	Cam CAL 213
Rondo alla Turca from Sonata in A Major, K.331 (t) (Collections)	LSSO – V LM 2042(1955) (NBCSO)

Third Movement from Symphony no. 40
in G Minor
(Beethoven: Second Movement from
Symphony no. 8 in F Major)

PO – V 74609(1919)

V 6243
HMV DB 385

Ottokar Novacek
'Moto perpetuo' (t)
(Harl McDonald: 'The Arkansas
Traveler')
(Collections)

PO – V 18069(1940)
HMV DB 5966

Cam CAE 192
Cam CAL 123

(De Falla: Ritual Fire Dance from 'El
Amor Brujo')
(Collections)

AAYO – AC 11879D(1941)

NaPO – AC M 34543(1976)
AC MT 34543
AC MA 34543
CBS 73589
CBS 40-73589

Jacques Offenbach
Barcarole from 'The Tales of Hoffmann'
(t)
(Schubert: Moment musicale no. 3 in
F Minor)
(Collections)

HBSO – V 11-9174(1945)
HMV DB 10130

Cam CAL 153

Carl Orff
'Carmina Burana'
Soloists: Virginia Babikian,
Clyde Hager, and Guy Gardner
With the Houston Chorale

HSO – Cap PAR 8470(1958)
Cap SPAR 8470
Regal SREG 2032
S S 60236
S 4XG 60236

Niccolo Paganini
'Moto Perpetuo'
(Collections)

LSSO – Cap PAO 8415(1957)
Cap SPAO 8415
Cap L 9216
Cap SL 9216
Cap P 8650
Cap SP 8650
S S 60278
S 4XG 60278

Giovanni Palestrina
'Adoramus te Christe' (t)
(Bach: First Movement from Trio Sonata
no. 1 in E Flat Major)
(Wagner: Symphonic Synthesis from
'Tristan and Isolde')
(Frescobaldi: Gagliarda)
(Collections)

PO – V 11-8576(1934)
HMV DB 6260

V 15206
V 15207(ac)
HMV DA 1606
SA – UA UAL 7001(1958)
UA UAS 8001
Q PMC 7110E
Q P4C 7110E

(Collections)

Chorus – V WDM 1721(1952)
V LM 1721

'O bone Jesu'   Chorus – V WDM 1721(1952)
(Collections)   V LM 1721

Andrzej Panufnik
'Universal Prayer'   Harps – U RHS 305(1970)
Soloists: April Cantelo, Helen Watts,
John Mitchinson, and Roger Stalman
Organ: Nicolas Kynaston
With the Louis Halsey Singers

Vincent Persichetti
March from Divertimento for Band   LSSO – Cap SAL 8385(1956)
(Collections)   Cap SSAL 8385

Amilcare Ponchielli
'Dance of the Hours' from 'La   PO – Disney WDL 4101B(1939)
Gioconda'   Disney WDL S 4101B
(Tschaikovsky: Selections from 'The
Nutcracker')
(Collections)   Disney WDX 101
                            Disney STER 101
                            Buena Vista BVS 101
                            Buena Vista 101 VC
                            Buena Vista 101 VT

Francis Poulenc
Concerto Champetre for Harpsichord and   NYPO – IPA 106-07(1949)
Orchestra
(Other artistes)
Soloist: Wanda Landowska

Serge Prokofiev
Suite from 'Cinderella'   NYSO – Ev LPBR 6016(1958)
(Collections)   Ev SDBR 3016
                            Ev LPBR 6108
                            Ev SDBR 3108

Suite from 'Love for Three Oranges'   NBCSO – V 18497(1941)
                            HMV DB 6151
                            HMV DB 11130

'Peter and the Wolf'   AAYO – AC 11647-49D(1941)
Narrator: Basil Rathbone   AC 11650-52D(ac)
(Other artistes)   AC CL 671
                            AC ML 4038

Narrator: Bob Keeshan   NYSO – Ev LPBR 6043(1959)
(Orchestral Suite only)   Ev SDBR 3043

Suite from 'Romeo and Juliet'   NBCSOV LM 2117(1954)
(Schoenberg: 'Verklärte Nacht')
(Menotti: Suite from 'Sebastian')
                          V ARL 1-2715
                          V ARK 1-2715
                          V ARS 1-2715

Symphony no. 5 in B Flat Major   USSRSO – Artia MK 1551(1958)
                            Bruno 14050

'The Ugly Duckling'   NYSO – Ev LPBR 6108(1958)
(Collections)   Ev SDBR 3108

Henry Purcell
Aria from 'Dido and Aeneas' (t)   LSSO – V 12-3087(1950)
(Bach: 'Komm', süsser Tod')   V 49-3087
(Collections)   V ERB 52
                                                           V LM 1875
                                                           HMV ALP 1387

(Collections)   RPO – Desmar DSM 1011(1975)
                                                   Desmar E 1047

Hornpipe from 'King Arthur'   LSSO – Cap P 8458(1958)
(Collections)   Cap SP 8458
                                                       S SIB 6094
                                                       S 4X2G 6094

Sergei Rachmaninov
Concerto no. 2 in C Minor for Piano   PO – V 8148-52(1929)
and Orchestra   V 16773-77(ac)
Soloist: Sergei Rachmaninov   HMV DB 1333-37
                                                          HMV DB 7427-31(ac)
                                                          V WCT 18
(Concerto no. 4 in G Minor for Piano   V LCT 1014
and Orchestra)

                                                          HMV ALP 1630
(Collection)   V LM 6123
(Collection)   V ARM 3-0296
Second and Third Movements only   PO – V 89166-71(1924)
Soloist: Sergei Rachmaninov   V 8064-66
                                                          HMV DB 747-49
(Collection)   V ARM 3-0260

Prelude in C Sharp Minor, op. 3,   CPO – L SPC 21130(1972)
no. 2 (t)   ED PFS 4351
(Collections)   ED KPFC 4351

Rhapsody on a Theme by Paganini for   PO – V 8553-55(1934)
Piano and Orchestra   V 8556-58(ac)
Soloist: Sergei Rachmaninov   HMV DB 2426-28
                                                          HMV DB 7812-14(ac)
(Concerto no. 1 in F Sharp Minor for   V WCT 1118
Piano and Orchestra)   V LCT 1118
(Collection)   V LM 6123
(Collection)   V ARM 3-0296

Symphony no. 3 in A Minor   NaPO – Desmar DSM 1007(1975)
(Vocalise, op. 34, no. 14)   Desmar E 1046

Vocalise, op. 34, no. 14   LSSO – V ERA 182(1953)
(Collections)   V LM 2042
(Collections)   LSSO – Cap PAO 8415(1957)
                                                       Cap SPAO 8415
                                                       Cap L 9216
                                                       Cap SL 9216
                                                       Cap P 8650
                                                       Cap SP 8650
                                                       S S 60278
                                                       S 4XG 60278

(Collections)
Soloist: Anna Moffo
(Symphony no. 3 in A Minor)

ASO – V LM 2795(1965)
    V LSC 2795
NaPO – Desmar DSM 1007(1975)
    Desmar E 1046

Maurice Ravel
Alborado del Gracioso
(Collections)

ONRF – Cap P 8463(1958)
    Cap SP 8463
    S S 60102
    HMV CC SXL P 30263
    HMV CC TC SXL P 30263

Bolero

AAYO – AC 17205-06D(1940)
    AC 17236-37D(ac)

Suite no. 2 from 'Daphnis and Chloé'
(Collections)
With the London Symphony Orchestra
Chorus

(Collection)

LSO – L SPC 21059(1970)
    ED PFS 4220
    L SPC 21112
    L M 521112
    L M 821112
    ED DPA 519-20
    ED KDPC 519-20

Fanfare from 'L'Eventail de Jeanne'
(Franck: Symphony in D Minor)

(Collections)

HRPO – L SPC 21061(1970)
    L M 94061
    E D PFS 4218
    ED SPA 159
    ED KCSP 159

Rapsodie Espagnole

(Collections)

PO – V 8282-83(1934)
    HMV DB 2367-68
    Cam CAL 118
    V DMM 4-0341

(Debussy: 'Nocturnes')

LSO – Cap P 8520(1959)
    Cap SP 8520
    S S 60104

Ottorino Respighi
'Pines of Rome'
(Collections)

SA – UA UAL 7001(1958)
    UA UAS 8001

Silvestre Revueltas
'Sensemaya'
(Granados: Intermezzo from 'Goyescas')

LSSO – V 12-0470(1947)
    HMV DB 6915
    V 49-0882

Nikolai Rimsky-Korsakov
Capriccio Espagnol
(Collections)

NPO – L SPC 21117(1973)
    L M 521117
    ED PFS 4333
    ED KPFC 4333

Prelude to Act 3 of 'Ivan the Terrible'
(Dukas: 'L'Apprenti Sorcier')
(Bloch: 'Schelomo')
(Collections)

PO – V 17502(1939)
    HMV DB 6039
    HMV DB 6057
NaPO – AC M 34543(1976)
    AC MT 34543
    AC MA 34543
    CBS 73589
    CBS 40-73589

Russian Easter Overture	PO – V 7018-19(1929)
	HMV D 1676-77
(Tschaikovsky: 'Capriccio Italien')	V L 7002
(Wagner: Prelude and Good Friday	Cam CAL 163
Spell from 'Parsifal')	
(Collections)	V VCM 7101
	NBCSO – V 11-8426-27(1942)
	HMV DB 6173-74
(Collections)	LSSO – V ERB 1816(1953)
	V LM 1816
	Q PMC 7026E
	Q P4C 7026E
(Khachaturian: Symphony no. 3)	CSO – V LSC 3067(1968)
	V R8S 1122
(Collections)	V VCS 7077
	V RK 5072
	V R8S 5072
'Scheherazade'	PO – V 6738-42(1927)
	V 7037-41(ac)
	HMV D 1436-40
	HMV D 7032-36(ac)
(Collections)	V DMM 4-0341
	PO – V 8698-8703(1934)
	V 16672-77(ac)
	HMV DB 2522-27
	HMV DB 7875-80(ac)
	PhO – V WDM 1732(1951)
	V LM 1732
	HMV ALP 1339
	LSO – L PM 55002(1964)
	L SPC 21005
	L M 94005
	L M 95005
	ED LK 4658
	ED PFS 4062
	RPO – V ARL 1-1182(1975)
	V ARK 1-1182
	V ARS 1-1182
First Movement only	LSO – L SPC 21111(1964)
(Collections)	L M 521111
	L M 821111
Third Movement only	PO – V 74691(1921)
(Fourth Movement)	V 6246
Fourth Movement only	PO – V 74593(1919)
(Third Movement)	V 6246
'Dance of the Tumblers' from 'Snow	PO – V 74849(1923)
Maiden'	
(Tschaikovsky: Second Movement from	V 6431
Symphony no. 5 in E Minor)	
'Flight of the Bumble Bee' from Act 3 of	AYYO – AC 19005D(1941)
'The Tale of Czar Saltan' (t)	

(Tschaikovsky: Humoreske, op. 10, no. 2)
(Collections)
                    NaPO – AC M 34543(1976)
                               AC MT 34543
                               AC MA 34543
                               CBS 73589
                               CBS 40-73589

Gioacchino Rossini
Overture to 'William Tell'
(Collections)
                    NaPO – Pye PCNHX 6(1976)
                               Pye ZCPNH 6

Camille Saint-Saëns
'Le Carnaval des Animaux'
(Tschaikovsky: Chant sans Paroles in
A Minor, op. 40, no. 6)
Pianos: Mary Binney Montgomery and
Olga Barabini
                    PO – V 7200-02(1929)
                               V 7203-05(ac)
                               HMV D 1992-94
                               HMV D 7417-19(ac)

Pianos: Sylvan Levin and Jeannie Behrend
                    PO – V 18047-49(1939)
                               HMV DB 5942-44
(Tschaikovsky: Suite from 'The Nutcracker')
                               HMV DB 8897-99(ac)
                               Cam CAL 100

'Dance macabre'
                    PO – V 6505(1925)
                               HMV DB 961
                               HMV D 1121
(Collections)
                               V DMM 4-0341
                    PO – V 14162(1936)
                               HMV DB 3077
(Collections)
                               Cam CAL 254
                               V VCM 7101
(Collections)
                    NaPO – Pye PCNH 4(1975)
                               Pye ZCPHG 4

Bacchanal from 'Samson and Delilah'
(Chabrier: Espana Rhapsody)
                    PO – V 74671(1920)
                               V 6241
                               HMV DB 384

(Berlioz: Hungarian March from
'Damnation of Faust')
(Collections)
                    PO – V 6823(1927)
                               HMV D 1807
                               V VCM 7101
Scenes from 'Samson and Delilah'
Soloists: Jan Peerce, Risé Stevens,
and Robert Merrill
With Robert Shaw Chorale
                    NBCSO – V LM 1848(1954)
                               HMV ALP 1308

Excerpts only
                               V ERB 49

Erik Satie
Gymnopedies no. 1 and 2
                    PO – V 1965(1937)
                               HMV DA 1688

Arnold Schoenberg
'Gurrelieder'
Soloists: Jeanette Vreeland,
Rose Bampton, Poul Althouse,
Robert Bett, Abrasha Robofsky,
and Benjamin de Loache
                    PO – V 7524-37(1932)
                               V 7538-51(ac)
                               HMV DB 1769-82
                               HMV DB 7293-7306(ac)
                               V L 11609-15

With Princeton Glee Club, Fortnightly Club, and Mendelssohn Club	V 11-8061-74(ac) V LCT 6012 Va AVM 2-2017
'Song of the Wood Dove' from 'Gurrelieder' (Other artistes) Soloist: Martha Lipton	NYPO – AC ML 2140(1949)
'Verklärte Nacht' (Vaughan Williams: Fantasy on a Theme by Thomas Tallis) (Prokofiev: Suite from 'Romeo and Juliet') (Loeffler: 'A Pagan Poem')	LSSO – V WDM 1739(1952) V LM 1739 HMV ALP 1205 V LM 2117 LSSO – Cap P 8433(1957) Cap SP 8433 S S 60080

Franz Schubert

'Ave Maria' – together with Moussorgsky's 'A Night on the Bare Mountain' (Beethoven: Symphony no. 6 in F Major) Soloist: Julietta Novis (Collections)	PO – Disney WDL 4101C(1939) Disney WDL S 4101C Disney WDX 101 Disney STER 101 Buena Vista BVS 101 Buena Vista 101 VC Buena Vista 101 VT
Deutsche Tänze, op 33 (t)	PO – V 74814(1923) LSSO – V 10-1519(1949) V 49-0814
(Johann Strauss: Waltz from 'Die Fledermaus') (Ballet Music no. 2 in G Major from 'Rosamunde') (Collections)	V ERA 67 HMV 7ER 5043 V LM 1238
Moment musicale no. 3 in F Minor (t) (Grieg: 'Anitra's Dance' from 'Peer Gynt') (Ballet Music no. 2 in G Major from 'Rosamunde') (Collections)	PO – V 66098(1922) V 799 PO – V 1312(1927) Cam CAE 188 Cam CAL 123 V DMM 4-0341
(Offenbach: Barcarole from 'The Tales of Hoffmann') (Collections)	HBSO – V 11-9174(1945) HMV DB 10130 LSO – L SPC 21130(1972) ED PFS 4351 ED KPFC 4351
Overture to 'Rosamunde' (Collections)	NaPO – Pye PCNHX 6(1976) Pye ZCPNH 6
Ballet Music no. 2 in G Major from 'Rosamunde' (Moment musicale no. 3 in F Minor)	PO – V 1312(1927)

(Collections)	Cam CAL 123
Earlier recording	PO – V DMM 4-0341(1927)
(Collections)	
Suite from 'Rosamunde'	LSSO – V WDM 1730(1952)
(Wagner: Prelude to Act 1 and	V LM 1730
Symphonic Synthesis from Act 3	
of 'Parsifal')	
(Tschaikovsky: Suite from 'The Nut-	HMV ALP 1193
cracker')	
Ballet Music no. 2 in G Minor only	HMV 7ER 5043
(Deutsche Tänze, op. 33)	
Symphony no. 8 in B Minor	PO – V 74894-99(1924)
	V 6459-61
	HMV DB 792-94
	PO – V 6663-65(1927)
	V 7050-52(ac)
	HMV D 1779-81
	HMV D 7375-77(ac)
	V L 11645-46
(Collections)	V DMM 4-0341
(Beethoven: Symphony no. 7 in A Major)	Pa 5
	AAYO – AC 11675-77D(1941)
	AC 11678-80D(ac)
(Beethoven: Symphony no. 5 in C Minor)	LPO – L SPC 21042(1969)
	L M 94042
	L M 95042
	ED PFS 4197
(Collections)	ED D94D2
	ED K94K2

Robert Schumann

'Träumerei' from 'Kinderszenen' (t)	AAYO – AC 11982D(1941)
(Tschaikovsky: Solitude, op. 73, no. 6)	
Symphony no. 2 in C Major	LSSO – V WDM 1614(1950)
	V LM 1194

Alexander Scriabin

Etude in C Sharp Minor, op. 2, no. 1 (t)	ASO – Van VCS 10095(1971)
(Tschaikovsky: Symphony no. 4 in	Van VSQ 30001
F Minor)	Van 7175-30001H
'Poeme d'Extase', op. 54	PO – V 7515-18(1932)
('Prometheus', op. 60)	V 17195-98(ac)
	HMV DB 1706-07
	V L 11616
(Amirov: 'Azerbaijan Mugam')	HSO – Ev LPBR 6032(1959)
	Ev SDBR 3032
(Collections)	CPO – L SPC 21117(1972)
	L M 521117
	ED PFS 4333
	ED KPFC 4333
	ED D94D2
	ED K94K2

'Prometheus', op. 60 PO – V 7515-18(1932)
('Poeme d'Extase', op. 54) V 17195-98(ac)
Piano: Sylvan Levin HMV DB 1708-09
With the Curtis Institute Chorus V L 11617

Dimitri Shostakovitch
Suite from 'The Age of Gold' CSO – V LSC 3133(1968)
(Symphony no. 6)
Polka only V VCS 7077
(Collections) V RK 5072
  V R8S 5072

Entr'acte from 'Lady Macbeth of SA – UA UAL 7004(1958)
Minsk' UA UAS 8004
(Collections)

Prelude in E Flat Minor, op. 34, PO – V 8928(1935)
no. 14 (t) V 16697(ac)
(Stravinsky: Suite from 'The Firebird') HMV DB 2884
  HMV DB 8224(ac)
(Symphony no. 1 in F Major) V 7888
  V 7889(ac)
(Stravinsky: Suite from 'The Firebird') AAYO – AC 11524D(1940)
  AC 11525D(ac)
(Bach: Chorale 'Ein feste Burg') AC 12903D
(Collections) SA – UA UAL 7004(1958)
  UA UAS 8004
(Collections) NaPO – AC M 34543(1976)
  AC MT 34543
  AC MA 34543
  CBS 73589
  CBS 40-73589

Symphony no. 1 in F Major PO – V 7884-88S(1933)
  V 7889-93S(ac)
(Prelude in E Flat Minor, op. 34, V 7884-88
no. 14) V 7889-93(ac)
(Tschaikovsky: Chant sans Paroles HMV DB 2203-07
in A Minor, op. 40, no. 6) HMV DB 7687-91(ac)
  HMV DB 3847-51S
  HMV DB 8695S-99(ac)
  V L 11744-46
(Collections) SA – UA UAL 7004(1958)
  UA UAS 8004
Symphony no. 5 PO – V 15737-42(1939)
  V 15995-16000(ac)
  HMV DB 3991-96
  HMV DB 8933-38(ac)
  NYSO – Ev LPBR 6010(1958)
  Ev SDBR 3010

Symphony no. 6 PO – V 18391-95(1940)
(Harl McDonald: 'The Arkansas V 18396-400(ac)
Traveler')
(Suite from 'The Age of Gold') CSO – V LSC 3133(1968)

235

Symphony no. 11	HSO – Cap PBR 8448(1958)
	Cap SPBR 8448
	Cap SPBO 8700
	S S 60228
	Ev 3310

Jean Sibelius

'Finlandia'	PO – V 74698(1921)
(Moussorgsky: Prelude to Act 4 of	V 6366
'Khovantchina')	HMV DB 599
	PO'– V 7412(1930)
	HMV DB 1584
('The Swan of Tuonela')	V L 11656
(Wagner: Magic Fire Music' from Act 3	Cam CAE 101
of 'Die Walküre')	
(Collections)	Cam CAL 120
	V VCM 7101
(Collections)	LSSO – Cap P 8399(1956)
	Cap SP 8399
	S SIB 6094
	S 4X2G 6094
'Valse triste' from Kuolema'	PO – V 14726(1936)
(Berceuse from 'The Tempest')	HMV DB 6009
(Franck: 'Panis Angelicus' from Messe	HMV DB 3318
Solennelle, op. 12)	
(Berceuse from 'The Tempest')	Cam CAE 188
(Collections)	Cam CAL 123
(Berceuse from 'The Tempest')	LSSO – V 12-1191(1949)
	HMV DB 21334
	V 49-1168
	HMV 7R 101
(Collections)	V LM 1238
	V ERB 7024
	V LRM 7024
'Maiden with the Roses' from	NYPO – AC 12938D(ac)(1948)
'Svanhvide'	
(Tschaikovsky: 'Francesca da Rimini')	
'The Swan of Tuonela'	PO – V 7380(1929)
	HMV D 1997
('Finlandia')	V L 11656
(Collections)	V VCM 7101
	LSSO – V 12-0585(1947)
	HMV DB 21555
	V 49-0461
(Collections)	V ERB 7024
	V LRM 7024
	V LM 151
	V LM 9029
(Collections)	LSSO – Cap P 8399(1956)
	Cap SP 8399
	Cap SP 8673
	S SIB 6094
	S 4X2G 6094

(Symphony no. 1 in E Minor)	NaPO – AC M 34548(1976)
	AC MT 34548
	AC MQ 34548
	CBS 76666
	CBS 40-76666
Symphony no. 1 in E Minor	LSSO – V WDM 1497(1950)
	HMV DB 21264-67
	HMV DB 9616-19(ac)
	V LM 1125
	HMV ALP 1210
('The Swan of Tuonela')	NaPO – AC M 34548(1976)
	AC MT 34548
	AC MQ 34548
	CBS 76666
	CBS 40-76666
Symphony no. 2 in D Major	NBCSO – V LM 1854(1954)
	HMV ALP 1440
Symphony no. 4 in A Minor	PO – V 7683-86(1932)
	V 7687-90(ac)
	V L 11638-39
(Collection)	V SRS 3001
Berceuse from 'The Tempest'	PO – V 14726(1937)
('Valse triste' from 'Kuolema')	HMV DB 6009
(Dukas: 'L'Apprenti Sorcier')	HMV DB 3534
('Valse triste' from Kuolema')	Cam CAE 188
(Collections)	Cam CAL 123
('Valse triste' from 'Kuolema')	LSSO – V 12-1191(1950)
	HMV DB 21334
	V 49-1168
	HMV 7R 101
(Collections)	V LM 1238
	V ERB 7024
	V LRM 7024

Bedrich Smetana

Overture to 'The Bartered Bride'	RCAVSO – V LM 2471(1960)
(Collections)	V LSC 2471
'The Moldau'	RCAVSO – V LM 2471(1960)
(Collections)	V LSC 2471
	V VCS 7077
	V RK 5072
	V R8S 5072

John Stafford Smith

'The Star-Spangled Banner' (t)	AAYO – AC 17204D(1940)
(Berlin: 'God Bless America')	

John Philip Sousa

'El Capitan'	PO – V 1441(1929)
('The Stars and Stripes Forever')	HMV E 556
'The Stars and Stripes Forever'	PO – V 1441(1929)
('El Capitan')	HMV E 556
(Collections) (t)	NaPO – Pye PCNH 4(1975)
	Pye ZCPHG 4

William Grant Still
Scherzo from Afro-American Symphony   AAYO – AC 11992D(1940)
(Bach: Little Fugue in G Minor)

Johann Strauss
'On the Beautiful Blue Danube' (t)   PO – V 74627(1919)
(Weber: 'Invitation to the Dance')   V 6237
('Tales from the Vienna Woods')   PO – V 6584(1926)
                                                         HMV DB 1014
                                                         HMV D 1218

('Tales from the Vienna Woods')   PO – V 15425(1939)
                                                         HMV DB 3821
(Collection)   V LM 6074
('Tales from the Vienna Woods')   LSSO – V 12-1160(1949)
                                                         HMV DB 21346
                                                         V 49-1076
                                                         HMV 7R 169

('Tales from the Vienna Woods') (– t)   NBCSO – V ERA 259(1955)
(Collections)   (LSSO)V LM 2042
(Collections)   LSSO – Cap P 8399(1956)
                                                         Cap SP 8399
                                                         Cap SPAO 8694
                                                         S SIB 6094
                                                         S 4X2G 6094

Waltz from 'Die Fledermaus' (t)   HBSO – V 10-1310(1946)
                                                         V 49-0279
(Schubert: Deutsche Tänze. op. 33)   V ERA 67

'Tales from the Vienna Woods' (t)   PO – V 6584(1926)
('On the Beautiful Blue Danube')   HMV DB 1014
                                                         HMV D 1218

('On the Beautiful Blue Danube')   PO – V 15425(1939)
                                                         HMV DB 3821
(Collections)   Cam CAL 153
(Collection)   Cam CAL 282
('On the Beautiful Blue Danube')   LSSO – V 12-1160(1949)
                                                         HMV DB 21346
                                                         V 49-1076
                                                         HMV 7R 169

('On the Beautiful Blue Danube') (– t)   NBCSO – V ERA 259(1955)
(Collections)   (LSSO)V LM 2042
(Collections)   NaPO – Pye PCNH 4(1975)
                                                         Pye ZCPHG 4

Richard Strauss
'Death and Transfiguration'   PO – V 8288-90(1934)
                                                         V 8291-93(ac)
                                                         HMV DB 2324-26
                                                         HMV DB 7872-74(ac)
                                                   AAYO – AC 11728-30D(1941)
                                                         AC 11731-33D(ac)
                                                   NYCSO – V 11-8826-28(1945)
                                                         V 11-8829-31(ac)
                                                         HMV DB 6320-22
                                                         HMV DB 9266-68(ac)

(Other artistes)	Cam CAL 189
'Don Juan' (Collections)	NYSO – Ev LPBR 6023(1958) Ev SDBR 3023
'Dance of the Seven Veils' from 'Salome'	PO – V 74729-30(1921) V 6240 HMV DB 383
(Eichheim: 'Japanese Nocturne')	PO – V 7259-60(1929) HMV D 1935-36
(Collections) (Collections)	Cam CAL 254 NYSO – Ev LPBR 6023(1958) Ev SDBR 3023
Gavotte from Suite for Winds in B Flat Major (Collections)	LSSO – Cap SAL 8385(1956) Cap SSAL 8385
'Till Eulenspiegels lustige Streiche' (Collections)	NYSO – Ev LPBR 6023(1958) Ev SDBR 3023

Igor Stravinsky

Suite from 'The Firebird'	PO – V 6492-93(1924) HMV DB 841-42
(Moussorgsky: Prelude to Act 4 of 'Khovantchina') 'Dance of the Firebird' only (Moussorgsky: Prelude to Act 4 of 'Khovantchina') (Shostakovitch: Prelude in E Flat Minor, op. 34, no. 14)	PO – V 6773-75(1927) V 7047-49(ac) HMV D 1427 PO – V 8926-28(1935) V 16697-99(ac) HMV DB 2882-84 HMV DB 8224-26(ac)
(Shostakovitch: Prelude in E Flat Minor, op. 34, no. 14) Tschaikovsky: Humoreske, op. 10, no. 2)	AAYO – AC 11522-24D(1940) AC 11525-27D(ac) NBCSO – V 11-8423-25(1942) V 11-8312-14(ac) LSSO – V 12-1311-13(ac)(1950) V LM 44
(Collections) (Collection) (Suite from 'Petrouchka')	V LM 9029 V LM 6113 BPO – Cap PAO 8407(1956) Cap SPAO 8407 Cap STK 80329 S S 60229 Cap SP 8673
Berceuse and Finale only (Collections) (Collections)	LSO – L SPC 21026(1967) L M 94026 ED LK 4927 ED PFS 4139
Infernal Dance only (Collections)	L SPC 21111 L M 521111 L M 821111
Berceuse and Finale only	L SPC 21112

(Collections)	L M 521112
	L M 821112
'Fireworks', op. 4	PO – V 1112(1922)
(Liadov: 'Dance of the Amazon', op. 65)	
'L'Histoire du soldat (French)	LSSO – Van VRS 1165(1966)
Soloists: Madeleine Milhaud	Van VSD 71165
(narrator), Martial Singher (the Devil),	Van VCS 10121
and Jean Pierre (English)	Van VRS 1166
Aumont (the Soldier)	Van VSD 71166
Orchestral Suite only	Van VCS 707-08
(Collections)	Van ZCVB 707-08
Pastorale (t)	PO – V 1998(1939)
(Chopin: Prelude no. 24 in D Minor,	
op. 28)	
(Collections)	RPO – L SPC 21041(1969)
	L M 94041
	L M 95041
	ED PFS 4189
	ED SPA 159
	ED KCSP 159
'Petrouchka'	PO – V 15467-70(1937)
	V 16111-14(ac)
	HMV DB 3511-14
	HMV DB 8633-36(ac)
(Borodin: Polovtsian Dances from 'Prince	Cam CAL 203
Igor')	
	LSSO – V WDM 1568(1950)
	V LM 1175
	HMV ALP 1240
Suite from 'Petrouchka'	BPO – Cap PAO 8407(1956)
(Suite from 'The Firebird')	Cap SPAO 8407
	Cap STK 80329
	S S 60229
(Kodaly: Suite from 'Hary Janos')	HRO – LSS LS 2(1967)
'Le Sacre du Printemps'	PO – V 7227-30(1929)
	V 7231-34(ac)
	HMV D 1919-22
	HMV D 7326-29(ac)
(Bach: Toccata and Fugue in D Minor)	PO – Disney WDL 4101A(1939)
	Disney WDL S 4101A
(Collections)	Disney WDX 101
	Disney STER 101
	Buena Vista BVS 101
	Buena Vista 101 VC
	Buena Vista 101 VT

Ambroise Thomas

Gavotte from Act 2 of 'Mignon'	PO – V 66172(1923)
(Gounod: Waltz from Act 2 of 'Faust')	V 944
	HMV DA 562
(Debussy: 'Dance sacré et Dance profane')	PO – V 7456(1929)

Virgil Thomson
'The Plow That Broke the Plains' HBSO – V 11-9520-21(1946)
                                         V 11-9522-23(ac)
('The River')   SA – Van VRS 1071(1960)
                                     Van VSD 2095
(Collections)   Van VCS 707-08
                                     Van ZCVB 707-08

'The River'   SA – Van VRS 1071(1960)
('The Plow That Broke the Plains')   Van VSD 2095

Peter Tschaikovsky
'Aurora's Wedding'   LSSO – V ERB 4(1953)
(Collections)   V LM 1774
                                     NaPO – AC M 34560(1976)
                                         AC MT 34560
                                         CBS 76665
                                         CBS 40-76665

'Capriccio Italien'   PO – V 6949-50(1929)
                                         HMV D 1739-40
                                         HMV DB 6005-06
(Rimsky-Korsakov: Russian Easter   V L 7002
Overture)
(Collections)   LPO – P 6500 766(1973)
                                         P 7300 332

Chant sans Paroles in A Minor, op. 40, PO – V 1111(1924)
no. 6 (t)
(Chopin: Prelude no. 4 in E Minor,
op. 28)
(Saint-Saëns: 'Le Carnaval des Animaux') PO – V 7202(1928)
                                         V 7203(ac)
                                         HMV D 1994
                                         HMV D 7417(ac)
                                         HMV DB 2207
(Shostakovitch: Symphony no. 1 in   HMV DB 7687(ac)
F Major)
(Collections)   LSO – L SPC 21130(1972)
                                         ED PFS 4351
                                         ED KPFC 4351

'Letter Scene' from 'Eugen Onegin' LSSO – V WDM 1610(1951)
(Villa-Lobos: Bachiana Brasileira no. 5) V LM 142
Soloist: Licia Albanese   HMV BLP 1075

Polonaise from 'Eugen Onegin'   LSSO – V LM 2042(1953)
(Collections)
(Collections)   LPO – P 6500 766(1973)
                                         P 7300 332

Waltz from 'Eugen Onegin'   LPO – P 6500 766(1973)
(Collections)   P 7300 332

'Francesca da Rimini'   NYPO – AC 12938-40D(ac)(1947)
(Sibelius: 'Maiden with the Roses' from
'Svanhvide')

(Khachaturian: 'Masquerade' Suite)	AC ML 4071
('Romeo and Juliet')	AC ML 4381
	EC 33 CX 1030
('Hamlet' Overture)	NYSO – Ev LPBR 6011(1958)
	Ev SDBR 3011
(Serenade for Strings in C Major)	LSO – P 6500 921(1974)
	P 7300 364
'Hamlet' Overture	NYSO – Ev LPBR 6011(1958)
('Francesca da Rimini')	Ev SDBR 3011
Humoreske, op. 10, no. 2 (t)	AAYO – AC 19005D(1941)
(Rimsky-Korsakov: 'Flight of the Bumble Bee' from Act 3 of 'The Tale of Czar Saltan')	
(Stravinsky: Suite from 'The Firebird')	NBCSO – V 11-8425(1942)
	V 11-8312(ac)
(Solitude, op. 73, no. 6)	HBSO – V 11-9187(1945)
(Collections)	Cam CAL 153
(Solitude, op. 73, no. 6)	LSSO – V ERA 182(1953)
(Collections)	V LM 1774
(Collections)	NaPO – AC M 34543(1976)
	AC MT 34543
	AC MA 34543
	CBS 73589
	CBS 40-73589
'Marche slave'	PO – V 6513(1925)
	HMV DB 898
	HMV D 1046
	HBSO – V 11-9388(1945)
(Collections)	Cam CAL 153
(Collections)	LSO – L SPC 21026(1967)
	L M 94026
	ED LK 4927
	ED PFS 4139
	ED SPA 159
	ED KCSP 159
	ED D94D2
	ED K94K2
	LSO – L SPC 21090-91(1972)
	ED OPFS 3-4
	ED KPFC 3-4
	L SPC 21108
	L M 521108
	L M 821108
	Ace SDD 454
Suite from 'The Nutcracker'	PO – V 6615-17(1926)
	V 7072-74(ac)
	HMV DB 1003-05
	HMV D 1214-16
	HMV D 7390-92(ac)
	V L 7004
	PO – V 8662-64(1934)

	V 16669-71(ac)
	HMV DB 2540-42
	HMV DB 7902-04(ac)
(Saint-Saëns: 'Le Carnaval des Animaux')	Cam CAL 100
Excerpts only	Cam CAE 187
	LSSO – V 12-3061-63(ac)(1950)
	V EPR 46
	V LM 46
(Debussy: 'Children's Corner')	V LM 9023
	V ANL 1-2604E
	V ANS 1-2604E
(Schubert: Suite from 'Rosamunde')	HMV ALP 1193
Excerpts only	V ERA 247
'Dance of the Sugar Plum Fairy' only	V 10-1487
(Mozart: German Dances, K.605, no. 3)	V 49-0553
'Waltz of the Flowers' only	HMV DB 21547
	V 49-3346
(Humperdinck: Overture to 'Hänsel and	HMV 7ER 5016
Gretel')	
(Collections)	V 12-1208-12(ac)
	V WDM 1394
	V LM 1083
	HMV ALP 1133
	Va VIC 1020
(Collections)	LPO – P 6500 766(1973)
	P 7300 332
Selections from 'The Nutcracker'	PO – Disney WDL 4101B(1939)
(Ponchielli: 'Dance of the Hours' from	Disney WDL S 4101B
'La Gioconda')	
(Collections)	Disney WDX 101
	Disney STER 101
	Buena Vista BVS 101
	Buena Vista 101 VC
	Buena Vista 101 VT
'Dance of the Flutes' from 'The Nut-	PO – V 66128(1922)
cracker'	
(Boccherini: Minuet from String Quintet	V 798
in E Major, op. 13, no. 5)	
Overture '1812'	PO – V 7499-7500(1930)
	HMV DB 1663-64
(Collections)	RPO – L SPC 21041(1969)
With the John Alldis Choir, the	L M 94041
Welsh National Opera Chorus, and	L M 95041
the Band of the Grenadier Guards	ED PFS 4189
	L SPC 21108
	L M 521108
	L M 821108
	Ace SDD 454
'Pater Noster'	NSOL – V LM 2593(1961)
(Collections)	V LSC 2593
With the Norman Luboff Choir	

'Romeo and Juliet'   PO – V 6995-97(1928)
(De Falla: Dance no. 1 from 'La Vida   V 6900-02(ac)
Breve')   HMV DB 1947-49
(Waltz from Serenade for Strings in   NYPO – AC 13068-70D(ac)(1948)
C Major)
(Wagner: 'Siegfried's Rhine Journey' and   AC ML 4273
'Funeral Music' from 'Die Götter-
dämmerung')
('Francesca da Rimini')   AC ML 4381
                                                         EC 33 CX 1030
(Moussorgsky: Symphonic Synthesis from   OSR – L SPC 21032(1968)
'Boris Godunov')   L M 94032
                                                         L M 95032
                                                         ED PFS 4181
(Collections)   L SPC 21108
                                                         L M 521108
                                                         L M 821108
                                                         Ace SDD 454

Serenade for Strings in C Major   LSO – P 6500 921(1974)
('Francesca da Rimini')   P 7300 364

Waltz only   NYPO – AC 13068D(ac)
('Romeo and Juliet')

Suite from 'The Sleeping Beauty'   LSSO – V 12-0190-95(1947)
                                                         V 12-0196-0201(ac)
                                                         V 18-0118-23
                                                         HMV DB 9499-9504(ac)
                                                         V LM 1010
                                                         HMV ALP 1002

(Suite from 'The Swan Lake')   NPO – L PM 55006(1965)
                                                         L SPC 21008
                                                         L M 94008
                                                         L M 95008
                                                         ED LK 4807
                                                         ED PFS 4083
                                                         ED KPFC 4083
                                                         ED EPFC 4083
Waltz only   L SPC 21108
(Collections)   L M 521108
                                                         L M 821108
                                                         Ace SDD 454
                                                         ED SPA 159
                                                         ED KCSP 159

Solitude, op. 73, no. 6 (t)   PO – V 14947(1937)
(Franck: Andante from 'Grand Piece
Symphonique')
(Wagner: Prelude to Act 3 of   HMV DB 3255
'Tannhäuser')
(Schumann: 'Träumerei' from   AAYO – AC 11982D(1941)
'Kinderszenen')
(Humoreske, op. 10, no. 2)   HBSO – V 11-9187(1945)
(Collections)   Cam CAL 153

(Humoreske, op. 10, no. 2)	LSSO – V ERA 182 (1953)
(Collections)	V LM 1774
(Collections)	NaPO – Pye PCNH 4 (1975)
	Pye ZCPHG 4
Andante cantabile from String Quartet	LSSO – V 11-9574(1947)
no. 1 in D Major (t)	V 49-0296
(Excerpts from the Second Movement	
of Symphony no. 5 in E Minor)	
(Collections)	LSSO – Cap P 8458(1958)
	Cap SP 8458
	Cap L 9216
	Cap SL 9216
	Cap P 8650
	Cap SP 8650
	S S 60278
	S 4XG 60278
Scenes from 'The Swan Lake'	NBCSO – V LM 1894(1954)
	HMV ALP 1443
	Q PMC 7007E
Selections from 'The Swan Lake'	LSSO – V 12-1208-12(ac)(1950)
(Collections)	V WDM 1394
	V LM 1083
	HMV ALP 1133
	Va VIC 1020
	V ERB 7022
	V LRM 7022
'Queen of the Swans' only	V 49-3368
Suite from 'The Swan Lake'	NPO – L PM 55006(1965)
(Suite from 'The Sleeping Beauty')	L SPC 21008
	L M 94008
	L M 95008
	ED LK 4807
	ED PFS 4083
	ED KPFC 4083
	ED EPFC 4083
Excerpts	L SPC 21111
(Collections)	L M 521111
	L M 821111
Excerpts	L SPC 21112
(Collections)	L M 521112
	L M 821112
Waltz only	L SPC 21108
(Collections)	L M 521108
	L M 821108
	Ace SDD 454
Dance and Finale only	ED SPA 159
(Collections)	ED KCSP 159
Symphony no. 4 in F Minor	PO – V 6929-33(1928)
	V 17251-55(ac)
	HMV DB 1793-97
	HMV DB 7281-85(ac)

	NBCSO – V 11-8100-04(1941)
	V 11-8105-09(ac)
(Scriabin: Etude in C Sharp Minor, op. 2, no. 1)	ASO – Van VCS 10095(1971)
	Van VSQ 30001
	Van 7175-30001H
Third Movement only (Collections)	LSSO – Cap SAL 8385(1956)
	Cap SSAL 8385
	Cap SP 8673
	S SIB 6094
	S 4X2G 6094
Symphony no. 5 in E Minor	PO – V 8589-94(1934)
	V 8595-8600(ac)
	HMV DB 2548-53
	HMV DB 7905-10(ac)
	Cam CAL 201
	LSSO – V LM 1780(1953)
	NPO – L PM 55015(1966)
	L SPC 21017
	L M 95017
	ED LK 4882
	ED PFS 4129
	ED KPFC 4129
	ED EPFC 4129
	Ace SDD 493
(With extra record of rehearsals)	IFYO-CC GOCLP 9007S(1973)
Second Movement only	PO – V 74846-48(1923)
(Rimsky-Korsakov: 'Dance of the Tumblers' from 'Snow Maiden')	V 6430-31
Excerpts from Second Movement (Andante cantabile from String Quartet no. 1 in D Major)	LSSO – V 11-9574(1947)
	V 49-0296
Symphony no. 6 in B Minor	AAYO – AC 11444-49D(1940)
	AC 11450-55D(ac)
	HBSO – V 11-9475-80(1945)
	V 11-9481-86(ac)
	Cam CAL 152
	LSO – V ARL 1-0426(1973)
	V ARK 1-0426
	V ARS 1-0426
	V ARD 1-0426
	V ART 1-0426
Third Movement only	PO – V 74713(1921)
(Brahms: Third Movement from Symphony No. 3 in F Major)	V 6242
Joaquin Turina	
'La Oracion del Torero', op. 8 (Collections)	LSSO – Cap P 8458(1958)
	Cap SP 8458
	Cap SPAO 8694
	S SIB 6094
	S 4X2G 6094
Ralph Vaughan Williams	
Fantasy on 'Greensleeves'	NYPO – AC 12977D(ac)(1949)

(Symphony no. 6 in E Minor) (Collection)	AC BM 13
Fantasy on a Theme by Thomas Tallis (Schoenberg: 'Verklärte Nacht')	LSSO – V WDM 1739(1952) V LM 1739 HMV ALP 1205
(Collections)	RPO – Desmar DSM 1011(1975) Desmar E 1047
Symphony no. 6 in E Minor (Fantasy on 'Greensleeves') (Messiaen: 'L'Ascension') (Other Artistes)	NYPO – AC 12977-80D(ac)(1949) AC ML 4214 CBS M 61432
Second Movement from Symphony no. 8 in D Minor (Collections)	LSSO – Cap SAL 8385(1956) Cap SSAL 8385
Overture to 'The Wasps' (Collection)	NYSO – Ev SDBR 3327(1959)

Heitor Villa-Lobos

Mohinda from Bachiana Brasileira no. 1 (Collections)	NYSO – Ev LPBR 6016(1958) Ev SDBR 3016
Bachiana Brasileira no. 5 Soloist: Licia Albanese (Tschaikovsky: 'Letter Scene' from 'Eugen Onegin')	LSSO – V 12-3277(1951) HMV DB 4322 V WDM 1610 V LM 142 HMV BLP 1075
(Collections) Soloist: Anna Moffo	ASO – V LM 2795(1965) V LSC 2795
'Uirapuru' (Collections)	NYSO – Ev LPBR 6016(1958) Ev SDBR 3016

Antoni Vivaldi

Concerto Grosso in D Minor, op. 3, no. 11 (t) (Collections)	PO – V 14113-14(1934) HMV DB 6047-48 LSSO – V WDM 1721(1952) V LM 1721
(Collections) (–t)	LSSO – Bach BGS 70696(1967) Van S 363 Van VCS 707-08 Van ZCVB 707-08
Concertos for Violin and Orchestra, op. 8, no. 1-4 Soloist: Hugh Bean Harpsichord: Charles Spinks	NPO – L PM 55013(1966) L SPC 21015 L M 94015 L M 95015 ED LK 4873 ED PFS 4124 ED KPFC 4124 ED EPFC 4124

Richard Wagner

Symphonic Synthesis from 'Die Götterdämmerung' (t) Soloist: Agnes Davies	PO – V 7843-47(1933) V 7848-52(ac) HMV DB 2126-30

Without soloist	LSO – V ARL 1-1317(1974) V ARK 1-1317 V ARS 1-1317
'Siegfried's Rhine Journey' and 'Funeral Music' from 'Die Götterdämmerung' (Tschaikovsky: 'Romeo and Juliet')	NYPO – AC ML 4273(1949)
(Collections)	LSO – L PM 55014(1966) L SPC 21016 L M 94016 L M 95016 ED LK 4851 ED PFS 4116 ED SPA 537 ED KCSP 537
Finale from 'Die Götterdämmerung' (Overture to 'Rienzi')	PO – V 6625(1927) HMV DB 1036 HMV D 1227
(Collections)	V VCM 7101
Prelude to Act 1 of 'Lohengrin'	PO – V 6490(1924) HMV DB 839 PO – V 6791(1927) HMV D 1463
(Collections)	Cam CAL 120
Prelude to Act 3 of 'Lohengrin' (Prelude to Act 1 of 'Die Meistersinger')	PO – V 17568(1940) V 18464(ac) HMV DB 5853 HMV DB 6041
Prelude to Act 1 of 'Die Meistersinger' (Prelude to Act 3 of 'Lohengrin')	PO – V 17567-68(1936) V 18464-65(ac) HMV DB 5852-53 HMV DB 6040-41
(Collections)	LSO – L SPC 21090-91(1972) ED OPFS 3-4 ED KPFC 3-4
Prelude to Act 3 of 'Die Meistersinger'	PO – V 1584(1931) HMV DA 1291
Prelude to Act 3, 'Dance of the Apprentices', and 'Entry of the Masters' from 'Die Meistersinger' (Collections)	RPO – V ARL 1-0498(1973) V ARK 1-0498 V ARS 1-0498
Prelude to Act 1 of 'Parsifal'	PO – V 14728-29(1936) V 16464-67(ac) HMV DB 3269-70
(Rimsky-Korsakov: Russian Easter Overture) (Schubert: Suite from 'Rosamunde')	Cam CAL 163 LSSO – V WDM 1730(1952) V LM 1730
'Good Friday Spell' from Act 3 of 'Parsifal'	PO – V 14730-31(1936) V 16464-67(ac)

(Rimsky-Korsakov: Russian Easter
Overture)
    HMV DB 3271-72
    Cam CAL 163

(Symphonic Synthesis from Act 3)
    HSO – Ev LPBR 6031(1959)
    Ev SDBR 3031

Symphonic Synthesis from Act 3
of 'Parsifal' (t)
    PO – V 8617-18(1934)
    HMV DB 2272-73

(Schubert: Suite from 'Rosamunde')
    LSSO – V WDM 1730(1952)
    V LM 1730

('Good Friday Spell' from Act 3)
    HSO – Ev LPBR 6031(1959)
    Ev SDBR 3031

Symphonic Synthesis from 'The
Rheingold' (t)
    PO – V 7796-98(1933)
    V 7799-7801(ac)
    HMV DB 1976-78
    V L 11643-44

'Entrance of the Gods into Valhalla'
from 'The Rheingold'
(Collections)
    SA – V LM 2555(1961)
    V LSC 2555
    Va VICS 1301
    V VCS 7077
    V RK 5072
    V R8S 5072
    V AGL 1-1336

(Collections)
    LSO – L PM 55014(1966)
    L SPC 21016
    L M 94016
    L M 95016
    ED LK 4851
    ED PFS 4116
    ED SPA 537
    ED KCSP 537

Overture to 'Rienzi'
    PO – V 74602-03(1919)
    HMV 3-0520-21
    V 6239
    HMV DB 382

(Finale from 'Die Götterdämmerung')
    PO – V 6624-25(1927)
    HMV DB 1035-36
    HMV D 1226-27

(Brahms: Symphony no. 1 in C Minor)
    CC GOCLP 9009H

('Wotan's Farewell' and 'Magic Fire
Music' from Act 3 of 'Die Walküre')
    NYPO – AC ML 2153(1947)
    EC 33 C 1026

(Collections)
    RPO – V ARL 1-0498(1973)
    V ARK 1-0498
    V ARS 1-0498

Symphonic Synthesis from 'Siegfried' (t)
    PO – V 14845-47(1934)
    V 16423-25(ac)
    HMV DB 3678-80

Soloists: Agnes Davies and Frederick
Jagel
'Waldweben' from Act 2 of 'Siegfried'
    HBSO – V 11-9418(1946)
    HMV DB 21238

(Collections)
    Cam CAL 153

(Collections)	LSO – L PM 55014(1966)
	L SPC 21016
	L M 94016
	L M 95016
	ED LK 4851
	ED PFS 4116
	ED SPA 537
	ED KCSP 537
Overture to 'Tannhäuser' (Dresden)	PO – V 74758-59 + 74768(1921)
	HMV DB 386
('Entry of the Guests' from Act 2)	V 6244 + 6478
Overture and Bacchanal from	PO – V 7262-64(1929)
'Tannhäuser' (Paris)	V 7265-67(ac)
	HMV D 1905-07
	HMV D 7372-74(ac)
	V L 11669-70S
With Women's Chorus	PO – V 15310-12(1937)
	V 16159S-63(ac)
	HMV DB 3775-77
With Women's Chorus	LSSO – V 12-1184-87(ac)(1950)
(Prelude to Act 3)	V WDM 1383
(Wesendonck Songs)	V LM 1066
(Collections)	SA – V LM 2555(1961)
With Women's Chorus	V LSC 2555
	Va VICS 1301
	V AGL 1-1336
'Entry of the Guests' from Act 2 of	PO – V 6478(1924)
'Tannhäuser'	
(Overture to 'Tannhäuser')	
Prelude to Act 3 of 'Tannhäuser'	PO – V 15313-14S(1936)
	V 16159S-63(ac)
(Tschaikovsky: Solitude, op. 73, no. 6)	HMV DB 3254-55
(Overture and Bacchanal from	LSSO – V 12-1184-87(ac)(1950)
'Tannhäuser')	V WDM 1383
'Pilgrims' Chorus' from Act 3 of	NSOL – V LM 2593(1961)
'Tannhäuser'	V LSC 2593
(Collections)	V VCS 7077
With the Norman Luboff Choir	V RK 5072
	V R8S 5072
Symphonic Synthesis from 'Tristan and	PO – V 7621-24(1932)
Isolde' (t)	V 7625-28(ac)
(Prelude, Liebesnacht, and Liebestod)	HMV DB 1911-14
	HMV DB 7399-7402
	V L 11636-37
(Palestrina: 'Adoramus te Christe')	PO – V 15202-06(1937-1939)
	V 15207-11(ac)
	V 16232S-36(ac)
Prelude omitted	HMV DB 3087-89
Different version	V 15202-06S
(Prelude, Liebesnacht, Liebestod, and	V 15207S-11(ac)
End of Act 2)	

| | LSSO – V WDM 1567(1950) |
| | V LM 1174 |

Prelude and Liebestod from 'Tristan and Isolde'
(Collections)

RPO – V ARL 1-0498(1973)
V ARK 1-0498
V ARS 1-0498

Love Music from Act 2 and 3 of 'Tristan and Isolde' (t)
(De Falla: 'El Amor Brujo')

AAYO – AC 11431-33D(1940)
AC 11434-36D(ac)
PO – AC ML 5479(1960)
AC MS 6147
CBS BRG 61288
CBS SBRG 61288
O Y 32368

(Collection)

AC MGP 17

Prelude to Act 3 of 'Tristan and Isolde'
(Collections)

SA – V LM 2555(1961)
V LSC 2555
Va VICS 1301
V AGL 1-1336

Symphonic Synthesis from Act 3 of 'Die Walküre' (t)
Soloist: Lawrence Tibbett

PO – V 8542-45(1934)
V 8546-49(ac)
HMV DB 2470-73
HMV DB 7955-58(ac)

'Ride of the Valkyries' from Act 3 of 'Die Walküre'
('Wotan's Farewell' and 'Magic Fire Music' from Act 3)
(Collections)

PO – V 74684(1921)
HMV 3-0632
V 6245
HMV DB 387
SA – V LM 2555(1961)
V LSC 2555
Va VICS 1301
V AGL 1-1336
V VCS 7077
V RK 5072
V R8S 5072

(Collection)

V LSC 5007
V R8S 1187

(Collections)

LSO – L PM 55014(1966)
L SPC 21016
L M 94016
L M 95016
ED LK 4851
ED PFS 4116
ED SPA 537
ED KCSP 537
ED SPA 159
ED KCSP 159

(Collection)

ED DPA 519-20
ED KDPC 519-20

'Wotan's Farewell' and 'Magic Fire Music' from Act 3 of 'Die Walküre'
('Ride of the Valkyries' from Act 3)

PO – V 74736(1921)
HMV 3-0723
V 6245
HMV DB 387

(Overture to Rienzi') (t)	NYPO – AC 12897-98D(1947)
	AC ML 2153
	EC 33 C 1026
(Collections) (t)	HSO – Ev LPBR 6070(1960)
	Ev SDBR 3070
'Magic Fire Music' from Act 3 of 'Die Walküre'	PO – V 15800(1939)
	HMV DB 3942
	HMV DB 6024
(Sibelius: 'Finlandia')	Cam CAE 101
(Collections)	Cam CAL 120
	V VCM 7101
(Collections)	RPO – V ARL 1-0498(1973)
	V ARK 1-0498
	V ARS 1-0498
Wesendonck Songs	LSSO – V 12-0351-53(1950)
Soloist: Eileen Farrell	V 12-0354-56(ac)
(Overture and Bacchanal from	V LM 1066
'Tannhäuser')	
(Other artistes)	Va AVM 1-1413
No. 3, 4, and 5 only	PO – V 18403-04(1940)
Soloist: Helen Traubel	
(Collections)	V DMM 4-0341

Ben Weber

Symphony on Poems by William Blake	LSSO – V LM 1785(1952)
(Harrison: Suite for Violin, Piano, and Orchestra)	
Soloist: Warren Galjour	
(Goeb: Symphony no. 3)	CRI 120

Carl Maria von Weber

'Invitation to the Dance'	PO – V 74598(1919)
(Johann Strauss: 'On the Beautiful Blue Danube')	V 6237
	PO – V 6643(1927)
	HMV D 1285
(Brahms: Symphony no. 3 in F Major)	LSS LS 1
	PO – V 15189(1937)
	HMV DB 3699
(Collections)	Cam CAE 192
	Cam CAL 123
(Collection)	Cam CAL 282
	AAYO – AC 11481D(1940)
(Collections)	LSSO – V 12-1208-12(ac)(1950)
	V WDM 1394
	V LM 1083
	HMV ALP 1133
	Va VIC 1020
	V ERB 7022
	V LRM 7022

J. S. Bach   PO – AC ML 5713
                                                AC MS 6313
Brandenburg Concerto no. 5 in D Major   O Y 33228
Chorale Prelude 'Ich rufe zu dir' (t)   CBS 30061
Chorale Prelude 'Nun kommt der Heiden   CBS 40-30061
Heiland' (t)
Chorale Prelude 'Wir glauben all' an
einen Gott' (t)

Stokowski – Encore   NaPO – AC M 34543
                                                AC MT 34543
Albeniz: 'Fete dieu a Seville' from   AC MA 34543
'Iberia' (t)   CBS 73589
Chopin: Mazurka no. 25 in B Minor,   CBS 40-73589
op. 33, no. 4 (t)
Chopin: Prelude no. 24 in D Minor,
op. 28 (t)
Debussy: 'Soirée dans Grenade' from
'Estampes' (t)
Debussy: 'Clair de Lune' from 'Suite
Bergamasque' (t)
Novacek: 'Moto perpetuo' (t)
Rimsky-Korsakov: Prelude to Act 3 of
'Ivan the Terrible' (t)
Rimsky-Korsakov: 'Flight of the Bumble Bee'
from Act 3 of 'The Tale of Czar Saltan' (t)
Shostakovitch: Prelude in E Flat Minor,
op. 34, no. 14 (t)
Tschaikovsky: Humoreske, op. 10,
no. 2 (t)

In Dulci Jubilo   LSSO – Bach BGS 70696
                                                Van S 363
J. S. Bach: Chorale from Cantata
no. 147 (t)
J. S. Bach: Aria from Cantata no. 208 (t)
J. S. Bach: Sinfonia from Christmas
Oratorio
Corelli: Concerto Grosso in G Minor,
op. 6, no. 8
Vivaldi: Concerto Grosso in D Minor,
op. 3, no. 11

Dukas: 'L'Apprenti Sorcier'   PO – Cam CAL 118
Moussorgsky: 'A Night on the Bare
Mountain' (t)
Ravel: Rapsodie Espagnole

Concert Classics   PO – Cam CAL 120
                                                Cam CAE 101

J. S. Bach: Fugue no. 2 in C Minor from
'Wohltemperiertes Klavier' I (t)
Boccherini: Minuet from String Quintet
in E Major, op. 13, no. 5 (t)
Handel: Sinfonia from 'Messiah'
Haydn: Serenade from Quartet in
F Major, op. 3, no. 5 (t)
Sibelius: 'Finlandia'
Wagner: Prelude to Act 1 of 'Lohengrin'
Wagner: 'Magic Fire Music' from Act 3
of 'Die Walküre'

Concert Gems

PO – Cam CAL 123
Cam CAE 188
Cam CAE 192

Brahms: Hungarian Dance no. 1
in G Minor (t)
Debussy: 'Clair de Lune' from 'Suite
Bergamasque' (t)
Ippolitov-Ivanow: 'Procession' from
'Caucasian Sketches'
Novacek: 'Moto perpetuo' (t)
Schubert: Moment musicale no. 3 in
F Minor (t)
Schubert: Ballet Music no. 2 in G Major
from 'Rosamunde'
Sibelius: 'Valse triste' from 'Kuolema'
Sibelius: Berceuse from 'The Tempest'
Weber: 'Invitation to the Dance'

Concert Favourites

HBSO – Cam CAL 153

Clarke: 'A Trumpet Voluntary' (t)
Offenbach: Barcarole from 'The Tales of
Hoffmann' (t)
Johann Strauss: 'Tales from the Vienna   PO
Woods' (t)
Tschaikovsky: Humoreske, op. 10, no. 2 (t)
Tschaikovsky: 'Marche slave'
Tschaikovsky: Solitude, op. 73, no. 6 (t)
Wagner: 'Waldweben' from Act 2 of
'Siegfried'

Bloch: 'Schelomo'   PO – Cam CAL 254
Saint-Saëns: 'Dance macabre'
Richard Strauss: 'Dance of the Seven Veils'
from 'Salome'

Landmarks of a Distinguished Career

LSSO – Cap P 8399
Cap SP 8399

J. S. Bach: Toccata and Fugue in
D Minor (t)

Debussy: 'Prelude a l'apres-midi d'un
faune'
Debussy: 'Clair de Lune' from 'Suite
Bergamasque' (t)
Sibelius: 'Finlandia'
Sibelius: 'The Swan of Tuonela'
Johann Strauss: 'On the Beautiful Blue
Danube'

The String Orchestra

LSSO – Cap P 8458
    Cap SP 8458

J. S. Bach: Air from Suite no. 3 in
D Major for Orchestra (t)
Theodore Berger: Rondino giocoso
Boccherini: Minuet from String Quintet
in E Major, op. 13, no. 5 (t)
Gluck: Ballet Music from 'Orpheus and
Euridice'
Handel: Tamburina from 'Alcina'
Purcell: Hornpipe from 'King Arthur'
Tschaikovsky: Andante cantabile from
String Quartet no. 1 in D Major (t)
Turina: 'La Oracion del Torero', op. 8

Debussy: 'Iberia' (No. 2 of 'Images' III
Ibert: 'Escales'
Ravel: Alborado del Gracioso

ONRF – Cap P 8463
    Cap SP 8463
    S S 60102
    HMV CC SXLP 30263
    HMV CC TC SXLP 30263

J. S. Bach – Stokowski

LSSO – Cap P 8489
    Cap SP 8489

Chorale 'Ein feste Burg' (t)
Sinfonia from Christmas Oratorio
Bourré from English Suite no. 2
in A Minor (t)
'Komm', süsser Tod' (t)
Little Fugue in G Minor (t)
Sarabande from Partita no. 1 in
B Minor (t)
Passacaglia and Fugue in C Minor (t)

Music for Strings

LSSO – Cap PAO 8415
    Cap SPAO 8415

J. S. Bach: 'Mein Jesus, was für
Seelenweh' (t)
J. S. Bach: Prelude from Partita no. 3 in
E Major (t)
Borodin: Nocturne from String Quartet
no. 2 in D Major
Gluck: Lento and Sicilienne from
'Armide'

Gluck: Lento from 'Ifigenia in Aulis'
Paganini: 'Moto perpetuo'
Rachmaninov: Vocalise, op. 34, no. 14

The Orchestra   LSSO – Cap SAL 8385
                                                     Cap SSAL 8385

Barber: Adagio for Strings
Dukas: Fanfare from 'La Péri'
Farberman: First Part of 'Evolution'
Moussorgsky: Last Two Movements from
'Pictures at an Exhibition' (Ravel)
Persichetti: March from Divertimento for
Band
Richard Strauss: Gavotte from Suite for
Winds in B Flat Major
Tschaikovsky: Third Movement from
Symphony no. 4 in F Minor
Vaughan Williams: Second Movement
from Symphony no. 8 in D Minor

Sound of Strings   LSSO – Cap L 9216
                                                     Cap SL 9216

J. S. Bach: Air from Suite no. 3 in
D Major for Orchestra (t)
Boccherini: Minuet from String Quintet
in E Major, op. 13, no. 5 (t)
Borodin: Nocturne from String Quartet
no. 2 in D Major
Paganini: 'Moto perpetuo'
Rachmaninov: Vocalise, op. 34, no. 14
Tschaikovsky: Andante cantabile from
String Quartet no. 1 in D Major (t)

Plus Strings   LSSO – Cap P 8650
                                                     Cap SP 8650

J. S. Bach: Prelude from Partita
no. 3 in E Major (t)
J. S. Bach: Air from Suite no. 3 in
D Major for Orchestra (t)
Boccherini: Minuet from String
Quintet in E Major, op. 13, no. 5 (t)
Borodin: Nocturne from String Quartet
no. 2 in D Major
Gluck: Lento from 'Ifigenia in Aulis'
Gluck: Ballet Music from 'Orpheus
and Euridice'
Paganini: 'Moto perpetuo'
Rachmaninov: Vocalise, op. 34, no. 14
Tschaikovsky: Andante cantabile
from String Quartet no. 1 in
D Major (t)

The Best of Stokowski I   LSSO – Cap SP 8673

J. S. Bach: Little Fugue in G Minor (t)
Barber: Adagio for Strings
Debussy: 'Fêtes' from 'Nocturnes'   LSO
Debussy: 'Prelude a l'apres-midi d'un
faune'
Dukas: Fanfare from 'La Péri'
Sibelius: 'The Swan of Tuonela'
Stravinsky: Barceuse and Finale   BPO
from 'The Firebird'
Tschaikovsky: Third Movement from
Symphony no. 4 in F Minor

The Best of Stokowski II   LSSO – Cap SPAO 8694

J. S. Bach: Chorale 'Ein feste Burg' (t)
J. S. Bach: Toccata and Fugue in
D Minor (t)
Debussy: 'Clair de Lune' from 'Suite
Bergamasque' (t)
Moussorgsky: Last Two Movements from
'Pictures at an Exhibition' (Ravel)
Ravel: Alborado del Gracioso   ONRF
Johann Strauss: 'On the Beautiful Blue
Danube'
Turina: 'La Oracion del Torero', op. 8

The Stokowski String Sound   RPO – Desmar DSM 1011
                                                    Desmar E 1047
Dvorak: Serenade for Strings in
E Major
Purcell: Aria from 'Dido and
Aeneas' (t)
Vaughan Williams: Fantasy on a
Theme by Thomas Tallis

'Fantasia'   PO – Disney WDX 101
                                                    Disney STER 101
J. S. Bach: Toccata and Fugue in   Buena Vista BVS 101
D Minor (t)   Buena Vista 101 VC
Beethoven: Symphony no. 6 in F Major   Buena Vista 101 VT
Dukas: 'L'Apprenti Sorcier'
Moussorgsky: 'A Night on the Bare
Mountain' (t)
Ponchielli: 'Dance of the Hours' from
'La Gioconda'
Schubert: 'Ave Maria'
Stravinsky: 'Le Sacre du Printemps'
Tschaikovsky: Selections from 'The
Nutcracker'

Leopold Stokowski 1882-1977

	ED D94D2
	ED K94K2
J. S. Bach: Toccata and Fugue in	CPO
D Minor (t)	
Beethoven: Overture to 'Egmont'	NPO
Debussy: 'Prelude a l'apres-midi d'un	LSO
faune'	
Elgar: Enigma Variations	CPO
Schubert: Symphony no. 8 in B Minor	LPO
Scriabin: 'Poeme d'Extase', op. 54	CPO
Tschaikovsky: 'Marche slave'	LSO

The Phase Four World of Leopold Stokowski

	ED SPA 159
	ED KCSP 159
Moussorgsky: Last Two Movements	NPO
from 'Pictures at an Exhibition' (t)	
Ravel: Fanfare from 'L'Eventail de	HRPO
Jeanne'	
Stravinsky: Pastorale (t)	RPO
Tschaikovsky: 'Marche slave'	LSO
Tschaikovsky: Waltz from 'The Sleeping	NPO
Beauty'	
Tschaikovsky: Dance and Finale from	NPO
'The Swan Lake'	
Wagner: 'Ride of the Valkyries'	LSO
from Act 3 of 'Die Walküre'	

Prokofiev: Suite from 'Cinderella'	NYSO – Ev LPBR 6016
Villa-Lobos: Mohinda from Bachiana	Ev SDBR 3016
Brasileira no. 1	
Villa-Lobos: 'Uirapuru'	

Music by Richard Strauss

	NYSO – Ev LPBR 6023
	Ev SDBR 3023
Don Juan'	
'Dance of the Seven Veils' from 'Salome'	
'Till Eulenspiegels lustige Streiche'	

Thomas Canning: Fantasy on a Hymn	HSO – Ev LPBR 6070
by Justin Morgan	Ev SDBR 3070
Chopin: Mazurka no. 13 in A Minor,	
op. 7, no. 4 (t)	
Chopin: Prelude no. 24 in D Minor.	
op. 28 (t)	
Chopin: Waltz no. 7 in C Sharp Minor,	
op. 64, no. 2 (t)	
Wagner: 'Wotan's Farewell' and 'Magic	
Fire Music' from Act 3 of 'Die Walküre' (t)	

Debussy: No. 2, 5, and 6 from 'Children's	NYSO – Ev LPBR 6108
Corner'	Ev SDBR 3108

Prokofiev: Suite from 'Cinderella'
Prokofiev: 'The Ugly Duckling'

Wagner Programme   LSO–L PM 55014
                                                    L SPC 21016
'Siegfried's Rhine Journey' and 'Funeral   L M 94016
Music' from 'Die Götterdämmerung'   L M 95016
'Entrance of the Gods into Valhalla'   ED LK 4851
from 'The Rheingold'   ED PFS 4116
'Waldweben' from Act 2 of 'Siegfried'   ED SPA 537
'Ride of the Valkyries' from Act 3 of   ED KCSP 537
'Die Walküre'

Moussorgsky: 'A Night on the Bare   LSO–L SPC 21026
Mountain' (t)   L M 94026
Stravinsky: Suite from 'The Firebird'   ED LK 4927
Tschaikovsky: 'Marche slave'   ED PFS 4139

Borodin: Polovtsian Dances from 'Prince   RPO–L SPC 21041
Igor'   L M 94041
Stravinsky: Pastorale (t)   L M 95041
Tschaikovsky: Overture '1812'   ED PFS 4189

Berlioz: 'Dance of the Sylphs'   LSO–L SPC 21059
from 'Damnation of Faust'   ED PFS 4220
Debussy: 'La Mer'
Ravel: Suite no. 2 from 'Daphnis and
Chloé'

Sixtieth Anniversary Concert   LSO–L SPC 21090-91
                                                    ED OPFS 3-4
Brahms: Symphony no. 1 in C Minor   ED KPFC 3-4
Debussy: 'Prelude a l'apres-midi d'un
faune'
Glazunow: Concerto in A Minor for
Violin and Orchestra
Tschaikovsky: 'Marche slave'
Wagner: Prelude to Act 1 of 'Die
Meistersinger'

J. S. Bach Programme   CPO–L SPC 21096
                                                    L M 521096
Chorale from Cantata no. 4 (t)   L M 821096
Chorale Prelude 'Wir glauben all'   ED PFS 4278
an einen Gott' (t)
'Mein Jesus, was für Seelenweh' (t)
Passacaglia and Fugue in C Minor (t)
Toccata and Fugue in D Minor (t)
Prelude no. 8 in E Flat Minor from
'Wohltemperiertes Klavier' I (t)

Tschaikovsky Fantasia	L SPC 21108
	L M 521108
	L M 821108
	Ace SDD 454

'Marche slave'	LSO
Overture '1812'	RPO
'Romeo and Juliet'	OSR
Waltz from 'The Sleeping Beauty'	NPO
Waltz from 'The Swan Lake'	NPO

Debussy Fantasia	L SPC 21109
	L M 521109
	L M 821109
	Ace SDD 455

'La Mer'	LSO
'Prelude a l'apres-midi d'un faune'	LSO
Prelude no. 10 I ('La Cathédrale engloutie') (t)	NPO

Moussorgsky Fantasia	L SPC 21110
	L M 521110
	L M 821110
	Ace SDD 456

Symphonic Synthesis from 'Boris Godunov (t)	OSR
'A Night on the Bare Mountain' (t)	LSO
'Pictures at an Exhibition' (t)	NPO

Russian Fantasia	L SPC 21111
	L M 521111
	L M 821111

Borodin: Polovtsian Dances from 'Prince Igor'	RPO
Glazunow: Concerto in A Minor for Violin and Orchestra	LSO
Rimsky-Korsakov: First Movement of 'Scheherazade'	LSO
Stravinsky: 'Infernal Dance' from 'The Firebird'	LSO
Tschaikovsky: Excerpts from 'The Swan Lake'	NPO

Ballet Fantasia	L SPC 21112
	L M 521112
	L M 821112

Berlioz: 'Dance of the Sylphs' from 'Damnation of Faust'	LSO
Elgar: 'Nimrod' from Enigma Variations	CPO
Ravel: Suite no. 2 from 'Daphnis and Chloé'	LSO
Stravinsky: Berceuse and Finale from 'The Firebird'	LSO

Tschaikovsky: Excerpts from 'The Swan Lake'   NPO

Dvorak: Slavonic Dance in E Minor, op. 72, no. 2   CPO – L SPC 21117
                                                      L M 521117
Rimsky-Korssakov: Capriccio Espagnol   NPO – ED PFS 4333
                                          ED KPFC 4333
Scriabin: 'Poeme d'Extase', op. 54

Stokowski Encores   L SPC 21130
                          ED PFS 4351
                          ED KPFC 4351

Byrd: Pavane and Gigue 'Earl of Salisbury' (t)   LSO
Chopin: Mazurka no. 13 in A Minor, op. 17, no. 4 (t)   LSO
Clarke: 'A Trumpet Voluntary' (t)   LSO
Duparc: 'Extase' (t)   LSO
Dvorak: Slavonic Dance in E Minor, op. 72, no. 2   CPO
Elgar: 'Nimrod' from Enigma Variations   CPO
Rachmaninov: Prelude in C Sharp Minor, op. 3, no. 2 (t)   CPO
Schubert: Moment musicale no. 3 in F Minor (t)   LSO
Tschaikovsky: Chant sans Paroles in A Minor, op. 40, no. 6 (t)   LSO

Tschaikovsky Programme   LPO – P 6500 766
                               P 7300 332

'Capriccio Italien'
Polonaise and Waltz from 'Eugen Onegin'
Suite from 'The Nutcracker'

Stokowski Spectacular   NaPO – Pye PCNH 4
                             Pye ZCPHG 4

Berlioz: Hungarian March from 'Damnation of Faust'
Brahms: Hungarian Dance no. 1 in G Minor (t)
Chabrier: Espana Rhapsody
Haydn: Serenade from Quartet in F Major, op. 3, no. 5 (t)
Ippolitov-Ivanow: 'Procession' from 'Caucasian Sketches'
Moussorgsky: Prelude to Act 4 of 'Khovantchina' (t)
Saint-Saëns: 'Dance macabre'
Sousa: 'The Stars and Stripes Forever' (t)
Johann Strauss: 'Tales from the Vienna Woods'
Tschaikovsky: Solitude, Op. 73, no. 6 (t)

261

Stokowski Overtures

NaPO – Pye PCNHX 6
Pye ZCPNH 6

Beethoven: Leonore Overture no. 3
Berlioz: Roman Carnival Overture
Mozart: Overture to 'Don Giovanni'
Rossini: Overture to 'William Tell'
Schubert: Overture to 'Rosamunde'

Beethoven: Symphony no. 7 in A Major
Frescobaldi: Gagliarda (t)
Palestrina: 'Adoramus te Christe' (t)

SA – Q PMC 7110E
Q P4C 7110E

Wagner Programme

RPO – V ARL 1-0498
V ARK 1-0498
V ARS 1-0498

Prelude to Act 3, 'Dance of the
Apprentices', and 'Entry of the Masters'
from 'Die Meistersinger'
Overture to 'Rienzi'
Prelude and Liebestod from 'Tristan and
Isolde'
'Magic Fire Music' from Act 3 of 'Die
Walküre'

J. S. Bach Programme

LSO – V ARL 1-0880
V ARK 1-0880
V ARS 1-0880
V ARD 1-0880
V AGL 1-3656
V AGK 1-3656

Sinfonia from Cantata no. 156 (t)
Chorale 'Ein feste Burg' (t)
Chorale Prelude 'Wachet auf' (t)
'Komm', süsser Tod' (t)
Little Fugue in G Minor (t)
Chaconne from Partita no. 2 in
D Minor (t)
Prelude from Partita no. 3 in E Major (t)
Air from Suite no. 3 in D Major for
Orchestra (t)

First Edition

PO – V DMM 4-0341

J. S. Bach: Chorale Prelude 'Ich rufe
zu dir' (t)
J. S. Bach: Bourré from English Suite
no. 2 in A Minor (t)
J. S. Bach: Toccata and Fugue in
D Minor (t)
Beethoven: Symphony no. 7 in A Major
Bloch: 'Schelomo'
Borodin: Polovtsian Dances from 'Prince
Igor'
Debussy: 'Soirée dans Grenade' from
'Estampes' (t)
Debussy: 'Nuages' from 'Nocturnes'
Debussy: 'Fêtes' from 'Nocturnes'

Debussy: 'Prelude a l'apres-midi d'un
faune'
Debussy: Prelude no. 10 I (t)
Ravel: Rapsodie Espagnole
Rimsky-Korsakov: 'Scheherazade'
Saint-Saëns: 'Dance macabre'
Schubert: Moment musicale no. 3 in
F Minor (t)
Schubert: Ballet Music no. 2 in G Major
from 'Rosamunde'
Schubert: Symphony no. 8 in B Minor
Wagner: Wesendonck Songs, no. 3, 4
and 5

Berlioz: 'Dance of the Sylphs'   LSSO – V LM 151
from 'Damnation of Faust'
Granados: Intermezzo from 'Goyescas'
Ibert: 'Escales'
Sibelius: 'The Swan of Tuonela'

Heart of the Ballet   LSSO – V 12-1208-12
                                  V WDM 1394
Adam: Selections from 'Giselle'   V LM 1083
Chopin: Selections from 'Les Sylphides'   HMV ALP 1133
Delibes: Selections from 'Sylvia'   Va VIC 1020
Tschaikovsky: 'Waltz of the Flowers'
from 'The Nutcracker'
Tschaikovsky: Selections from 'The Swan
Lake'
Weber: 'Invitation to the Dance'

Stokowski Conducts Bach I   LSSO – V WDM 1512
                                  V LM 1133
Bourrée from English Suite no. 2 in   V ERA 89
A Minor (t)   V ERA 244
'Mein Jesus, was für Seelenweh' (t)
Chaconne from Partita no. 2 in
D Minor (t)
Passacaglia and Fugue in C Minor (t)
Siciliano from Sonata no. 4 in C Minor (t)

Music by Debussy   LSSO – V WDM 1560
                                  V LM 1154
'Nocturnes'   V ERA 47
'Prelude a l'apres-midi d'un faune'   HMV 7ER 5011
'Clair de Lune' from 'Suite
Bergamasque' (t)

Stokowski Conducts Bach II   LSSO – V WDM 1569
                                  V LM 1176
Chorale from Cantata no. 4 (t)   V ERA 89
Chorale from Cantata no. 147 (t)   HMV 7ER 5004

Aria from Cantata no. 208 (t)
Chorale Prelude 'Wir glauben all' an
einen Gott' (t)
'Komm', süsser Tod' (t)
Little Fugue in G Minor (t)
Suite no. 2 in B Minor for Orchestra

Chopin: Prelude no. 4 in E Minor, op. 28 (t)	LSSO – V LM 1238
	V ERA 124
Chopin: Prelude no. 24 in D Minor, op. 28 (t)	HMV 7ER 5046
	V ERA 67
Grainger: English and Irish Folk Tunes	HMV 7ER 5043

Grainger: English and Irish Folk Tunes
('Country Gardens', 'Early in the
Morning', 'Handel in the Strand',
'Londonderry Air', 'Mock Morris Dances',
'Molly on the Shore', and 'Shepherd's
Hey')
Mozart: German Dances, K.605, no. 3
Schubert: Deutsche Tänze, op. 33 (t)
Sibelius: 'Valse triste' from 'Kuolema'
Sibelius: Berceuse from 'The Tempest'

Early Italian Music LSSO – V WDM 1721
V LM 1721

Cesti: 'Tu mancavi a tormentarmi' (t)
Frescobaldi: Gagliarda (t)
Gabrieli: Canzona quarti toni a 15
Gabrieli: 'In Ecclesiis Benedicite
Domino' (t)
Lully: Nocturne from 'Le Triomphe de
l'Amour'
Lully: March from 'Thésée'
Palestrina: 'Adoramus te Christe'
Palestrina: 'O bone Jesu'
Vivaldi: Concerto Grosso in D Minor,
op. 3, no. 11 (t)

Music by Tschaikovsky LSSO – V ERB 4
V LM 1774
V ERA 182

'Aurora's Wedding'
Humoreske, op. 10, no, 2 (t)
Solitude, op. 73, no. 6 (t)

Russian Music LSSO – V ERB 1816
V LM 1816
Q PMC 7026E
Q P4C 7026E
HMV 7ER 5060

Borodin: 'In the Steppes of Central Asia'
Gliere: 'Russian Sailors' Dance' from
'The Red Poppy'
Moussorgsky: Suite from 'Khovantchina'
Moussorgsky: 'A Night on the Bare
Mountain' (t)
Rimsky-Korsakov: Russian Easter Overture

Restful Music	LSSO – V ERB 52
	V LM 1875
Bach: 'Mein Jesus, was für Seelenweh' (t)	HMV ALP 1387
Bach: Siciliano from Sonata no. 4 in	V ERA 244
C Minor (t)	
Bach: Sarabande from Suite no. 2 in	
B Minor for Orchestra	
Beethoven: Second Movement from	NBCSO
Symphony no. 6 in F Major	
Bizet: Adagietto from Suite no. 1 from	
'L'Arlesienne'	
Cesti: 'Tu mancavi a tormentarmi' (t)	
Frescobaldi: Gagliarda (t)	
Lully: Nocturne from 'Le Triomphe de	
l'Amour'	
Purcell: Aria from 'Dido and Aeneas' (t)	
In the Lighter Vein	LSSO – V LM 2042
	V ERA 182
Bach: Toccata and Fugue in D Minor (t)	V ERA 259
Bach: Prelude no. 24 in B Minor from	HMV 7ER 5016
'Wohltemperiertes Klavier' I (t)	
Beethoven: Turkish March from 'The	NBCSO
Ruins of Athens'	
Humperdinck: Prelude to 'Hänsel and	
Gretel'	
Mozart: Rondo alla Turca from Sonata in	NBCSO
A Major. K.331 (t)	
Rachmaninov: Vocalise, op. 34, no. 14	
Johann Strauss: 'On the Beautiful Blue	NBCSO
Danube'	
Johann Strauss: 'Tales from the Vienna	NBCSO
Woods'	
Tschaikovsky: Polonaise from 'Eugen	
Onegin'	
Rhapsodies	RCAVSO – V LM 2471
	V LSC 2471
Enesco: Romanian Rhapsody no. 1	
Liszt: Hungarian Rhapsody no. 2	
Smetana: Overture to 'The Bartered	
Bride'	
Smetana: 'The Moldau'	
The Sound of Wagner and Stokowski	SA – V LM 2555
	V LSC 2555
'Entrance of the Gods into Valhalla' from	Va VICS 1301
'The Rheingold'	V AGL 1-1336
Overture and Bacchanal from	
'Tannhäuser' (Paris)	
Prelude to Act 3 of 'Tristan and Isolde'	
'Ride of the Valkyries' from Act 3 of	
'Die Walküre'	

Inspiration

NSOL – V LM 2593
V LSC 2593

Anonymous: 'Deep River'
Anonymous: 'Praise God from Whom All
Blessings Flow'
Bach: Chorale from Cantata no. 147 (t)
Bach: Aria from Cantata no. 208 (t)
Beethoven: 'Die Ehre Gottes aus der
Natur', op. 48, no. 4
Gluck: 'O Saviour, Hear Me' from
Orpheus and Euridice'
Handel: Largo from 'Xerxes'
Humperdinck: 'Evening Prayer' from
'Hänsel and Gretel'
Tschaikovsky: 'Pater Noster'
Wagner: 'Pilgrims' Chorus' from Act 3
of 'Tannhäuser'

Anna Moffo – Leopold Stokowski

ASO – V LM 2795
V LSC 2795

Canteloube: 'Songs of the Auvergne'
Rachmaninov: Vocalise, op. 34, no. 14
Villa-Lobos: Bachiana Brasileira no. 5

Berlioz: 'Dance of the Sylphs'
from 'Damnation of Faust'
Granados: Intermezzo from 'Goyescas'
Ibert: 'Escales'
Sibelius: 'The Swan of Tuonela'
Stravinsky: Suite from 'The Firebird'

LSSO – V LM 9029

Chopin: Selections from 'Les Sylphides'
Delibes: Selections from 'Sylvia'
Tschaikovsky: Selections from 'The Swan
Lake'
Weber: 'Invitation to the Dance'

LSSO – V ERB 7022
V LRM 7022

Debussy: 'Prelude a l'apres-midi d'un
faune'
Sibelius: 'Valse triste' from 'Kuolema'
Sibelius: 'The Swan of Tuonela'
Sibelius: Berceuse from 'The Tempest'

LSSO – V ERB 7024
V LRM 7024

Music by Bach

LSSO – V ERB 7033
V LRM 7033
HMV BLP 1074

'Komm', süsser Tod' (t)
Passacaglia and Fugue in C Minor (t)
Toccata and Fugue in D Minor (t)

**Stokowski and the Philadelphia
Orchestra**

PO – V VCM 7101

J. S. Bach: Passacaglia and Fugue in

266

C Minor (t)
J. S. Bach: Toccata and Fugue in
D Minor (t)
Berlioz: Hungarian March from
'Damnation of Faust'
Gliere: 'Russian Sailors' Dance' from
'The Red Poppy'
Ippolitov-Ivanow: 'Procession' from
'Caucasian Sketches'
Liszt: Hungarian Rhapsody no. 2
Moussorgsky: 'A Night on the Bare
Mountain' (t)
Rimsky-Korsakov: Russian Easter
Overture
Saint-Saëns: 'Dance macabre'
Saint-Saëns: Bacchanal from 'Samson and
Delilah'
Sibelius: 'Finlandia'
Sibelius: 'The Swan of Tuonela'
Wagner: Finale from 'Die Götter-
dämmerung'
Wagner: 'Magic Fire Music' from Act 3 of
'Die Walküre'

Stokowski's Greatest Hits	V VCS 7077
	V RK 5072
	V R8S 5072
J. S. Bach: Chorale from Cantata no. 147 (t)	NSOL
J. S. Bach: Aria from Cantata no. 208 (t)	NSOL
Enesco: Romanian Rhapsody no. 1	RCAVSO
Handel: Water Music Suite (t)	RCAVSO
Handel: Largo from 'Xerxes'	NSOL
Liszt: Hungarian Rhapsody no. 2	RCAVSO
Rimsky-Korsakov: Russian Easter Overture	CSO
Shostakovitch: Polka from 'The Age of Gold'	CSO
Smetana: 'The Moldau'	RCAVSO
Wagner: 'Entrance of the Gods into Valhalla' from 'The Rheingold'	SA
Wagner: 'Pilgrims' Chorus' from Act 3 of 'Tannhäuser'	NSOL
Wagner: 'Ride of the Valkyries' from Act 3 of 'Die Walküre	SA

| **Stokowski Plays Bach** | LSSO – S S 60235 |
| | S 4XG 60235 |

Chorale 'Ein feste Burg' (t)
Sinfonia from Christmas Oratorio
'Komm', süsser Tod' (t)
Little Fugue in G Minor (t)

Sarabande from Partita no. 1 in
B Minor (t)
Passacaglia and Fugue in C Minor (t)
Toccata and Fugue in D Minor (t)

Stokowski and Strings   LSSO – S S 60278
                             S 4XG 60278

J. S. Bach: Prelude from Partita no. 3 in
E Major (t)
J. S. Bach: Air from Suite no. 3 in
D Major for Orchestra (t)
Boccherini: Minuet from String Quintet
in E Major, op. 13, no. 5 (t)
Borodin: Nocturne from String Quartet
no. 2 in D Major
Gluck: Lento from 'Armide'
Gluck: Ballet Music from 'Orpheus and
Euridice'
Paganini: 'Moto perpetuo'
Rachmaninov: Vocalise, op, 34, no. 14
Tschaikovsky: Andante cantabile from
String Quartet no. 1 in D Major (t)

The Art of Leopold Stokowski   LSSO – S SIB 6094
                                   S 4X2G 6094

J. S. Bach: 'Mein Jesus, was für
Seelenweh' (t)
J. S. Bach: Toccata and Fugue in
D Minor (t)
Barber: Adagio for Strings
Debussy: 'Prelude a l'apres-midi d'un
faune'
Debussy: 'Clair de Lune' from 'Suite
Bergamasque' (t)
Dukas: Fanfare from 'La Péri'
Gluck: Sicilienne from 'Armide'
Gluck: Lento from 'Ifigenia in Aulis'
Moussorgsky: Last Two Movements from
'Pictures at an Exhibition' (Ravel)
Purcell: Hornpipe from 'King Arthur'
Sibelius: 'Finlandia'
Sibelius: 'The Swan of Tuonela'
Johann Strauss: 'On the Beautiful Blue
Danube'
Tschaikovsky: Third Movement from
Symphony no. 4 in F Minor
Turina: 'La Oracion del Torero', op. 8

Italian Music   SA – UA UAL 7001
                    UA UAS 8001

Cesti: 'Tu mancavi a tormentarmi' (t)
Frescobaldi: Gagliarda (t)

Gabrieli: Sonata pian e forte
Palestrina: 'Adoramus te Christe' (t)
Respighi: 'Pines of Rome'

Music by Shostakovitch   SA–UA UAL 7004
                                          UA UAS 8004

Entr'acte from 'Lady Macbeth of Minsk'
Prelude in E Flat Minor, op. 34, no. 14 (t)
Symphony no. 1 in F Major

The Best of Stokowski   Van VCS 707-08
                                          Van ZCVB 707-08

J. S. Bach: Chorale from Cantata   LSSO
no. 147 (t)
J. S. Bach: Aria from Cantata no. 208 (t) LSSO
Mozart: Excerpts from Serenade no. 10 in ASO
B Flat Major, K. 361
Stravinsky: Orchestral Suite from   LSSO
'L'Histoire du soldat'
Virgil Thomson: 'The Plow That Broke   SA
the Plains'
Vivaldi: Concerto Grosso in D Minor,   LSSO
op. 3, no. 11

First Performances

Abbreviations

A . . . . American Premiere
UK . . . . English Premiere
W . . . . World Premiere

Orchestras

AAYO . . . . . All American Youth Orchestra
ASO . . . . . . American Symphony Orchestra
CBSSO . . . . CBS Symphony Orchestra
CiSO . . . . . . Cincinnati Symphony Orchestra
ClSO . . . . . . Cleveland Symphony Orchestra
CSO . . . . . . Chicago Symphony Orchestra
DSO . . . . . . Detroit Symphony Orchestra
FRSO . . . . . Frankfurt Radio Symphony Orchestra
HBSO . . . . . Hollywood Bowl Symphony Orchestra
HSO . . . . . . Houston Symphony Orchestra
LSSO . . . . . Leopold Stokowski Symphony Orchestra
MSO . . . . . . Mexico Symphony Orcestra
NBCSO . . . NBC Symphony Orchestra
NPO . . . . . . New Philharmonia Orchestra
NSO . . . . . . New Symphony Orchestra
NYCSO . . . New York City Symphony Orchestra
NYPO . . . . . New York Philharmonic Orchestra
PO . . . . The Philadelphia Orchestra

PSO . . . . Pittsburgh Symphony Orchestra
RHDO . . . . Robin Hood Dell Orchestra
RPO . . . . . . Royal Philharmonic Orchestra
SA . . . . Symphony of the Air

Isaac Albeniz/Stokowski
'Fête dieu a Seville' from 'Iberia' (W)   PO – March 20th, 1925

Fikret Amirov
Azerbaijan Mugam (A)   HSO – March 16th, 1959

Anonymous
'Etenraku' (Ritual Japanese Music) (A)   PO – December 27th, 1935

Anonymous/Stokowski
Russian Christmas Music (W)   PO – December 16th, 1932
Two Ancient Liturgical Melodies (W)   PO – December 27th, 1935

George Antheil
Symphony no. 4 (W)   NBCSO – February 13th, 1944

Fernandez Arbos
'Guajiras' (A)   PO – November 28th, 1913

Richard Arnell
Ceremonial and Flourish for Brass (A)   HSO – March 18th, 1957

Tor Aulin
Concerto no. 3 in C Minor for Violin and   CiSO – December 10th, 1909
Orchestra, op. 14 (A)
Soloist: Maud Powell

George Auric
Nocturne (A)   PO – January 26th, 1923

Jacob Avshalomov
'The Taking of T'ung Kuan' (W)   DSO – November 20th, 1952

J. S. Bach/Stokowski
Chorale from Cantata no. 4 (W)   PO – March 19th, 1915
Sinfonia from Cantata no. 29 (W)   PO – November 22nd, 1940
Chorale from Cantata no. 147 (W)   LSSO – August 8th, 1950
Sinfonia from Cantata no. 156 (W)   PO – November 22nd, 1940
Aria from Cantata no. 208 (W)   LSSO – August 8th, 1950
Chorale 'Ein feste Burg' (W)   PO – October 6th, 1933
Chorale Prelude 'Aus der Tiefe rufe ich' (W)   PO – March 28th, 1924
Chorale Prelude 'Christ lag in Todesbanden (W)   PO – March 15th, 1931
Chorale Prelude 'Ich rufe zu dir' (W)   PO – December 30th, 1926
Chorale Prelude 'Nun kommt der Heiden   PO – October 9th, 1931
Heiland' (W)
Chorale Prelude 'Wachet auf, ruft uns die   PO – March 19th, 1915
Stimme' (W)
Chorale Prelude 'Wir glauben all' an einen   PO – March 28th, 1924
Gott' (W)
Sinfonia from Christmas Oratorio (W)   PO – December 25th, 1914
Bourrée from English Suite no. 2 in A Minor (W) PO – January 10th, 1936
Sarabande from English Suite no. 3 in   PO – April 6th, 1934
G Minor (W)

Great Fugue in G Minor (W)	PO – December 30th, 1926
'Komm', süsser Tod' (W)	PO – March 3rd, 1933
Little Fugue in G Minor (W)	PO – December 12th, 1930
'Mein Jesus, was für Seelenweh' (W)	PO – April 16th, 1937
Sarabande from Partita no. 1 in B Minor (W)	PO – April 6th, 1934
Chaconne from Partita no. 2 in D Minor (W)	PO – December 19th, 1930
Prelude from Partita no. 3 in E Major (W)	PO – April 6th, 1934
Passacaglia and Fugue in C Minor (W)	PO – February 10th, 1922
'Es ist vollbracht' from Passion According to St John (W)	PO – October 12th, 1934
Chorale from Passion According to St Matthew (W)	PO – November 6th, 1936
Prelude and Fugue in E Minor (W)	PO – December 10th, 1937
Andante from Solo Sonata no. 2 in A Minor (W)	AAYO – July 11th, 1941
Siciliano from Sonata no. 4 in C Minor (W)	PO – April 28th, 1933
Air from Suite no. 3 in D Major for Orchestra (W)	PO – November 30th, 1923
Adagio from Toccata, Adagio, and Fugue in C Major (W)	PO – April 28th, 1933
Toccata and Fugue in D Minor (W)	PO – February 12th, 1925
First Movement from Trio Sonata no. 1 in E Flat Major (W)	PO – November 24th, 1939
Fugue no. 2 in C Minor from 'Wohltemperiertes Klavier' I (W)	PO – October 7th, 1932
Prelude no. 8 in E Flat Minor from 'Wohltemperiertes Klavier' I (W)	PO – April 8th, 1927
Prelude no. 24 in B Minor from 'Wohltemperiertes Klavier' I (W)	PO – April 8th, 1927

Matthias Bamert
'Matrajana' (W)   ASO – December 12th, 1971

Samuel Barlow
'Babar' (W)   PO – November 23rd, 1936

Maurice Baron
Ode to Democracy (W)   NYPO – January 22nd, 1949
With Schola Cantorum, New York

Hans Barth
Quartertone Concerto for Piano and   PO – March 28th, 1930
Orchestra (W)
Soloist: Hans Barth

Marion Bauer
Sun Splendor, op. 19 (W)   NYPO – October 25th, 1947

John Beach
'New Orleans Street Cries at Dawn' (W)   PO – April 22nd, 1927

Nathalie Bender
Soliloquy for Oboe and Orchestra (W)   HSO – March 18th, 1957

Poul Ben-Haim
Concerto for Piano and Orchestra (A)   ASO – November 11th, 1963
Soloist: Amiram Rigai

Robert Russell Bennett
Overture to an Imaginary Drama (W)   NYPO – November 26th, 1949

Symphony 'Abraham Lincoln' (W)	PO – October 24th, 1931

Alban Berg

'Wozzeck' (A)	PO – March 19th, 1931

With Anne Roselle, Ivan Ivantzoff,
Bruno Korell, and Ivan Steschenko
Assistant Conductors: Henri Elkan and
Sylvan Levin

Arthur Bliss

Introduction and Allegro (A)	PO – October 19th, 1928
Melée Fantasque (A)	PO – February 27th, 1925

Johannes Brahms/Stokowski

Hungarian Dance no. 1 in G Minor (W)	PO – March 22nd, 1934

Walter Braunfels

Variations on a Theme by Berlioz (A)	PO – October 14th, 1921

Havergal Brian

Symphony no. 28 in C Minor (W)	NPO – October 6th, 1973

Benjamin Britten

Concerto no. 1 in D Major for Piano and Orchestra, op. 13 (A)	NYPO – November 24th, 1949

Soloist: Jacques Abram

Max Bruch

Concerto for Two Pianos and Orchestra, op. 88 (W)	PO – December 29th, 1916

Soloists: Rose and Ottilie Sutro

Ferruccio Busoni

Indian Fantasy for Piano and Orchestra, op. 44 (A)	PO – February 19th, 1915

Soloist: Ferruccio Busoni

Diderik Buxtehude/Stokowski

Sarabande and Courant (W)	PO – December 12th, 1930

William Byrd/Stokowski

Pavane and Gigue ('Earl of Salisbury') (W)	PO – April 6th, 1937

John Alden Carpenter

'A 'Pilgrim Vision' (W)	PO – November 26th, 1920

Julian Carrillo

Concerto for Violin, Guitar, Cello, Piccolo, Harp, and Orchestra (W)	PO – March 4th, 1927
Horizontes for Violin, Cello, and Harp (W)	PSO – November 30th, 1951
Sonido 13 for Violin, Horn, Guitar, Piccolo, Cello, and Harp (W)	MSO – January 2nd, 1931

Pablo Casals/Stokowski

'O Vos Omnes' (W)	ASO – April 15th, 1970

Marc Antonio Cesti/Stokowski

'Tu mancavi a tormentarmi' (W)	LSSO – February 28th, 1952

Abram Chasins

Concerto no. 2 in F Sharp Minor for	PO – March 3rd, 1933

Piano and Orchestra (W)
Soloist: Abram Chasins

Carlos Chavez
'HP' (A)   PO – March 31st, 1932

Frederic Chopin/Stokowski
Mazurka no. 13 in A Minor, op. 17,   PO – November 20th, 1936
no. 4 (W)
Mazurka no. 25 in B Minor, op. 33,   PO – November 18th, 1937
no. 4 (W)
Prelude no. 4 in E Minor, op. 28 (W)   PO – November 16th, 1922
Prelude no. 24 in D Minor, op. 28 (W)   PO – April 9th, 1937
Waltz no. 7 in C Sharp Minor, op. 64,   HSO – November 14th, 1955
no. 2 (W)

Jeremiah Clarke/Stokowski
'A Trumpet Voluntary' (W)   PO – December 26th, 1924

Aaron Copland
Dance Symphony (W)   PO – April 15th, 1931

Henry Cowell
American Piper (W)   NYPO – January 22nd, 1949
Concerto for Coto and Orchestra (W)   PO – December 18th, 1964
Soloist: Kimio Eto
Pastoral and Fiddler's Delight (W)   AAYO – July 26th, 1940
Persian Set (W)   LSSO – April 18th, 1957
Symphony no. 6 (W)   HSO – November 14th, 1955
Symphony no. 12 (W)   HSO – March 28th, 1960
Tales from Our Countryside (W)   AAYO – May 11th, 1941
Soloist: Henry Cowell

Henry Walford Davies
'A Solemn Melody' (A)   HSO – October 30th, 1956

William Dawson
Negro Folk Symphony (W)   PO – November 16th, 1934

Claude Debussy/Stokowski
'Soirée dans Grenade' from   PO – April 6th, 1937
'Estampes' (W)
Prelude no. 10 I ('La Cathédrale   PO – February 5th, 1926
engloutie') (W)
'Clair de Lune' from 'Suite   PO – April 6th, 1937
Bergamasque' (W)

Arcady Dubensky
Concerto Grosso for Three Trombones, Tuba,   NYPO – November 3rd, 1949
and Orchestra (W)
Fugue for Eighteen Violins (W)   PO – April 1st, 1932
The Raven' (W)   PO – December 9th, 1932
Narrator: Benjamin de Loache
Tom Sawyer Overture (W)   PO – November 29th, 1935

George Dyson
Overture to the Cantata 'Canterbury Pilgrims' (A) NYPO – February 10th, 1949

Henry Eichheim
'Bali' (W)   PO – December 1st, 1933

Edward Elgar
Symphony no. 2 in E Flat Major (A)   CiSO – November 24th, 1911

George Enesco
Suite no. 2 for Orchestra (A)   PO – February 19th, 1926

Oscar Espla
'Don Quixote Verlando les Armas' (A)   HSO – April 10th, 1956

Manuel de Falla
'El Amor Brujo' (A)   PO – April 15th, 1922

Gregor Fitelberg
Polish Rhapsody (A)   PO – November 4th, 1921

Cesar Franck/Stokowski
'Panis Angelicus' from Messe Solennelle, op. 12 (W) PO – December 27th, 1935

Girolamo Frescobaldi/Stokowski
Gagliarda (W)   PO – October 24th, 1934

Anis Fuleihan
Concerto for Thereminvox and Orchestra (W)   NYCSO – February 26th, 1945
Soloist: Clara Rockmore

Giovanni Gabrieli/Stokowski
'In Ecclesiis Benidicite Domino' (W)   NYPO – April 6th, 1950
With Schola Cantorum and the Westminster
Choir, New York

Serge de Gastyne
'Attala' (W)   HSO – November 3rd, 1958

Roger Goeb
Symphony no. 3 (W)   LSSO – April 27th, 1952

Morton Gould
Chorale and Fugue in Jazz (W)   PO – January 2nd, 1936

Enrique Granados
Excerpts from 'Goyescas' (W)   PO – March 10th, 1916

Alexander Gretchaninow
Symphony no. 5 in G Minor, op. 153 (W)   PO – April 5th, 1939

Charles Griffes
'The White Peacock' (W)   PO – December 19th, 1919

Gene Gutche
'Djengis Khan' (A)   ASO – March 23rd, 1969

George Frederic Handel/Stokowski
Overture in D Minor (W)   PO – December 11th, 1925
Dead March from 'Saul' (W)   PO – October 6th, 1933

Lou Harrison
Suite for Violin, Piano, and Orchestra (W)   LSSO – January 11th, 1952
Soloists: Anahid and Maro Ajemian

Siegmund von Hausegger
'Wieland der Schmied' (A)   PO – October 17th, 1913

Hans Werner Henze
Quattro Poemi (W)   FRSO – May 31st, 1955

Paul Holmes
'Fable' (W)   HSO – April 10th, 1956

Alan Hovhaness
'Ad Lyram', op. 143 (W)   HSO – March 12th, 1957
Soloists: Melba Petzold, Ruth Porter,
Alvan Messer, and Henry Bennick
With the Houston Chorale
'Meditation on Orpheus', op. 155 (W)   HSO – October 20th, 1958
'Meditation on Zeami' (W)   ASO – October 5th, 1964
'Mountain Bell' (W)   ASO – October 5th, 1964
'Mysterious Mountain', op. 132 (W)   HSO – October 31st, 1955
'Praise the Lord with Psaltry' (W)   ASO – December 22nd, 1968
With the Camerata Singers
Symphony no. 3 (W)   SA – October 14th, 1956
Symphony no. 15 (W)   ASO – March 28th, 1963
'As on the Night' from Triptych, op. 100 (W)   HSO – December 17th, 1956
Soloist: Lois Townsend
With the Houston Chorale
'Visions from a High Rock', op. 123 (W)   DSO – February 17th, 1955

Stevan Hristic
Six Balkan Dances (A)   RHDO – June 29th, 1961

Michail Ippolitov-Ivanow
Caucasian Sketches, op. 10 (UK)   NSO – May 18th, 1909
Caucasian Sketches, op. 10 (A)   CiSO – December 10th, 1909

Charles Ives
Orchestral Set no. 2 (UK)   LSO – June 18th, 1970
Robert Browning Overture (W)   SA – October 14th, 1956
Symphony no. 4 (W)   ASO – April 26th, 1965
With Schola Cantorum, New York

Norman Dello Joio
Concert Music for Orchestra (W)   NYPO – March 14th, 1948

Aram Khachaturian
Festive Poem (W)   HSO – November 28th, 1955
Russian Fantasy (A)   NYPO – April 1st, 1948
Symphony no. 3 (A)   CSO – February 15th, 1968

Leon Kirchner
Toccata for Strings, Winds, and Percussion (W)   SA – October 4th, 1956

Kenneth Leighton
Overture 'Primavera Romana' (W)   RPO – August 4th, 1951

Dimitri Levidis
Poeme Symphonique pour Solo d'Ondes Musicales PO – December 12th, 1930
et Orchestre (A)
Soloist: Dimitri Levidis

Rolf Liebermann
Furioso for Orchestra (A)   DSO – December 9th, 1950

Gustav Mahler
'Das Lied von der Erde' (A)   PO – December 15th, 1916
Soloists: Tilly Koenen and Johannes Sembach
Symphony no. 8 in E Flat Major (A)   PO – March 2nd, 1916

Soloists: Inez Barbour, Adelaide Fischer,
Florence Hinkle, Susanna Dercum, Margaret
Keyes, Reinald Werrenrath, Lambert Murphy,
and Clarence Whitehall
With the Philadelphia Orchestra Chorus, the
Philadelphia Choral Society, Mendelssohn Club,
and the Fortnightly Club

Gian Francesco Malipiero
'Pause del Silenzio' (W)   PO – April 1st, 1927

Bohuslav Martinu
Concerto no. 4 for Piano and Orchestra (A)   SA – October 4th, 1956
Soloist: Rudolf Firkusny

Daniel Gregory Mason
Symphony no. 1 in C Minor, op. 11 (A)   PO – February 18th, 1916

William Mayer
Octagon for Piano and Orchestra (W)   ASO – March 21st, 1971
Soloist: William Masselos

Robert McBride
'Show Piece' (W)   PO – December 10th, 1937

Harl McDonald
Concerto for Two Pianos and Orchestra (W)   PO – April 2nd, 1937
Soloists: Jeannie Behrend and Alexander Kelberine
'Festival of Workers' (W)   PO – November 24th, 1933
Symphony no. 1 (Sante Fé Trail) (W)   PO – November 16th, 1934
Symphony no. 2 (Rhumba Symphony) (W)   PO – October 4th, 1935

Nikolai Medtner
Concerto no. 1 in C Minor for Piano and   PO – October 31st, 1924
Orchestra, op. 33 (A)
Soloist: Nikolai Medtner

Gian-Carlo Menotti
Triple Concerto (W)   ASO – October 6th, 1970

Olivier Messiaen
'Hymne au Saint Sacrement' (W)   NYPO – March 13th, 1947
'Trois Petite Liturgies de la Presence Divine' (A) NYPO – November 17th, 1949

Nikolai Miakowsky
Symphony no. 5 in D Major, op. 18 (A)   PO – January 2nd, 1926
Symphony no. 6 in E Flat Minor, op. 23 (A)   PO – November 26th, 1926

Darius Milhaud
'Saudades de Brazil' (A)   NYPO – January 2nd, 1947

Ernest Moeran
'In the Mountain Country' (A)   NYPO – January 27th, 1949

Alexander Mossolov
'Soviet Iron Foundry' (A)   PO – October 23rd, 1931

Modeste Moussorgsky/Stokowski
Symphonic Synthesis from 'Boris Godunov' (W)   PO – October 25th, 1935
Prelude to Act 4 of 'Khovantchina' (W)   PO – October 27th, 1922
'A Night on the Bare Mountain' (W)   PO – December 6th, 1940
'Pictures at an Exhibition' (W)   PO – November 15th, 1939

W. A. Mozart/Stokowski
Turkish March from Sonata in A Major, K.331 (W) LSSO – February 9th, 1955

Paul Nordoff
Fugue (W)   PO – April 9th, 1937

Ottokar Novacek/Stokowski
'Moto perpetuo' (W)   PO – November 27th, 1940

Carl Orff
Trionfo di Afrodite (A)   HSO – April 2nd, 1956
With the Houston Chorale

Leo Ornstein
Concerto no. 2 for Piano and Orchestra (W)   PO – February 13th, 1925
Soloist: Leo Ornstein

Ignaz Paderewski
Symphony in B Minor (A)   PO – January 15th, 1915

Giovanni Palestrina/Stokowski
'Adoramus te Christe' (W)   PO – February 16th, 1923

Andrzej Panufnik
Epitaph for the Victims of Katyn (A)   ASO – November 17th, 1968
Sinfonia Eligiaca (W)   HSO – November 11th, 1957
Sinfonia Sacra (A)   ASO – December 10th, 1966
Symphony of Peace (A)   DSO – February 17th, 1955
Tragic Overture (W)   NYPO – March 24th, 1949
Universal Prayer (W)   LSSO – May 24th, 1970
Soloists: Meredith Rung, Jan Reiman, Timothy
Seitz, and Thomas van Vranken
With the Westminster Choir College
Universal Prayer (UK)   LSSO – June 20th, 1971
Soloists: April Cantelo, Helen Watts, Ian Partridge,
and Roger Stalman
With Louis Halsey Singers and Cantanti Camerati
of Richmond

Walter Piston
Suite no. 1 for Orchestra (W)   PO – April 1st, 1932

Francis Poulenc
Concerto in D Minor for Two Pianos and   PO – December 27th, 1935
Orchestra (A)
Soloists: Jeannie Behrend and Alexander Kelberine

Serge Prokofiev
Alexander Nevsky Cantata (A)   NBCSO – March 7th, 1943
Soloist: Jeannie Tourel
With the Westminster Choir
'Le Pas d'Acier', op. 41 (A)   PO – April 10th, 1931
Symphony no. 6 in E Flat Minor, op. 111 (A)   NYPO – November 24th, 1949

Henri Rabaud
Symphony no. 2 in E Minor, op. 5 (A)   PO – October 24th, 1913

Sergei Rachmaninov
'The Bells', op. 35 (A)   PO – February 6th, 1920
Soloists: Florence Hinkle, Arthur Hackett, and
Frederick Patton

With the Philadelphia Orchestra Chorus
Concerto no. 4 in G Minor for Piano and   PO – March 18th, 1927
Orchestra, op. 40 (W)
Soloist: Sergei Rachmaninov
Rhapsody for Piano and Orchestra, op. 43 (W)   PO – November 7th, 1934
Soloist: Sergei Rachmaninov
Symphony no. 3 in A Minor, op. 44 (W)   PO – November 6th, 1936
Three Russian Folksongs for Chorus and Orchestra, PO – March 18th, 1927
op. 41 (W)
With the Philadelphia Orchestra Chorus

Sergei Rachmaninov/Stokowski
Prelude in C Sharp Minor, op. 3, no. 2 (W)   PO – December 17th, 1962

Maurice Ravel
Concerto in G Major for Piano and Orchestra (A) PO – November 4th, 1932
Soloist: Sylvan Levin

Silvestre Revueltas
'Sensemaya' (W)   NYCSO – February 26th, 1945

William Rice
Concerto for Wind and Percussion (W)   HSO – October 30th, 1956

Wallingford Riegger
Study in Sonority for Ten Violins, op. 7 (W)   PO – October 30th, 1929
Symphony no. 3, op. 42 (UK)   RPO – May 27th, 1951

Nikolai Rimsky-Korsakov
Excerpts from 'The Invisible City of Kitezh' (A) PO – October 26th, 1923

Bernard Rogers
Two American Frescoes (W)   PO – November 20th, 1936

Albert Roussel
Evocation no. 2 (A)   PO – January 2nd, 1914

Carl Ruggles
Organum (W)   NYPO – November 24th, 1949
Organum (UK)   RPO – June 4th, 1951

Camille Saint-Saëns
Marche Heroique, op. 34 (A)   PO – March 24th, 1920

Ernest Schelling
Legende Symphonique (A)   PO – October 31st, 1913
A Victory Ball (W)   PO – February 23rd, 1923

Florent Schmitt
Rapsodie Viennoise, op. 53 (A)   PO – November 28th, 1913

Arnold Schoenberg
Chamber Symphony, op. 9 (A)   PO – November 5th, 1915
Concerto for Piano and Orchestra, op. 42 (W)   NBCSO – February 6th, 1944
Soloist: Eduard Steuermann
Concerto for Violin and Orchestra, op. 36 (W)   PO – December 6th, 1940
Soloist: Louis Krasner
'Die Glückliche Hand', op. 18 (A)   PO – April 11th, 1930
Soloist: Ivan Ivantzoff
With the Curtis Institute Chorus
'Gurrelieder' (A)   PO – April 8th, 1932

Soloists: Jeanette Vreeland, Rose Bampton, Poul
Althouse, Robert Bett, Abrasha Robofsky, and
Benjamin de Loache
With the Princeton Glee Club, Fortnightly Club,
and Mendelssohn Club
Variations for Orchestra, op. 31 (A)   PO – October 18th, 1929

Franz Schubert/Stokowski
Deutsche Tänze, op. 33 (W)   PO – October 13th, 1922
Moment musicale no. 3 in F Major (W)   PO – January 20th, 1922

Robert Schumann/Stokowski
'Träumerei' from 'Kinderscenen', op. 15 (W)   AAYO – July 11th, 1941

Cyril Scott
Concerto for Piano and Orchestra (W)   PO – November 5th, 1920
Soloist: Cyril Scott

Alexander Scriabin
'The Divine Poem', op. 43 (A)   PO – November 19th, 1915

Alexander Scriabin/Stokowski
Etude in C Minor, op. 2, no. 1 (W)   NYCSO – December 14th, 1944

José Serebrier
Poeme Elegiaco (W)   ASO – October 7th, 1963
Symphony no. 1 (W)   HSO – November 4th, 1957

Rodion Shchredin
Suite from 'The Humpbacked Horse' (A)   HSO – November 18th, 1957

Dimitri Shostakovitch
Concerto for Piano, Trumpet, and Orchestra,   PO – December 12th, 1934
op. 35 (A)
Soloist: Eugene List
Symphony no. 1 in F Major, op. 10 (A)   PO – November 2nd 1928
Symphony no. 3, op. 20 (A)   PO – December 30th, 1932
Symphony no. 6, op. 54 (A)   PO – November 29th, 1940
Symphony no. 11, op. 103 (A)   HSO – April 7th, 1958

Dimitri Shostakovitch/Stokowski
Prelude in E Flat Minor, op. 34, no. 14 (W)   PO – December 27th, 1935

Jean Sibelius
'Song of the Earth', op. 93 (A)   HSO – December 6th, 1955
With the Houston Chorale
Symphony no. 5 in E Flat Major, op. 82 (A)   PO – October 21st, 1921
Symphony no. 6 in D Minor, op. 104 (A)   PO – April 23rd, 1926
Symphony no. 7 in C Major, op. 105 (A)   PO – April 3rd, 1926

Elie Siegmeister
'Prairie Legend' (W)   NYPO – January 18th, 1947
Symphony no. 1 (W)   NYPO – October 30th, 1947

John Stafford Smith/Stokowski
'The Star Spangled Banner' (W)   AAYO – July 21st, 1940

Alexander Steinert
Rhapsody for Clarinet and Orchestra (W)   HBSO – July 22nd, 1945

Robert Stevenson
Two Peruvian Preludes (W)   RHDO – June 28th, 1962

William Grant Still
Symphony in G Minor (W)   PO – December 10th, 1937

Leopold Stokowski
Dithyrambe (W)   PO – November 15th, 1917

Johann Strauss/Stokowski
'On the Beautiful Blue Danube' (W)   PO – April 22nd, 1925
'Tales from the Vienna Woods' (W)   PO – December 18th, 1925
Waltzes from 'Die Fledermaus' (W)   HBSO – August 23rd, 1946

Richard Strauss
Alpensymphonie, op. 64 (A)   PO – April 28th, 1916
Metamorphosen (A)   CBSSO – March 19th, 1947

Igor Stravinsky
'Le Sacre du Printemps' (A)   PO – March 3rd, 1922
'The Song of the Nightingale' (A)   PO – October 19th, 1923
Symphonie d'Instruments a Vent (A)   PO – November 23rd, 1923

Igor Stravinsky/Stokowski
Pastorale (W)   PO – November 16th, 1934

Karol Szymanowski
Concerto no. 1 for Violin and Orchestra,   PO – November 28th, 1924
op. 35 (A)
Soloist: Angel Reyes
Symphony no. 3, op. 27 (A)   PO – November 19th, 1926

Germaine Tailleferre
Concerto for Piano and Orchestra (A)   PO – March 20th, 1925
Soloist: Germaine Tailleferre

Virgil Thomson
Shipwreck and Love Scene from Byron's 'Don   NYPO – April 11th, 1968
Juan' (W)
Soloist: Richard Kness

Michael Tippett
Ritual Dances from 'A Midsummer Marriage' (A)   HSO – November 5th, 1956

Peter Tschaikovsky/Stokowski
Chant sans Paroles in A Minor, op. 40,   PO – April 28th, 1924
no. 6 (W)
Humoreske, op. 10, no. 2 (W)   AAYO – July 10th, 1941
Solitude, op. 73, no. 6 (W)   PO – November 6th, 1936
Andante Cantabile from String Quartet no. 1 in   PO – January 11th, 1930
D Major (W)

Edgar Varese
Ameriques (W)   PO – April 9th, 1926
Arcana (W)   PO – April 8th, 1927
Integrales (W)   PO – March 1st, 1925

Ralph Vaughan Williams
Symphony no. 6 in E Minor (A)   NYPO – January 27th, 1949
Symphony no. 7 (A)   ClSO – December 9th, 1954
Symphony no. 9 in E Minor (A)   SA – September 25th, 1958

Tomas Luis de Victoria/Stokowski
'Jesu Dulcis Memoria' (W)   NYPO – January 3rd, 1947

Antonio Vivaldi/Stokowski
Concerto Grosso in D Minor, op. 3, no. 11 (W)   PO – October 20th, 1922

Richard Wagner/Stokowski
Symphonic Synthesis from 'Die   PO – April 29th, 1932
Götterdämmerung' (W)
Symphonic Synthesis from Act 3 of 'Parsifal' (W)   PO – January 19th, 1934
Symphonic Synthesis from 'The Rheingold' (W)   PO – March 3rd, 1933
Symphonic Synthesis from 'Siegfried' (W)   PO – December 16th, 1932
Symphonic Synthesis from 'Tristan and   PO – April 15th, 1932
Isolde' (W)
Symphonic Synthesis from 'Die Walküre' (W)   PO – April 28th, 1933

Anton Webern
Passacaglia, op. 1 (A)   PO – March 4th, 1927
Symphony for Small Orchestra, op. 21 (A)   PO – October 23rd, 1931

Karl Weigl
Symphony no. 5 (W)   ASO – October 27th, 1968

Charles Marie Widor
Symphony no. 6 (A)   PO – March 27th, 1919
Organ: Charles Courboin

Arnold Zemachsen
Chorale and Fugue in D Minor, op. 4 (W)   PO – November 21st, 1930

Efrem Zimbalist
'Daphnis and Chloe' (W)   PO – January 2nd, 1932

First Stage Productions in USA

Alban Berg
'Wozzeck'   PO – March 19th, 1931
With Anne Roselle, Bruno Korell, Sergei
Radamsky, Abrasha Robofsky, Albert Mahler,
Edwina Eustis, Ivan Ivantzoff, Ivan Steschenko,
Gabriel Leonoff, Benjamin de Loache, Louis
Purdey, and Evelyn Smith
Assistant Conductors: Henri Elkan and Sylvan
Levin
Direction: Wilhelm von Wymetal, Jr.
Scenography: Robert Edmond Jones
In collaboration with the Philadelphia Grand Opera
Company

Carlos Chavez
'HP'   PO – March 31st, 1932
Solo Dancers: Alexis Dolinoff, Douglas Coudy,
Thomas Cannon, Rosalie Betz, Dorothie Littlefield,
Dorothea Renninger, Lorraine Gamson, Sophie
Fadum, Dorothy Jackson, Erich von Wymetal,
Louis Purdey, Kenneth Howard, Martha
Fitzpatrick, Stella Claussen, Anna McCue, and
Mary Woods

Choreography: Catherine Littlefield
Direction: Wilhelm von Wymetal, Jr.
Scenography: Diego Rivera
In collaboration with the Philadelphia Grand Opera
Company

Carl Orff
'Carmina Burana'   NYCSO – September 24th, 1959
Soloists: Reri Grist, John Alexander, and John
Reardon
Direction: Robert Irving

Serge Prokofiev
'Le Pas d'Acier'   PO – April 10th, 1931
Solo Dancers: Edwin Strawbridge, Yeichi Nimura,
Pauline Koner, Grace Cornell, Ruth Wilton,
Martha Eaton, John Glenn, and Mary Rivoire
Choreography: Edwin Strawbridge
Scenography: Lee Simonson
In collaboration with the League of Composers

Arnold Schoenberg
'Die Glückliche Hand'   PO – April 11th, 1930
Soloist: Ivan Ivantzoff
With the Curtis Institute Chorus
Direction: Rouben Mamoulian
Scenography: Robert Edmond Jones
In collaboration with the League of Composers

Igor Stravinsky
'Les Noces'   LSSO – April 25th, 1929
Pianists: Aaron Copland, Marc Blitzstein, Louis
Gruenberg, and Frederick Jacobi
Scenography: Robert Edmond Jones
In collaboration with the League of Composers

'Oedipus Rex'   PO – April 10th, 1931
Soloists: Margaret Matzenauer, Paul Althouse,
M. Rudinov, Sigurd Nilssen, Daniel Healy, and
Wayland Rudd
With the Princeton University Glee Club
Scenography: Robert Edmond Jones
In collaboration with the League of Composers

'Le Sacre du Printemps'   PO – April 11th, 1930
Solo Dancer: Martha Graham
Choreography: Leonide Massine
Scenography: Nicholas Roerich
In collaboration with the League of Composers

Index

284

287

288